Atonement

THE ATONEMENT AND OURSELVES

THE ATONEMENT
AND OURSELVES

BY

P. L. SNOWDEN
VICAR OF HEPWORTH

LONDON
SOCIETY FOR PROMOTING
CHRISTIAN KNOWLEDGE
NEW YORK: THE MACMILLAN COMPANY
1919

TO HIS SISTER

C. A. S.,

HIS STEADFAST SUPPORTER
DURING MANY STRENUOUS AND EXACTING YEARS,
THE AUTHOR
DEDICATES THIS BOOK.

PREFACE

THIS book is in some sense a war book. Ten weeks of
national service in the form of labouring for a party
of tree-fellers near York offered the opportunity for
beginning to write it, and to a certain extent influenced
its form. After a couple of weeks' practice the labour of
cross-cutting became sufficiently easy and mechanical
to allow one to work out minor problems in the subject
which had first aroused my interest twenty years
previously when getting up Dr. Dale's great book on
the Atonement for my Priest's examination. The
dinner-hour, spent sitting in the sunshine on a carpet
of pine-needles with one's back to a log or tree-trunk,
afforded opportunity for putting one's working thoughts
into the form of rough notes; and the unoccupied hours
of long summer evenings spent in the pleasant cottage
of the farm labourer, a true gentleman of the soil, with
whom I lodged, enabled me to elaborate and arrange
the day's notes.

This work was necessarily done away from my own
books, but in addition to the advantages of these favourable surroundings and leisure, I enjoyed the run of the
vicarage library, and found there some material which
served my purpose.

The work, which in this way I had found opportunity
to begin, was continued on my return home, where,
amidst the claims of one's usual parochial work, it
became rather more toilsome; but books and notes

drawn up at an earlier period made it possible to complete what had been begun.

It would not be a complete account of the origins of this book unless I acknowledged the help received from friends and relatives who, with no claim upon them to do so, have yet been good enough to criticize the MS. for me. Though not seeing my way to accept their suggestions save in minor details, yet their criticisms showed me the need for working out more fully certain points which I had previously taken almost for granted, or dismissed in a sentence or two; and though this has made the book considerably longer, yet I believe it has made it a more complete whole.

There is one point in connection with the argument of it on which perhaps something needs to be said. Though not the most noticeable, yet one of the most profound and far-reaching results of the great war has been its effect upon the moral outlook of mankind. Five, or even two, years ago, when this book was begun, the world's estimate of the relative values of mercy and justice was very different from what it is now. At that time the claims of penal justice were often felt to require defence or explanation to an extent which at present it is difficult to realize. The change of view is so striking as almost to be incredible were it not that pre-war writings bear witness to the fact. A few years ago desire for the retributive punishment of evil was regarded as the outcome of an imperfect morality hardly distinguishable in its ethical quality from vengeance; whereas the moral beauty of mercy required no explanation, and its largest claims passed everywhere unquestioned.

It was in a moral atmosphere of this kind, and in instinctive protest against it, that this book was conceived and written; but German statecraft and methods of warfare have borne their natural fruit, and especially in the last few months have altered all that. The coldest justice now recognizes that the instinct which demands punishment for sin and reparation for injury is one of pure morality. Yet man's memory is short, and the existence and effect of the former moral outlook may usefully be placed on record against the time when our natural tendency towards moral easefulness inclines us once more to take lenient moral views and to forget the hardly-learnt lessons of these last years.

Its statement will also explain the emphasis and weight of argument which at the time of writing it was felt were needed to support the status and claims of justice in the scheme of divine holiness.

Moreover, as one looks round and tries to estimate the moral and religious tendencies of the age, one still feels that our greatest present need is for a fresh outpouring of the Holy Ghost to bring home to men's consciences a truer perception of the guilt of sin; and that divine providence probably intends one chief and great result of the war to be the increase of moral seriousness in the world. The soil is now prepared, and men will be more ready to listen to religious teaching of this kind. In recent years the Church has shrunk from adequate teaching upon the claims of God's justice because, being unable to show how such claims could be satisfied, it was felt to amount to a religion of despair. As a result of this failure both the fear and the love of God have been dying out in the world, for experience proves that a person cannot be deeply loved unless his character is one which on due occasion calls for fear also.

If, in addition to this increased realization of the seriousness and danger of sin, the Church can impress upon men that the only way of salvation is by achieving a real union with Christ; that mere acceptance of His

teaching, or His morality, or faith in His life and death
are not in themselves sufficient, but only valuable
in so far as they lead on to and produce a union with
Him, with *His* very Personality who said—not " I
teach," but—" I *am* the Way"; so that men come to
realize that the equivalent to the old question, " Are
you saved ?" is " Are you one with Christ ?"—if, and
when, this ideal is generally grasped, I believe it will
produce that respect for, vitality in, and enthusiasm
for Christianity which is mankind's greatest need.
It is therefore my hope that by drawing attention
to (1) the status and claims of divine justice, and (2) to
the reality and profound nature of the union with
Christ which the New Testament language involves,
that this book may do something to quicken both the
fear and love of God, and so help forward the longed-for
revival of religion.

In sending it out to the public I am conscious that in
some matters it is an attempt to express inexpressible
truths, and that I possess very inadequate literary
equipment for a task which in any case would have been
too great for me. An industrial education not being the
best preparation for work of this kind, all I have been
able to aim at has been to try to make my meaning as
clear as possible. I ask therefore that the theory of
the Atonement it contains may not be judged by the
quality of its scholarship, nor its literary expression,
but by what is felt to be its substantial truth. In writing
it I have been impressed by the providential manner
in which events have been moulded, thoughts suggested,
and my ordinary reading has happened to supply
matter just at the right time and just of the kind needed
for my purpose. This has been a great encouragement
to me in the work, and has led me to hope that it may
be found to provide some help, however slight, in the

difficult work of religious revival which lies before us.
It is a great thing to venture to hope for, but all effort
needs hope to inspire it, and God's goodness is often
greater than our hopes.

P. L. SNOWDEN.

HEPWORTH VICARAGE,
  HUDDERSFIELD,
    1918.

P.S.—In order to correct any misapprehensions arising
from criticisms in this book of some of the teaching
given by the Rev. E. L. Strong in his work on *The Incarnation of God*, I should like to say that there are few,
if any, books on Christian doctrine which I have found
more helpful or inspiring as a whole than this work,
and especially in connection with the doctrine after
which it is named.

CONTENTS

xv

PART IV

HOW OUR LORD SATISFIED THE REQUIREMENTS OF DIVINE HOLINESS

PART V

HOW OUR LORD'S SACRIFICE CONCERNS US: THE LAW OF IDENTIFICATION WITH DISTINCTION

APPENDICES

APPENDIX A

APPENDIX B

INDICES

THE
ATONEMENT AND OURSELVES

INTRODUCTION

THE tendency in recent years has been to take gentle
views of life and encourage lenient judgments. In the
home discipline has been softened by influences of
family affection. In public life the severities of law
have been relaxed in order to hamper individual liberty
as little as possible. Justice has learnt to wink: there
has been a demand that the effects of kindness should
be given full opportunity in every kind of home, school,
refuge, and institute. Liberty itself has had to give
way before the claims of material well-being and comfort, as represented by the demands upon individuals
of trade unions and masters' associations. In social
matters emphasis has been laid upon the influence of
environment as being almost irresistible in moulding
character, and as chiefly to blame for the errors of
mankind, which, for this reason, might be more truly
regarded as misfortunes than sins. The virtues of
gentleness and humanity have been emphasized; strictness has become unpopular, and severity generally
condemned.

All this has come about partly as a recoil from the
gloomy severities of a general type of religion which
was tinged with Calvinism, and the harshness of an
industrial life based upon the Manchester school of
laissez-faire and "unrestricted competition." It is
the result and the contribution to the general life of
undiluted severity and common sense. When children

1

were brought up to sit through the winter evenings at
the far edge of the circle of firelight, and only speak to
one another in whispers lest a stern father, whose
experience in life was chiefly that of struggle against
hard circumstance, should be disturbed, it was not
unnatural that later, when the struggles of their forbears
had succeeded in winning for them some of the sweets
of life, rapidly developing in recent years to a considerable degree of ease and comfort, they remembered the
restrictions of childhood, and determined that their own
children should be brought up under easier conditions
both of discipline and home comforts and pleasures than
they themselves experienced. This to a great extent
explains the milder views of recent times. Moreover,
the sins common to this age have not been of a strikingly
repellent character, and charity has been constantly
called upon to draw a veil even over these. When one
is aware of one's own faults it is natural not to be harsh
towards others, and there has been a ready response
to the appeal of charity by the good-natured people
who make up so large a part of mankind. No one is
capable of being altogether uninfluenced by the tendencies of the age, and even the most conscientious
men have responded, perhaps somewhat unduly, to the
charms of a charitable and lenient judgment.

There is reason to think that this general atmosphere
has, among other things, not been without influence in
shaping some of the more recent theories of the Atonement, in which the love of God has been presented as
His predominant characteristic, and the claims of
Divine Holiness have been somewhat overshadowed.
One has to look through a great mass of air in order to
see that its colour is blue, and in the same way it takes
a monstrous crime to enable us even approximately to
realize the true nature of sin and the consequent claims
of justice. The war has given us such a crime, and
to-day few would say that all which moral right demands
is that Germany should be reclaimed, and that there is

no need for her to provide reparation. We are all liable to assume that issues are less complex than they really are—that a single object alone is in view when, maybe, several are really being aimed at. For instance, with regard to the administration of justice, that in the punishment of a criminal the *only* object in view is his reclamation, that punishment is *only* remedial. But even though Germany were to express a sincere repentance for her sins against Belgium, and America or some other State were to come forward and make good all the material losses Belgium has suffered without any cost to her despoiler, no one would feel that under these circumstances the claims of justice had been fully satisfied. There would still be an almost universal feeling that Germany herself ought to make good the injuries she had caused, and, at any rate to that extent, suffer for her crimes; and that unless she did so the cause of justice would have been dishonoured in the world, and be in need of vindication.

In fact, the general instincts of morality demand that sin should suffer. There is something greater than peace, more clamant than mercy, and more exacting than love—namely, the holiness of God, which includes these and all His other virtues besides. Because holiness is so sacred a thing, being the sum-total of the whole moral character of God, it is right that even the happiness with which love longs to endow human souls should give way to it if necessary, and even misery take its place rather than that the divine standard of perfect holiness should be in the least degree impaired. There must not be the slightest falling away from perfection. It would be the greatest of all calamities should God's character be tinged with the least shadow of imperfection.

There is a certain kind of outlook upon life which, though it might not admit it even to itself, yet tacitly regards happiness, and even material prosperity, as the things of supreme value in life. Yet, when challenged, we all know that holiness is a greater thing than happiness; and God owes it, not only to Himself, but through Himself to the whole of existence, that the perfection of His holiness, which includes justice, should be maintained even at the cost, if need be, of eternal loss to erring souls. Divine Holiness is the supreme moral consideration. If that were lost, our whole religious world would fall in ruins.

An incident in the Archbishop of York's visit to America during the Great War helps one to realize this truth. On his return he recorded that the impression made upon him in a long interview with President Wilson was that here was a man who sought peace and ensued it with all his heart; a man who, by his training and by his connection with a country whose interests and history alike inclined it towards peaceful development, was devoted to that cause; a man who in his very soul hated war, and realized the unnameable suffering it involved better than most men did; but who yet judged it his duty to lead his country into a world-wide conflict because he knew that the causes of justice and liberty which were at stake were greater even than the blessing of peace. For this reason, passionately devoted as he was to peace, he had decided upon war as a moral and spiritual duty; and the conscience of the people of that great country, with everything to lose by his decision, with nothing but suffering and immense material loss to follow from it, had yet confirmed his choice.

Now, if this be true, if the voice of God speaking by the conscience of the American people declared that the anguish of a nation's suffering was not too great a price to pay, but even ought to be paid if necessary, in order to preserve the standards of justice and liberty in the world, then we can understand that the operation of vindicating law is a divine, moral necessity. To compare great things with things still greater, it becomes then conceivable that the crucifixion of our Lord and the infinite loss of impenitent sinners is not too great a price to pay, but a price which ought, if necessary, to be paid in order to vindicate and preserve the perfect standard of God's holiness.

We can understand, therefore, that the outlook which can see in the operation of such law nothing but a form of vengeance is due to a deficient moral conception. It is really an approach to the point of view for which some teachers have at different times made popular appeal by dressing up an imperfect morality in the guise of seeming charity, and which is well illustrated in Béranger's poem " Roger-Bontemps," whose " mistress's portrait decked the wall," whose " broken jug was emptied oft, Yet somehow always full," and who " held his philosophic school, Beneath the George and Dragon." In answer to the angry retorts of opponents, Jack " smiled, and drank his skinful," finding support for such a life and philosophy in reflecting upon God's mercies, and in his failure to see any sign of damnation in Nature:

> " I cannot see the smiling earth
> And think there's hell hereafter."[1]

A similar, though more serious, mixture of real charity with careless leniency is characteristic of this age even among some thoughtful people. Many still find it impossible to believe that a God of love, " after He hath killed hath power to cast into hell " (Luke xii. 5). They feel that love must cancel that power, even though it be the King of Love who declares otherwise. Yet surely such pseudo-charity as Béranger's will not satisfy the moral needs of a world purged in the fires of a universal war kindled by immorality, and in which one of the most inspiring motives of defence has been the claims of justice. With the awful and inevitable consequences of sin stamped upon their consciences by the evidence of a suffering world, men will surely feel the need of a higher standard, and turn for moral satisfaction

[1] Thackeray's translation in his *Paris Sketch-Book*.

to the purer ideals and more serious teaching of our Lord and His Apostles.

There seems likely, therefore, to be a reaction from theories of the Atonement based chiefly upon ideas of the sufficiency of penitence[1] and remedial punishment. The experience the world has gone through has caused its latent instincts, which were never quite silenced— nor could be so long as the denunciations of the Bible against sinners in both New and Old Testaments existed —to be awakened by the war, and it is roused to ask questions about the real nature and claims of divine morality.

In some minds a feeling is rising that there is need to ask in the most emphatic way possible, in order to challenge attention and compel an answer, whether justice is a virtue or not. If it is not, its claims can be ignored; but if it is a virtue, their satisfaction must be arranged for in any method of atonement for sin provided by an all-holy God; and any theory which, like some recent ones, fails to do so must, *ipso facto*, fall short of the truth. For otherwise God's holiness is limited, His perfection fails, and His nature is no longer infinite.

It is not a grateful work to oppose the claims of a merciful, if lenient, charity; but, after all, such claims depend for their validity upon their truth, and if based upon an imperfect or distorted view of God's character, such charity may be a mistaken kindness, and real love will restore the truth. It is, therefore, one chief object of this book to oppose the theory that remedial motives are the only ones which can inspire true justice, and to claim for Divine Holiness that it has other duties and objects in view in addition to the reclamation of the sinner. The attainment of these former as well as the latter appears to necessitate demands upon God's love

---

[1] The word " penitence " is used here and throughout the book in accordance with some recent custom, to mean only " sorrow for sin," and as not including the confession and restitution which, together with contrition, make up a complete repentance

and character which exceed the conceptions of recent theories of the Atonement, but which do not appear to be beyond our power to grasp.

There is reason to believe that the reassertion of these claims of justice and the exigeant character of true love is necessary at the present stage of our religious history, and will do more than anything else towards rehabilitating religion in the respect and interest of the nation. There is a general feeling abroad that one of the things which most need reconstructing after the war is men's conception of Christianity. The war itself has not quickened spiritual interest sufficiently to form a basis for religious revival, and nothing less than a quickened spiritual interest will form a sound foundation for such a movement. Intellectual interest, humanitarian considerations, the social instinct for fellowship, or ecclesiastical zeal, are none of them sufficient, either in themselves or collectively. Real spiritual interest produced by the power of the Holy Spirit working through realized truth can alone prove sufficient, and it is doubtful whether "the spiritual hunger" and "immense amount of interest" reported by the Committee appointed by the Archbishops to enquire into the evangelistic work of the Church is really much more than normal, though circumstances have attracted special attention to it.

A clergyman returning after several months' experience of the war in France under conditions giving him special facilities for meeting some of the best material from all parts of the army, reports that the spiritual heather is by no means on fire yet, and this represents a very general impression. At home, in spite of great and carefully planned efforts on the part of our religious leaders, our experience confirms this view. There may be deep movements at the bottom of the nation's spiritual life, but they have not become generally noticeable as yet. There is no general surface movement. The same Committee reports that in some ways evangelistic work has become even more difficult, rather than easier, during the war, and mentions several reasons for this, which may be put under the three headings of the competition of other interests, the lack of the right spirit, and the want of religious knowledge due to defective teaching. It is possible that if men possessed adequate religious knowledge it would inspire a zeal and earnestness which would enable the spirit of religion to compete successfully with the other rival interests mentioned; and in this case the reasons named by the Committee may be reduced to a single all-inclusive one —viz., the want of religious knowledge.

If this be granted, then, we can take a step farther in our investigation of the chief cause of religious indifference. For such a general failure of interest in a thing which is a general necessity to the welfare of the community, and is in itself, as a whole, sound, as our divinely instituted religion is, could not occur unless the fault lay somewhere at its centre. If the teaching and knowledge of its central truths were sound, imperfect ideas about its secondary doctrines would not affect it to such a degree. A fruit is in no danger of dropping so long as only its skin is injured and the core is sound. The awful catastrophe of this war, the severity of the wound it has inflicted upon the Christian world, the insulting and utter denial of Christian morality involved by its origin, and the methods introduced by its originators, and by them to some extent forced upon the world as a whole, suggest that the weakness of Christianity has been central, has lain at its heart rather than at unimportant outposts of doctrine. Therefore we must look for the cause of our weakness to a general failure to grasp the great truths which form the foundations of our religion: the personality and character of God, the Incarnation, Atonement, and Intercession of Christ, the work of the Holy Spirit, the last judgment, etc., rather than among secondary elements in our religious life.

Among these, the central doctrine of the Christian creed is the Cross: " Salvation in its widest sense . . . must always be the heart of the Gospel that we preach."[1] It follows, therefore, that very possibly it is especially *here*, in an inadequate knowledge or mistaken views of the doctrine of the Atonement, that our weakness lies. Reason suggests this, and the Committee from whose report the above statement is quoted find that facts support this deduction. They say: " It would seem, therefore, that while, as ever, repentance and remission of sins must be preached in Christ's name, we must at the same time remember that the fear and horror of judgment and the punishment of sin, which has been in all ages such a powerful incentive to repentance, is to-day perhaps weaker than ever before. The profound difficulty of finding a motive for repentance and amendment that will appeal to our generation lies at the root of much of our ineffective evangelism. . . . Safety was what men wanted. . . . To-day it is otherwise. . . . Men are not afraid of hell, because they have left behind the old thought of it, and have not yet realized that sin has inevitable and terrible results."[2]

One would have expected that the natural deduction from the above line of thought would have been: " We must therefore find a motive for repentance and amendment that will appeal to this generation, and make the evangelism of the Gospel effective by bringing home to men the inevitable and terrible results of sin." More than this, one would have thought that not only would this be the natural conclusion to come to, but that if it were true, as the Committee had just stated, that " the eternal element in the Christian Gospel is unchanging— salvation . . . must always be the heart of the Gospel," and " sin has inevitable and terrible results "—they would have found themselves forced to the conclusion that the great need of the times is to find some more

---

[1] *Cf.* the Report upon the Evangelistic Work of the Church, p. 11.
[2] *Ibid.*, pp. 12, 13.

effective way of reviving the fear of sin, of preaching the Cross, and uplifting it anew as the central doctrine of Christianity. If sin is as dangerous as ever it was the truth needs to be made as clear as ever it was.

It is therefore somewhat disappointing to find them turning aside from the quest for some method of satisfying the great need they have revealed in order to dwell upon the importance of issuing an " appeal to service " and " adventure " for God and His Christ, as being the most " arresting " appeal to-day, giving " meaning to life," and " sweeping a man out of himself into a larger world, and making him one with the purpose of God for whom he vaguely longs."

One cannot doubt that there is much truth in what is here said about the force of the appeal for service. Christianity has always been an appeal for service ever since our Lord first said, " Come, follow me," and " Go ye, preach and baptize "; and it is probable also that the world has reached a stage when, the generality of men having become more capable of service, more emphasis should be placed upon this aspect of religious life. No doubt, also, such appeals would be found arresting, and to some extent effective. But it does not follow, because the appeal for service is important, that therefore the fundamental object of Christianity can be neglected in the appeals made, or that we should acquiesce in its inadequate presentment. If now, " as ever, repentance and remission of sins must be preached in Christ's name," we are bound in solemn duty to find out how to preach it effectively, and ought to raise the Cross anew and rally round it in a new crusade for the " New Jerusalem " we hope to build " in England's green and pleasant land." For salvation is, after all, the main object of our religion. God sent His Son into the world that all men might through Him be *saved:*[1] He is named Jesus—*Saviour;*[2] in His last words to the Apostles He charged them that *remission of sins* should

---

[1] John iii. 17.   [2] Matt. i. 21.

be preached unto all nations.[1] Their great appeal
accordingly was, " *Save* yourselves from this untoward
generation";[2] and they preached everywhere *salvation*
by Christ. This was the great theme which by divine
command they presented to their hearers, and then
and ever since it has proved the most powerful lever
for Christian conversion. It cannot be denied that it
is indeed the central doctrine of the Gospel, the " good
news " itself. The Cross stands at the centre both of the
Christian creed and the Christian life. It is the symbol,
because it is the central fact, of Christianity. Salvation
is the Gospel, and therefore there is this very serious
consideration to be taken into account, that to be
unable to preach salvation effectively is to be unable to
preach the Gospel effectively.

For this reason very little thought is needed to make it
clear that it is impracticable to attempt to revive the
religious life of the nation on the basis of an appeal to
serve Christ as its main foundation. For such questions
must necessarily arise as, What form is the service to
take ? What object should it have in view ? What
does Jesus want us to do ? Why does He desire this
particular service ? And the true answer to all these
questions could only be that the real object in the
service of Christ is the salvation of men from sin for the
honour and glory of God, and in order to satisfy His love.
Here, then, lies an objection to the method of revival
suggested by the Committee which appears to be serious.
For how can a worker value salvation for others, and
labour for it in them, if he does not value it for himself ?

It seems, therefore, unlikely, if not impossible, that
we shall be able to revive religious life on the basis of
the appeal proposed. It would be trying to produce
fruit from a branch before it was properly rooted; and
it would prove equally impossible to organize revival
on any other secondary issue so long as the trouble lies
in a failure to appreciate the crucial importance of the

---

[1] Luke xxiv. 47.   [2] Acts ii. 40.

main object of religion. It is obviously useless to add
new attractions to the Christian building so long as the
foundations are insecure. What is needed is to find
some way of presenting the truths of the " inevitable
and terrible consequences of sin " and the necessity and
means of salvation in a way which will appeal to the
modern mind. The facts of the religious situation all
point to the conclusion that nothing less than this will
serve our need. Neither is it true to argue that such
a motive is immoral and unworthy of Christianity. For
there is a worthy as well as an ignoble fear—the " holy
fear "[1] of losing what is good. Nor is fear of suffering
in itself immoral. It cannot be, since it is a God-
implanted instinct. It is only cowardly when allowed
to drive a man into doing wrong. Our Lord Himself
employed it as a religious motive, and to overlook His
appeal is to ignore a whole section of His teaching. To
argue that God does not appeal to fear is tantamount
to saying that He does not punish, which clearly cannot
be maintained.

The history of the chief great Christian movements
of the past supports the view of the need to appeal to
the motive of man's need of salvation; for they have all
been inspired by the Cross, from the time that the
greatest missionary determined to know nothing among
his converts but " Jesus, and Him crucified " (1 Cor.
ii. 2), and revealed the source of the inspiration which
gave him power in his cry: " God forbid that I should
glory save in the Cross of our Lord Jesus Christ "
(Gal. vi. 14).

This same concentration upon the Cross as the means
of salvation from sin is found also in the case of St.
Francis of Assisi, the great revivalist of the thirteenth
century. We read how, in intense spiritual conflicts,
" seized with a real horror for the disorders of his youth,
he would implore mercy,"[2] until at last, after some years

---

[1] See the Bishop's prayer in the Confirmation Service.
[2] Sabatier, *Life of St. Francis*, Eng. Trans., p. 22.

of struggle, at the foot of the crucifix of St. Damien, he found the peace and acceptance by God he longed for; and how, later, even his very body was marked with the stigmata of the Cross as evidence of the nature and intensity of the conviction which drove him to his labours, and made them so marvellously fruitful. The Crusades were not, it is true, altogether or even mainly spiritual undertakings, but certainly religious feeling had a great deal to do with these vast movements, and the cross the crusaders bore on their shoulders expressed what was the most solemn and deepest motive inspiring them.[1] In the Reformation we find the same force at work in its central figure, Luther. The dominant thought in his mind was that which " is perhaps the most awful and imperious creation of Christianity—the sense of sin."[2] " I tormented myself to death," he said, " to make my peace with God, but I was in darkness, and found it not." The light came with the realization that forgiveness could only be found through faith in the crucified Christ, and it was no chance collision, but the natural result of this deep conviction of the need and true source of salvation which drove him to kindle the flame of the Reformation by his public denunciation of Tetzel's sale of pardons.

In our own land and in more recent times the Evangelical movements were inspired by the same motive. The awful consequences of sin and the love of God manifested in the salvation provided by the Cross were the two great thoughts animating the Evangelical revivalists; while later, in the Oxford Movement, which was ostensibly more concerned with questions relating

[1] Pope Urban II., at the famous Council at Clermont, promised absolution of even the most deadly sins and instant entrance into Paradise to every soldier who should fall in the attempt to deliver the Holy Land from the infidels. *Cf.* Dean Spence, *History of the Church of England*, vol. ii., p. 175.

[2] Quoted in Dean Spence's *History of the Church of England*, vol iii., p. 19.

to the outward organization of the Church, the title of one of Newman's sermons, "The Cross of Christ the Measure of the World," is in itself a sufficient indication of the place which the Atonement filled in the spiritual life of its leaders, and explains their emphasis on the doctrine of penance.

Human nature is in all ages the same, and therefore it is not unreasonable to suggest that this same interest in the Cross of Christ as the means for the salvation of the world, which history shows to have been the chief religious dynamic in past ages, will probably be found in this generation also to be the only sufficient motive for an adequate religious revival. Probably our greatest religious need is the discovery of some method adapted to meet the special mental outlook of the times, and which would forcibly bring home to men the terrible nature and consequences of sin, the difficulty of attaining salvation, and also the immensity of God's love in providing the Atonement in Christ.

But if this is really our great religious need, it is not at present being met. The old preaching of hell-fire and a transactional redemption have become impossible, and nothing practicable has been provided to replace it. A few years ago an educated layman said to his clergyman: "One never hears the doctrine of the Atonement taught now. Why don't you preach about it ?" The answer was: "Because it is not at all an easy subject to preach about. But I will lend you Moberly's book on it. When you have read it, perhaps you will understand." In due course the book was returned with the remark: "I had no idea there was such literature upon the subject; but I see now why you don't preach on it. It is too difficult." Again, in his book upon the Atonement Canon Wilson wrote: "Our preachers allude to it in symbol and word as if everyone understood their allusion; but they occupy themselves with other aspects of revelation or of life. This is a terrible loss." And later he asks: "But what doctrine of the Atonement is taught now ?   Who will answer ?   From many pulpits the answer would be, None; no theory is taught." And then, after enumerating a number of questions which rise in men's minds with regard to the doctrine, he adds: "That these questions should be imperfectly and inadequately answered is perhaps inevitable; but that they should so generally not be answered at all, but evaded, is, to my judgment, full of danger.   For here is the very centre of Christianity, and the source of its power."[1]

One feels that this is true, and that it is impossible for a religion to prosper, even though it represents the very truth of God, when, owing to the shifting of men's moral and mental outlook, it has become impossible to preach its central doctrine because its clergy have not yet found a suitable way of presenting it to the changed conditions of thought which obtain.   This weakness is one which lies at the very centre of the life of the Christian Church, and surely it is for this central trouble that we need first to seek and apply a remedy, rather than to evade its demands as too difficult, and pass on to concentrate our attention on satisfying other important but secondary needs.

It seems probable that in order to revive men's interest in and respect for religion it is necessary that three things should be brought home to them: (1) The inevitable and terrible consequences of sin; (2) the difficulty, in view of the reign of law, of attaining salvation from these consequences; and (3) the loving provision God has made for our salvation in the Atonement of our Lord Jesus Christ when combined with earnest moral and spiritual effort on our own part.

It is in the belief that the view of the Atonement presented in this book may to some extent serve these purposes that it has been written.   It contains a theory which in practice the writer has found to be practicable to preach, and which, after twenty years' trial, he at

[1] *The Gospel of the Atonement*, pp. 82, 83.

any rate has for himself found inspiring to contemplate. It is possible that what has helped him may help others also—at least, to some degree. To be able to do anything helpful at all in this matter would be a tremendous privilege, and is almost too much to hope for; yet when one perceives things which are felt, and, indeed, almost proved by long private experience of them to contain glimpses of truth, one dares, because one feels compelled, to proclaim them.

The discovery of great truths is often by advances tending to exaggeration first on one side and then on another, until at last a sufficient outlook has been attained to allow a fair survey of the whole field; and the full truth is then found either to occupy some central position between the extremes advanced, or, as in the science of astronomy, by the discovery of some fresh harmonizing fact, apparently conflicting views are found in a really marvellous way to fit in with one another to form a perfect whole. In the latter case, the apparently conflicting views of various thinkers which contribute to the final result are not essentially false, however distorted they may be, but only err on their negative side, like a picture-puzzle with some pieces omitted. They do but need certain additions to be made to them in order to take their rightful place as partial truths in the magnificent whole.

This will probably be found to represent the history of the investigation of most divine plans of operation. For these in their profundity will naturally stretch man's capacity for apprehension to the utmost, and only gradually be revealed in their perfection by the discovery of a piece here and another there, to be slowly fitted together to complete the whole.

So in the development of the doctrine of the Atonement, that theory will probably be the nearest to the full truth which finds most room for all the positive leading thoughts of the great teachers of the past, and tends to fit them into an harmonious whole, in which, to the disparagement of neither, the strictness of holy justice will be reconciled with the gentleness of love. For the law is fulfilled by Christ, not destroyed, and the " golden rule " is the law of love, which cannot be less than just, and must be fully satisfied. It is because the theory of the Atonement which follows is believed to be in harmony with this principle that it is presented with some hope that it may be found to approximate to the truth, and so satisfy the religious instincts of Christians.

In many respects it returns to earlier conceptions of the doctrine, and its general plan is drawn up to show that:

1. Divine Holiness requires the full moral and spiritual restoration of the sinner; to attain this, contrition alone for sin is not sufficient ; the law of justice requires reparation also.

2. Our Lord in the achievement of a perfect obedience suffered the penal consequences of sin.

3. By virtue of their union with Him, Christians are involved in Christ's sacrifice for sin, with all that such an identification involves of personal sanctification and complete reparation made to Almighty God, in this way satisfying all the law of holiness.

PART I

THE NATURE, STATUS, AND REQUIREMENTS OF DIVINE HOLINESS

CHAPTER I
THE NATURE AND CLAIMS OF HOLINESS

The Atonement and Ethics.

In presenting any theory of the Atonement it is clear that, since God is the source of all, it is to the characteristics of His nature we shall have to look in order to find the causes which led His plan for man's salvation to take the form revealed to us in the Christian religion.

This necessarily involves questions of ethics, but in this connection we must bear in mind that in considering such things as love, justice, and holiness, we are not dealing merely with abstract moral qualities, but with features in God's personal character.

This is an all-sufficient answer to those accustomed to say that abstract questions of holiness or justice do not appeal to them. For the duties and consequences imposed by these moral qualities are duties which God owes to Himself. They are not merely abstract questions, but deeply personal matters. The claims of love are the claims which God's love makes upon Him; the demands of justice are the demands of God's justice, which His self-respect compels Him to satisfy; the requirements of mercy and holiness are in the same way the requirements of *His* mercy and holiness. We cannot, therefore, consider such claims coldly as being divorced from personal feeling. If they do not interest

us, they ought to, for we are not dealing with philo-
sophical abstractions, but with living, personal forces,
and—if one may say so—the feelings of God.　It cannot
be defended, therefore, when men put aside the claims
of holiness or justice with regard to a sinner as being
merely abstract considerations, and as having no great
claim upon their interest compared with the question of
men's personal relation to God; for these characteristics
of His nature greatly concern God's personal relations
to themselves, and theirs to Him.

Bearing this truth in mind, we may next go on to
consider the moral characteristics of God, and what
they require from Himself and mankind.

Holiness God's Fundamental Characteristic.

From early times the doctrine of the Atonement has
been particularly connected with questions as to its
justice.　It is obvious, however, that any action of God,
any plan for man's redemption, must harmonize not
only with justice, but also with all the other attributes
of the divine character.

It is difficult to discuss so sacred a subject as the
moral attributes of God's being without some appearance of temerity; yet, as this is the only way in which
truth can be arrived at, and as the doctrine of the
Atonement necessarily involves the moral relations of
the Persons of the Holy Trinity, its consideration is
forced upon us.

The character of God as a whole is best summed up
by the word " holiness." But if used in this connection
it must not be taken in the technical, restricted sense
of " separateness from evil "; but in its ordinary present-
day significance as a kind of superlative of " goodness,"
so as to include all the virtues of God's character in their
perfect development.　God means " good," and His
holiness presents Him to us not only as the negation of
evil, but also as possessing all those good qualities of
which the lack of any would prove fatal to His claim

to perfect goodness. God is more than "pure." His
robe is not only clean from every stain, but is also of
"glistering whiteness," such as "no fuller on earth
could whiten it";[1] and St. John tells us that in the
Bible this whiteness symbolizes "righteousness", *i.e.*,
the due observance of all law—positive goodness.[2] A
thing is separated from foreign matter in order that it
may be pure in its own substance, and God is "separate
from evil" in order that He may be perfect in the
sanctity proper to His nature. The Holy Spirit of the
Father and the Son is not only the Spirit of purity: He
is also the *Spiritus Sanctus*—the source of all positive
Christian graces.

In God's being holiness may be viewed as filling the
fundamental position that consciousness does in personality; or we may say that God's consciousness is
conditioned by holiness. It presents everything to Him
from the point of view of holiness. Our consciousness
is mixed or neutral in its moral attitude towards the
realities presented to it. God's consciousness is predominantly moral, and His point of view is unswervingly
fixed by absolute right. There is, therefore, no neutral
attitude or mixed feelings with Him. His omniscience
enables His judgment to be decided, and whatever is
good He approves, and whatever is evil He abhors.

Holiness, then, is not properly a virtue. It is rather
a status, a condition of moral existence, a complete,
consistent character in itself, forming in the moral
sphere a whole class of qualities which includes all the
virtues, as evil includes all the vices. And therefore in
one word, and better than any other, it sums up the
character of God.

God's holiness, then, is the complete sum of all
perfect virtues, and as such we are told by the Apostle
of love in the New Testament, as well as by God's
Prophet in the Old, that it forms the basis of the heavenly

[1] Dan. x. 5; Matt. xvii. 2; Mark ix. 3, R.V.; Luke ix. 29.
[2] Rev. xix. 8.

worship. " They rest not day nor night, saying, Holy, holy, holy, Lord God Almighty."[1]

Philosophy suggests that the Unity of the Divine Character is Complex, consisting of Various Moral Qualities of Equal Standing, as being all necessary to God's Perfection.

God's holiness is also the basis of the moral unity of His character. If the highest kind of unity is " unity in diversity," or the " unity of plurality," as Lotze held,[2] then it would seem that this kind of plural unity must apply to God's character as well as to His being. Therefore we have ground for believing that its perfect unity does not consist in one predominant, all-absorbing virtue or characteristic, but in the perfect harmony of a plurality of virtues, all distinct from one another, and yet combining to complete His holiness, as the Three Persons of the Holy Trinity are united in the one Godhead.

Moreover, God being a consistent whole, it is reasonable to suppose that the same principles which obtain in the constitution of His being apply to His character in other respects also, so that the parallelism we have noted will probably extend farther, and the virtues composing the Divine Holiness may be supposed all to possess, as it were, an equality of rank within it, just as the Three Persons of the Holy Trinity are all equal to one another in the Godhead. Thus such virtues as love, justice, purity, mercy, and truth, have all an independent standing of their own in the sum of the qualities which compose holiness.

This view is supported by what we know of personality. If you take the manifestations of personality to

---

[1] *Cf.* Isa. vi. 3; Rev iv. 8.

[2] *Cf.* " That which is not only conceived by others as unity in multiplicity, but knows and makes itself good as such, is, simply on that account, the truest and most indivisible unity there can be." *Cf. Metaphys.* § 238, quoted in Dr. Illingworth's *Personality, Human and Divine*, Lecture II.

be action, knowledge, and feeling as the outcomes of will, intelligence, and the affections, then the directions which these things take will depend upon a still more fundamental characteristic—viz., the moral quality of the person possessing them, whether he is good or bad. It is God's goodness or holiness which makes His power beneficent, His knowledge wisdom, and His feeling to be love—which makes Him love what is right and hate what is evil. Love is not only feeling: it is good-feeling. It is His holiness which determines the directions of His energies. In the same way, the fundamental evil in Satan makes his power malevolent, his intelligence malicious, and his feeling towards men hatred. When, therefore, men surmise—as there seems to be a tendency, probably correct, to do—that it was God's feeling for man that inspired His plan of salvation, they must not forget that without His knowledge and power that feeling would have been inoperative, and also that it would not have taken the form of love unless He had been holy. It is His holiness, then, which is the decisive factor in God's relation towards creation. And His other characteristics co-operate in harmony, each perfect in its sphere, to carry out His goodwill.

The Bible supports the Above View, especially connecting Love, Truth, and Justice with the Persons of the Father, Son, and Holy Ghost respectively.

This conclusion suggested by philosophy is supported by the fact that the Bible connects particular virtues with particular Persons of the Holy Trinity. The Father, as His name indicates, is particularly connected with the love which moved Him to create the world and give His Son to save it; the Son, as the express image of the Father, is especially revealed to us as the truth and wisdom of God; and the Holy Ghost as the divine energy—*i.e.*, will in action. We have, then, here represented, in the three equal Persons of the Holy Trinity, the three constituent elements in personality—

the affections, the mind, and the will of God, whose character as a whole is holiness. His holiness in feeling issues in love; His holiness of mind in truth or wisdom; and His holiness in will or decision in justice of thought and action; and all three are equally necessary to the perfection of His holiness.

The statement that God's will in action takes the form of justice perhaps needs amplification. With God to will is equivalent to expression either in word or deed, for with perfect wisdom will has no indecision. God's mind cannot be a blank on anything nor His will undecided. Neutrality is also abhorrent to Him.[1] As light dispels darkness, so is He compelled by the holiness of His nature to oppose and condemn evil; and with His almighty power there is no need for delay in execution. With Him, therefore, to will with regard to anything is equivalent to taking up an attitude with regard to it, either of approving support or of disapproving hostility. And such attitude, being based upon perfect holiness, and in harmony with perfect love and wisdom, must be a just one. God's justice may be defined as the divine discrimination in favour of right, and is an integral activity of His being, as independent and essential to His perfection as His love. In other words, as God's feeling is love and His intelligence wisdom or truth, so His will is represented by justice. Love, truth, justice, are the three great fundamental virtues of God's personality, common to all the three Persons of the Holy Trinity, but proceeding especially from the Father, Son, and Holy Ghost respectively.

Since this is so, it appears unreasonable to believe that any of these primary virtues of God are dependent upon, or subordinate to, the others. As Father, Son, and Holy Ghost are all equal and distinct Persons, so their distinctive qualities of love, truth, and justice must also be equal in nature, since all have a share in completing God's holiness.

[1] Rev. iii. 16.

*As the Father has a Priority among Equals in the Holy
     Trinity, so also is Love the First among Equals in
     the Divine Character.*

Yet, just as the Father has a priority in the Godhead
as the fount of divine being, though the Son and the
Holy Ghost are equal with Him in the Godhead, so also
we can understand God's love has a priority among
God's virtues as the dynamic of divine energy, although
His justice and truth possess an equality with it.   But
to claim more than this for love, to claim for it a predominance over other virtues, would be an infringement
of their essential equality of nature, and would limit
and so mar their perfection.   God's justice and truth
cannot be limited by love.   They must be perfectly free
and complete in their action, or God's whole character
for holiness suffers.

Again, as the Father, Son, and Holy Ghost comprise
the Godhead, so also love, justice, truth, and the other
virtues of God, comprise His holiness, in perfect unity,
but must not have their distinct characters confused nor
confounded with one another.   In these matters there
is no doubt a certain danger in negatives; but just as,
in spite of the unity of the Holy Trinity, it is on the
whole more true and less dangerous to say that the
Father is not the Son, so also it will on the whole be
more true and less dangerous to say that God's justice
is not His love, than to say that His love is His justice.
This is, of course, not the same thing as to assert the
truism that His love is just, or that His justice is loving.

To view love as the all-inclusive virtue and basis of
the divine character is an over-subtlety of thought.
The direct, original aim of love is to bring blessing to
its object;[1] and though it may co-operate with other
virtues, and even stimulate and quicken their action, this
is not its original function.   To take the other view

[1] Happiness here, of course, involves holiness, for otherwise it would
not be true happiness.

necessarily modifies our conception of the purity of God's other qualities. For instance, to say that God's justice is only an aspect of His love colours the conception of justice. It inevitably suggests a bias, and limits the vigour of its action in certain directions. It is, as it were, to paint a picture of justice on toned paper, which, however attractive, cannot give the high lights in pure white. To speak of God's justice as "loving justice" to a certain extent qualifies it, but to speak of God's "holy love" or "holy justice" only extends the conception of both by bringing them into harmonious unity with His whole character.

Love is "Primus inter Pares" in the Divine Character.

While, therefore, in God's holiness love occupies a position of pre-eminence which accounts for St. John's statement "God is love," it is evident God is not *only* love. His love does not include all His other qualities. For love is an affection, and God is will and intelligence as well as affection. These latter may be loving, but they are not love. Even in the case of His affections it is arguable whether love is God's only virtue. Our Saviour teaches us that He is also wrath. He hates sin as light hates darkness. He possesses also other virtues which, while no doubt in perfect harmony with love, are not the same thing—*e.g.*, purity and justice. In His attributes, as well as in His Godhead, God's unity is that plurality-in-unity which is of a higher type than that of mere singularity in number.[1] So that though love is God's pre-eminent moral characteristic, it is not in Him an all-inclusive virtue. The final issue is between good and evil rather than between love and hate, and love does not dominate God's other virtues in the same way that His holiness regulates His whole being and action. God is perfectly one—a perfect harmony—and His attributes, as it were, all run in

[1] *Cf.* E. L. Strong, *The Incarnation of God*, pp. 2, 3.

parallel lines, each perfect in itself, and, because of their perfection, never clashing with one another, and absolutely independent of each other. They proceed in their action and attain their ends without having the satisfactions they require in any way limited by the requirements of any of the other virtues. God's love in no way clashes with the requirements of His justice, nor His justice with those of His love. He is always perfectly just and perfectly loving. It is a mistake to suppose any of His virtues ever subordinated to another in any degree. Each in perfect independence of the others, and with free play for its energies, attains its full satisfaction; and all support rather than restrict one another, for they all work together to complete the perfect whole of God's work and being. They are, therefore, like the sexes in this, that each is perfect and best in its own province; so that none are superior to the others, and each is necessary to complete the whole. Comparison, therefore, is out of place; and it is wrong, in thinking of the divine character, to exalt any one feature at the cost of another. When the judgment of God falls upon a sinner it is from His holiness that the sentence originally proceeds, and His love does but confirm it as just, righteous, and needful to the world's health. Again, when love triumphs in the restoration of a sinner to fellowship with God, His justice, as we shall see, supports and even requires reconciliation. When God is most just, He is also loving; and when He is most loving, He is perfectly just. His attributes agree in perfect harmony, yet each has its separate sphere and work.

Such a view is in no way derogatory to God's love. It still retains its priority of order as the original motive of creation and in God's plan of redemption; and, as men's conception of God's holiness deepens, their sense of the suffering of His love in its conflict with sin increases.

The Contrary View involves a Lack of Harmony in the Divine Character.

At the same time, to give the other virtues equality of nature or rank with love is necessary to the real unity of God's being. The other view is really to suppose the existence of a kind of friction in His character. It takes the idea of a difference of feeling between the Father and the Son on the matter of man's salvation—the idea of a mediating Son placating an angry Father—and transfers the dualism from the Persons to the very characteristics of God's moral nature, putting His love in opposition to His justice; and then gets over the difficulty of reconciling their rival claims by ignoring the requirements of His justice—of which our Lord said the Holy Ghost would convince the world[1]—or subordinating them to those of His love, a method the very popularity of which should make it suspect as a probable concession to natural inclination. This reduces justice to being a mere aspect of love without an independent life of its own. It subordinates its claims instead of satisfying them, and this lower valuation opens the way to mistaken conceptions. It is not, for instance, correct to say that justice is opposed to sin *because* God is love.[2] God's holiness would be opposed to sin even if there were no such thing as love. The fact is, God's self-revelation of His character as holiness is so pervasive, and has so familiarized us with the thought, that we have come to take it for granted. It has come to be so much the very atmosphere of our religion that we have come to overlook it, in the same way that we are generally oblivious to the physical atmosphere in which we live, and its absolute necessity to our existence.

[1] John xvi. 8.   [2] *Cf.* Strong, *The Incarnation of God*, p. 59.

CHAPTER II

THE LIMITATIONS OF DIVINE LOVE

God's Love is conditioned by His Holiness.

IF, in opposition to the view of the equality of the divine virtues, it be urged that if we are to be in harmony with St. John's teaching we must ascribe to God's love not only a pre-eminent, but also a predominating, position; if it be argued, " But we know that from all eternity the Persons of the Holy Trinity have been bound together by love, which must therefore be eternal and precede all other virtues "—if this be urged, then the answer is clear—viz., that all God's virtues must be equally eternal with Himself, even though some have lain dormant; and also that God's holiness must in any case be greater than His love, which only forms part of it. It is clear that if it had not been for God's holiness there would have been no need for His love to mediate an atonement. Man could have been received into divine communion without it.

Moreover, if this precedence be claimed for love, we must ask, What is love ? And directly its nature is considered, one is forced to the conclusion that it cannot exist apart from holiness, in the sense we have used the word. For love is a passion for goodness, so that there can be no such thing as love without some goodness in the thing loved. To speak of " the love of evil " is a contradiction in terms. Such a passion would necessarily be immoral. It would be lust, not love. Even God's infinite nature cannot love evil, but must hate and oppose it. He can only love what has in it some element or capacity for goodness, which, however minute, or even neutral, is capable of being developed into virtue. Therefore such capacity must exist—*i.e.*, there must be some potential goodness in a thing— before love can exist with regard to it; and divine love is infinite only in the true sense of being perfect, and not in the sense of being without limit. Again, love cannot exist without holiness: it becomes something different, and lower. But holiness can exist as truth, purity, justice, etc., without love. Therefore, though holiness is necessary to the very existence of love, love is only necessary to the completeness of holiness. It is because the Persons in the Holy Trinity have eternally possessed such holiness in infinite measure that they have eternally and infinitely loved one another.

The Limitations of Divine Love.

We have already noted that God cannot love evil, and if to " evil " we add sin, we have stated something equally incontrovertible which brings the list of things outside the range of God's love within the sphere of personality—for sin is admittedly a personal thing. It is clear, therefore, that there are elements in man- kind which God cannot love; and in any particular person there may be features of mind or will or affec- tions of this kind. God, therefore, is able to love men only because and in so far as they are distinguishable from their sins. From this point the possibility of God's love for a sinner becomes simply a question of degree, for the possibility is opened up of a personality being so sinful as a whole as to be outside the proper sphere of God's love.

To take an extreme case, granted the personality of the Devil, one may ask, " Does God, then, love Satan ?" for if not God's attitude towards him must be repre- sented by moral and spiritual qualities independent of love; God is not love so far as the Devil is concerned, and the still further question arises, "At what point does a personality pass beyond the reach of love ?"

By those who believe that love is the all-inclusive, fundamental quality of the divine character, the originating cause and explanation of all divine action, it may be—it has been—claimed that God even can and does love the Devil himself, that His love will follow a sinner in his deeps of sin into the lowest hell, and even seek out and wait for all the devils of hell. " This is the awful majesty of God ! This is His kingliness ! This is His eternal nature !"[1]

No doubt this is the conclusion demanded by logical consistency from these premises, and we must admit that there is something extremely attractive at first sight in the conception of the character of God as consisting of one single, dominant, all-inclusive quality— especially when that quality is love. Unitarianism bears witness to the force with which the conception of such simplicity—of such unity—appeals to the intellect. But yet the fact remains that with regard to the Godhead the Christian Church has been inspired to reject this conception of unity in relation to the divine nature as being more attractive than true; and philosophy has taught that the highest unity is that which is found in plurality—in unity with diversity. Moreover, such a view of all-inclusive love is difficult to reconcile with the teaching of a great deal of Scripture. God can be " all in all " (1 Cor. xv. 28), as St. Paul says in this same passage, by having all things put under His feet (verse 27)—i.e., by clear victorious rule over all, as well as through the conversion of the Devil by love.[2] However attractive such a conception may be to us, it may be due to our inability to grasp the utter, infinite vileness of evil, and it does not justify us in ignoring all that Bible teaching of which some part will be found in Appendix A at the end of this book, and which includes some of the most solemn sayings of our Lord Himself.

[1] *The Incarnation of God*, p. 161.

[2] In his recent book, *The Religion of the Church*, Bishop Gore prefers the alternative of annihilation to universalism as being the more in accordance with scripture.

Some of our Lord's Teaching touching upon the Possible Limitations of Salvation.

One passage not contained in this catena, and having special reference to the possible limitations of divine love, is His saying concerning Judas Iscariot, that it would have been good for him not to have been born,[1] and the statement in John xvii. 12 that he was lost, and a son of perdition. Apart from any natural interpretation which His hearers would put upon this last statement, it is difficult to see how it could have been good for Judas not to have been born if God seeks to save devils, and the lost even in the deepest hell,[2] and if the fruit of Christ's redemption is that it will ultimately enable all sinners to live God's life in perfect union with Himself.[3] In view of such a final consummation, how could it possibly have been better for Judas not to have been born than for him finally to attain this state of everlasting blessedness ? The implication involved in this saying of our Lord appears to be decisive against universalism. But this is only indirect implication, however clear, and there is other teaching by the same supreme authority of a direct character in the allegory given in Matt. xii. 43-45 and Luke xi. 24-26.

The context shows that our Lord had shortly before healed a demoniac, and His enemies claimed that He had done it by devilish power—through Beelzebub the chief of the devils. Our Lord refuted the assertion, and, after warning the Pharisees that there is a point at which persistent refusal to recognize the work of the Holy Spirit becomes an eternal and unforgiveable sin, spoke the allegory we have referred to. The authority for this passage is good, and its validity generally accepted.

[1] Matt. xxvi. 24; Mark xiv. 21.
[2] *The Incarnation of God*, pp. 161, 230.
[3] *Ibid.*, pp. 206, 208-209, 240, 243.

The circumstances show that our Lord's evident object was to support His solemn warning about the eternal and unforgiveable nature of the sin of blasphemy against the Holy Ghost. He describes the case of a man out of whom an evil spirit had been driven by divine grace, which had also cleansed his heart, swept the house, and furnished it with the spiritual gifts necessary to enable him to receive another and heavenly inmate. But the man had no desire for this holy Presence, and so presently the demon, represented as athirst for human souls, came back, and, finding the man's heart unoccupied, entered and dwelt there together with seven other spirits worse than himself, so that " the last state of that man was worse than the first."

The author of the article on " Number " in Dr. Hastings' *Dictionary of the Bible* says that the number " seven " in this passage only represents a round number meaning " a good many." But the arguments used are not convincing so far as this particular passage is concerned, where the whole setting and context conveys the impression that our Lord here used the figure " seven " with special and symbolical significance. This view is the one generally taken, and in this case it is agreed that the figure symbolizes finality and completeness. For instance, the *One-Volume Bible Commentary* says: " The return of the evil spirit with seven other spirits more wicked than himself represents the obstinate and final rejection of Christ by the nation," and adds that we are quite within our rights when we apply this teaching to the individual soul. This last appears to be evident when we remember that the nation, or class within it, to which the warning was addressed could only take advantage of it by individual repentance, and that the whole incident was connected with our Lord's healing of an individual demoniac.

But in whichever way we interpret the figure seven, it is unquestionable that our Lord meant to teach that

the man's spiritual condition was worse than before, so
that we have here described for us by the very highest
authority an instance of progressive deterioration; and
although it is possible that divine mercy might make
still further efforts for a soul's salvation, and cast out
even seven devils, and that such an effort, as in the
case of Mary Magdalene, might prove finally successful,
yet undoubtedly the whole passage points to a spiritual
condition increasingly critical, and the teaching was
deliberately intended by our Lord to be a solemn
warning as to the possibility of progressive spiritual
deterioration culminating in the eternal sin, unpardon-
able either in this world or the world to come (Matt.
xii. 32).

Some Warnings from the Epistles which tell against Universalism.

At any rate, His teaching seems to have been so
understood by His disciples, and the best comment on
the passage is found in the Epistle to the Hebrews, where
it is written that "as touching those who were once
enlightened, and tasted of the heavenly gift, and were
made partakers of the Holy Ghost, and tasted the good
word of God, and the powers of the age to come, and
then fell away, it is impossible to renew them again
unto repentance" (Heb. vi. 4-6);[1] and where repentance
is impossible all agree forgiveness is impossible also, so
that even St. John teaches that "there is a sin unto
death" for which he cannot see his way even to ask
our prayers (1 John v. 16). Coming from him, such
teaching is especially significant; and so far as the truth
of the doctrine of the limitation of divine love is concerned, it is difficult to see how it can be denied, except
by claiming a superiority in insight and knowledge in
these matters over that of our Lord Himself.

Yet there is undoubtedly an instinct in us which
makes it very difficult to accept the idea that anyone

[1] See also Heb. x. 26, 27, and 2 Pet. ii. 20, 21.

can be beyond the reach of God's love.   It is important, therefore, to realize that this is not due to any difficulty in believing that God hates evil, a thing which our whole conscience demands, but to the great difficulty we have in realizing that the evil in a man can so develop and infect his whole nature as to entirely identify him with it, so that he is nothing less than an impersonation of evil.   Our difficulty in imagining such a state seems to point to the rarity of it, but it cannot be denied that there is evidence pointing towards the possibility of Dr. Jekyll becoming Mr. Hyde.

The Teaching of Science points in the Same Direction.

In addition to the teaching of philosophy and Scripture on this point, we can add the suggestions of science as found in Bergson's teaching on the degradation of energy, which shows that evolution is not the only principle, nor progress the only movement, at work in the universe. There is also the activity of devolution and retrogression; of katabolism as well as anabolism.   While for each individual of the race there are paths which open the way to an eternally progressive life, there are also paths which lead to blind alleys ending in certain death.[1] Nor does it appear there is any reason for supposing that the forces of katabolism are any less permanent than those of anabolism.   This agrees with the teaching of the Bible, where, in its last pages, St. John, the Apostle of love, the seer of divine truths, and the revealer of the last things, gives us a vision of the Holy City provided with gates and surrounded by walls as an eternal barrier against the entrance of anything which defileth or worketh abomination—an everlasting defence against an everlasting enemy.

Meanwhile it is certain that God cannot love evil, and therefore it is clear that just as far as His omniscience and consistency recognize the Devil to be wholly evil, so far is it impossible for Him to love the pure evil of

[1] Cf. Evolution and the Need of Atonement, by S. A. MacDowall.

which the Devil's personality consists. God can only regard him with unqualified hostility. And this must also be His attitude towards all evil, including the evil in ourselves. He hates and cannot love it at all. The possibility of personality becoming identified with evil and the utter vileness of sin seem to be overlooked by those who conceive of God as loving the Devil. It is undoubtedly difficult to grasp, but the truth is that such a condition, which is as far beyond our powers of realization as is a state of perfect holiness, may not make any appeal to pity or love, but call only for utter abhorrence. This appears to be the dreadful truth, but in our present impure state, under which our moral sense is blunted to the true nature of evil, the more loving a man is, the more difficult does he find it to realize.

The Possibility of Complete and Irrevocable Self-Identification with Evil.

It is only another instance of the law of God's self-limitation, of the truth that His infinite nature is limited by the restrictions proper to His character. He is almighty, but He cannot commit sin, for His holiness forbids it; He is eternal, but He cannot regard the future as having already been, for His truth forbids it; He is all-loving, but He cannot love evil, for the purity of true love forbids it.

It follows that in the development of every soul a point might be reached at which it would cease to be within the sphere proper to God's love; and that point would be attained if it became so wholly evil as to afford no point of contact for true love. The possibility of such a state should not be overlooked. It cannot be positively denied that such a state is contemplated in our Lord's saying about the sin of blasphemy against the Holy Ghost, and it is not really loving to slur over these terrible possibilities. Nor need the consideration of them be feared in teaching upon the Atonement. God's love is large enough and His wisdom sufficient to provide for the requirements of His justice without injury to His love, and to do so is a greater and more loving thing than to ignore them.

The Consequent Attitude of Divine Love towards Sinners.

Leaving extreme cases, it would appear that God's feelings towards the generality of men must be mixed as their characters are mixed. We do not like to think that God's feelings towards us can be anything but unqualified love; but this is just an instance of the tendency in us to think that what is unpleasant cannot be true, and the fact must be as stated. We know that God has infinite love for the souls of men, and we can understand to some extent why. The Blessed Persons of the Holy Trinity have an infinite love for one another, for, being altogether holy, They are altogether lovable. And it is because of this, and because there is, first of all at any rate, something from Them existing in every human personality, that men are so greatly loved by Them. The Father loves men because each one bears in him something of the Son, the true Light that lighteth every man as he cometh into the world.[1] The Son loves men because they are the creative work of the Father, made in His own likeness; and both Father and Son love men because the Holy Spirit has been breathed into them as the breath of life, and they are temples of the Spirit.[2] It is because of these divine elements in man, and because he is capable of a development which can bring him into perfect union with Themselves, that the Persons of the Holy Trinity find man so lovable.

But there are also in men elements which God cannot love, and which He hates. There is evil in men which He cannot and does not love. " There is a righteous wrath which is not only compatible with the noblest of God-given impulses, but may be even of their essence."[3]

[1] Cf. John i. 9.　　　　　　　　[2] 1 Cor. iii. 16, 17; vi. 19.
[3] See Sermon by the Archbishop of Canterbury at St. Margaret's Church, Westminster, August 4, 1918.

If this is true of sinful man, much more is it true of God. The popular saying " God loves sinners " is found nowhere in the Bible. It has come from no recognized source, and it often creates so false an impression and has done such an immensity of harm that there is reason to think it may have had a far different origin. St. Paul's teaching that even " while we were yet sinners Christ died for us "[1] presents God's love in its right aspect, as existing, and prevailing *in spite of* sin; but this modern text suggests that God loves us *qua* sinners: that the sin and not our need appeals to Him. Put in this way, we recognize the fallacy of the suggestion, but often it is not detected, and the false impression created is very generally accepted as true teaching. It needs to be recognized and pressed home that so far as God loves sinners it is not the sin in them, but the good, and the potentiality for still more good, that He sees as part of them which He loves. And, on the other hand, that He hates the sin in them, and all that part of them which is identified with it, with a hatred proportionate to His love for the good in them which sin destroys. This must be so, and it is startling how strange we find the statement that there is part of us which God hates, and how much we are inclined to resent it. Yet the language of the Epistles leads one to think that the Apostles would not have felt it strange, and our resentment and surprise is perhaps the measure of our need for its clear re-statement.

Facts should be faced, and, as historically revealed, our Lord's feelings toward men do not appear to have been only, or sometimes even predominantly, those of love. We read of Him looking upon some with anger,[2] and the anger was not wholly loving anger. This last grieves over sin, and yearns over the sinner, and is exemplified in our Lord's outburst over Jerusalem. But in His denunciation of the Scribes and Pharisees a

---

[1] Rom. v. 8.   [2] Mark iii. 5.

note of hostility appears, which is nothing less than the penalty of retributory justice which has ceased to look for repentance. There is in it every moral element of force exerted in punishment.[1] As one reads His reiterated " Woes " upon them, it is not ingenuous to see in them nothing but the sternness of remedial love. There is even a clear note of hostility which reveals that just in proportion as God loves what is good in men, so He hates the evil in them and desires to destroy it. That is to say, God wishes to destroy that part of a man's personality which is sinful. The first man is of the earth earthy, and must die before God can create the new element, and perfect his manhood as He desires by the birth in him of the second man who is the Lord from heaven. The thought that God's love for man is increased *because of* his sins cannot be justified. Man's need may inspire God's action, but cannot deepen His love, which, as we have seen, is built upon very different foundations.

The Good Shepherd went after the sheep that was lost, not simply because something had gone astray, but because it was *His sheep* which had gone astray—that is, because He had lost something possessing qualities He was able to love. If it had been a scorpion or a serpent which had gone astray, He would not have gone after it; and when the wolf came He drove it away rather than sought to attract or tame it. Even infinite love is not all-embracing; it has its limitations.

We conclude, then, that the Persons of the Holy Trinity eternally loved one another because they had eternally been possessed of holiness, and this must therefore be God's fundamental characteristic, of which all His virtues form constituent parts, equally co-eternal with Him, and all essential to the perfection of His being.

[1] *Cf. Church and Nation*, Wm. Temple, p. 18.

Injury is caused to Religion by attributing Undue Prominence to Any of the Divine Attributes.

It is wrong, therefore, to exalt any one of the divine attributes at the cost of another. Such teaching must in the end injure religion, for it is contrary to the truth of God's being. It may well be that the marked tendency in recent times to exalt God's love into a predominating position, at the cost of depreciating His justice and holiness in public esteem in comparison with it, has had an injurious influence upon modern Christianity. The condition of religion in England at the present time supports such a conclusion. In select circles of religion and thought it may be different, but no one can mix with the great mass of people of all classes, and mark their easefulness in the things of God, without having it borne in upon him that their conceptions of God's holiness, and of what it requires of us, has been cheapened. The saying, " Never mind, for God loves sinners," or " for Christ died to save sinners," only too correctly hits off a great mass of common thought which is lying latent, if generally unexpressed; and though it is, of course, due to a miserably mistaken conception of the nature of true love, yet is it not just this apprehension of God's holiness which is needed in order to correct it, and maintain the true balance of reverent devotion ? Where God's holiness and justice are denied an equality of moral rank and independence as compared with His love, the inevitable result in human nature is that the general estimate of love becomes in turn debased to the level of mere benevolence and good-nature, and men lose not only reverence, but even respect, for God. If it were possible to examine into the origin of that sense of sin which accompanies all true conversion, we should probably find that it arises in the first place from a realization of the holiness of God, such as the revelation received by Isaiah at his call to the prophetical office, rather than from a perception of God's love. This comes later to deepen penitence, but a sense of guilt in comparison with God's purity is its first cause.

If there is to be a revival of religion, it seems clear there must be a reformation in the estimate of God's character, if only as to the holiness and exigeant quality of His love. Without anything approaching the harshness of Calvinism, the true balance of His character must be recovered in the mind of the Christian world, and this, not as a mere matter of expediency, but as a duty to religious truth. The doctrine of God's " holy fear " has become unpopular, if not discredited, in the general estimation, but we must try to recover it, and at least preserve such belief as remains in the holiness of His love in all its completeness—in its chaste austerity as well as in its tenderness.

God places Holiness First in revealing His Plan of Salvation.

It cannot be questioned but that this was God's way of training mankind. He revealed Himself to the Jews first as " holiness," and their whole religion was directed to impress upon them the truth that their God was a " holy " God. The fires and commandmants of Sinai; the laws of clean and unclean; the blood of the sin-offerings and other sacrifices; the white robes and lustrations of the priests; the Day of Atonement and the Passover, were all directed to teach the one great lesson—" The Lord your God is holy: be ye therefore holy."

And if some think that all this teaching of the Mosaic law is cancelled by St. John's more recent teaching in the New Testament that God is love, we may note that this cannot cancel the historic order of God's training of mankind, and that while it is nowhere said " God is love, love, love,"[1] yet both in the Old and New Testaments, by the Prophet Isaiah and by St. John himself,

[1] 1 John iv. 8.

the angelic hosts are represented as proclaiming " Holy, holy, holy, is the Lord of hosts, the Lord God Almighty."[1] It is true that the Trisagion is now generally, and rightly, viewed as foreshadowing the doctrine of the Holy Trinity. That is part of its true significance for us, but it could not have been so understood by Isaiah, nor the Jews for whom he wrote. By them, in accordance with the symbolism of the figure three, it would simply be understood to emphasize the perfect, fundamental holiness of God. That is what it would teach and be meant to teach them, as an eternal truth both for Christian and Jew alike. Moreover, all those passages which speak of God as " Light," in Whom is no darkness at all,[2] Whose first creation was light,[3] and Who is the Light of His last creation, the heavenly city;[4] and of our Lord Jesus Christ as the Light of the world,[5] the Sun of righteousness,[6] the true Light which lighteneth every man as he cometh into the world[7]—all these passages teach the same doctrine, that holiness is the fundamental characteristic of God. For the light they speak of is not only nor chiefly intellectual, but especially moral and spiritual: " it bears on the moral nature of God "[8]—i.e., it symbolizes holiness as opposed to the darkness of evil.[9]

When we remember, also, that all that weight of teaching which represents God as the Great Judge of the world is based upon His holiness as the necessary qualification for that office, it becomes clear that the

[1] Isa. vi. 3; Rev. iv. 8. This vision contains a full record of Isaiah's belief about God. He was possessed by " a burning sense of the awful earnestness of life, and the pitilessness of the divine providence in dealing with sin," as a consequence of the holiness and power of God. " The threefold repetition denotes emphasis or intensity (Jer. vii. 4)." See article on " Isaiah " by G. A. Smith in Hastings' *Dictionary of the Bible*, and *The One-Volume Bible Commentary* on the passage.

[2] 1 John i. 5.   [3] Gen. i. 3.   [4] Rev. xxi. 23, xxii. 5.

[5] Isa. lx. 1; Matt. iv. 16; Luke i. 79; John viii. 12, xii. 46

[6] Mal. iv. 2.   [7] John i. 9.

[8] *Cf.* Article " The Apostle John " (T. B. Strong) in Hastings' *Dictionary of the Bible.*

[9] Matt vi. 23; John i. 5, ii. 8-11, iii. 19-21, xii. 35, 36.

evidence centring from various quarters and pointing
to holiness as the fundamental characteristic of His
moral being is very considerable. It seems, therefore,
that the scriptural authority for regarding holiness as
the fundamental characteristic of God is at least as
authoritative as that cited in favour of love holding
this position; and when we come to later times we find
in the Church that the very nomenclature of Christianity is significant of the same doctrine. The accepted
name for God is " The *Holy* Trinity "; His Spirit is the
" *Holy* Spirit " or " *Holy* Ghost "; and the agent by
which He works in the world is " the *Holy* Catholic
Church," the members of which are called to *holiness*.
In agreement with all this He taught His followers to
ask for the realization of God's holiness as the very first
thing to pray for—" Hallowed be Thy Name."

It is true that the words " Our Father " precede this
petition in harmony with our Saviour's teaching upon
the fatherhood of God, which had brought the thought
of His love to the fore with an emphasis making it
practically, though not actually, a new revelation of
the divine character; yet we must not forget that fatherhood itself calls for reverent fear as well as for affection.
In the development of the child's character obedience
is based first upon respect and fear, as many a teacher
has been unwillingly forced by experience to discover.
Dr. Arnold's pupils feared him long before they learnt
to love him, and you could hardly have a more authoritative indication of the way in which moral feeling
naturally develops in human nature. And if it be
true that each individual is a microcosm of the race,
then it may be argued that this instance supports the
old maxim: " The fear of the Lord is the beginning of
wisdom."

But the truth is that this necessary fear of God was
taught during the last century in the wrong way. Only
inferior natures will submit to teaching which tries to
frighten them into obedience, as has been the too

common practice.   All that is best in us resents it and
rises into rebellion against it.   The right way to produce
in men a reverent fear of God is to bring home to them
the realization of His holiness as the basis of His
character.   When this is done there rises automatically
in their hearts a noble fear of offending His goodness,
and the way to a more just appreciation of His love is
opened out.

Some twenty years ago Archbishop Temple said that
the great difficulty religion was suffering under was that
the general standard of morality had become so im-
proved that men did not realize the evil of their commonplace sins, nor, consequently, their need of being saved
from them.   This was and is profoundly true, and the
only remedy for this state of things is to so raise the
conception of God's holiness as to make ordinary
commonplace sins appear in their true vileness, and
Christ's salvation at its true value, for this second is
dependent upon the first.

Again, the Archbishops' recent Committee of Enquiry
into the Evangelistic Work of the Church reports that
" there is to-day little or no conscious sense of sin . . .
and little conscious need of a Saviour," and they suggest
that this is " due to the lack of a positive ideal which
can *through very contrast produce the sense of sin*."   It
goes on to adopt the report from a Midland diocese
which says: " The root cause of the Church's weakness
is a seriously blurred sense of the majesty of God. . . .
The average man has come to believe in a God of
indolent good-nature, a God of no great importance
compared with, *e.g.*, education or modern science in the
practical affairs of life; a God towards whom anyone
can accord an otiose ' belief,' but a God who is simply
not worth being converted to."[1]   Nothing but a realization of the holiness of God can prevent our sense of
His love degenerating into belief in His leniency.

[1] P. 12.   The italics in the earlier quotation are not in the original.

The Interrelations of Holiness and Love.

We cannot realize the greatness of God's love until we realize the repellent guilt of our sins, to which His love nevertheless draws near; and we can only realize this by realizing and comparing it with God's holiness. It was the vision of the thrice-holy God which brought home to Isaiah the realization of his uncleanness (Isa. vi. 5); and it is the holiness of God which made the suffering of His sacrifice in conflict with evil so great and required His love to be perfect in order to undertake and complete His sin-bearing for us.

Love, as we have noticed, is the most persuasive of the forces attracting men to God, and there are two great avenues by which it makes its appeal, general and individual. The great general proofs of God's love are found in the doctrines of the Incarnation and the Cross of Christ; but these present themselves, at any rate at first, as proofs of God's love for the world at large rather than for the individual; as showing that " God so loved the world " rather than that He " so loves me." It is, therefore, to the second avenue that we must look for the realization of God's love for the individual, and this comes through his experience of God's forgiveness of his individual sins.

But until a man has some sense of God's holiness forgiveness does not seem so valuable a thing, or so hard for God to bestow. It seems to be an easy thing, not costing Him much, and therefore a thing to be granted readily if He is at all kindly disposed. Since it costs Him so little, and is so necessary for us, it is almost felt that He ought to forgive, and that no great debt of gratitude is incurred on our side.

So it is not until the nature of God's holiness is grasped, and the consequent difficulty and immensity of the gift of forgiveness, that the greatness of His love is realized. It is only when men perceive, however feebly, God's glorious moral perfection, the " glistering " whiteness of His robes, and the relative moral foulness of sin and God's intense shrinking from it—it is only then that they begin to have some perception of the effort required for their forgiveness, and the strength of the divine love which inspires it. But when a man does begin to feel this, and how, in spite of his constant preference for evil, shown by countless acts of defiant choice persisted in year after year, yet God has not turned from him, but through the years has still pursued and sought him; and how, at the first movement of sincere repentance, in spite of His horror and shrinking from sin, God has not shrunk from contact with his spiritual leprosy, but has welcomed him back to communion, touched him with His Holy Spirit, and even come to abide more fully in his heart in order to fill him with holy thoughts and desires otherwise impossible to him—it is when a man has experienced *this* that he begins to realize that " God is love," and can say, " God loves me." This is the experience which fills a man's heart with gratitude and draws out his answering love.[1]

So it is true of the spiritual history of the individual as well as of the world as a whole, that the realization of God's holiness comes prior to the revelation of His love. God's holiness is the background which shows up His love; and the love of God grows in proportion to our perception of His holiness and abhorrence of sin, and in proportion to our own hatred of it also. The only result of minimizing the requirements of God's holiness is to depreciate the achievements of His love. This explains why conversion is followed by a passionate love of God more often in the case of the notorious sinner than in that of the ordinary man. For the latter, however sincere, finds it more difficult to realize the vileness of his sins. The Cross, then, is the outward and visible sign of what it costs God to forgive. But it is *only* the

---

[1] This is our Lord's own teaching in the incident of Simon the Pharisee. It is those who realize themselves to have been greatly forgiven who greatly love.

outward and visible sign, and we cannot even approach a right conception of the quality of the love it stands for until we have penetrated to the inward struggle and triumph in God's heart which it represents. Herein is love, in that even while we are yet sinners, God loves us.

It follows that to do anything tending to depreciate our conception of God's holiness is to make it more difficult for us to love Him by lessening the achievement of His love for us. If the reaction against the un-balanced teaching upon hell has gone too far, as even those most anxious to base their religious teaching upon love alone are constrained to admit that it has,[1] it is because men have too much subordinated the holiness of God to His love. While a large part of mankind is only capable of being moved by the fear of punishment, it is little use speaking to them of the austerities of a quality of love they cannot apprehend, and especially when God's holiness is represented as occupying a position dominated by love. It is necessary to insist that the requirements of God's holiness and justice cannot be in any way limited by His love.

[1] *Cf. The Incarnation of God*, pp 71, 75.

CHAPTER III

THE NEED FOR RESTATING THE REQUIREMENTS OF DIVINE HOLINESS

WE have noticed that it was probably God's love that set His wisdom and power in motion to work for man's salvation, and His holy hatred of sin which in turn influenced His love; and man, being made in God's likeness, is moved by the same motives. If practical religion wanes it is because these motive powers, as the dynamics of religious life, have weakened or their order been reversed. It is when men hate sin that they want to save others from it. Holiness and love react upon one another as the prime motives to religious missionary effort. Indifference to sin, no less than want of love, is one of the great difficulties in the way of religious work for others, as well as in the pursuit of their own personal religion.

We may notice, also, in this connection that although the temperament of individuals varies, yet on the whole it is true that feelings of love and fear rather than reason are the main avenues by which religion gains entrance into men's lives. Of these, love is the more attractive virtue, yet possibly it is because it operates in our favour, rather than owing to any inherent superiority of its own, that we are inclined to value God's love so much above His other attributes. Possibly in His wider, unbiassed judgment it has little higher place than His purity or His justice.

The Need to revert to God's Order of Revelation.

It cannot be seriously argued that our general standard of spiritual development is so advanced that we can be sure that the fear of God as a motive to religious effort may be safely dispensed with, and lately we have had indications which point in the direction of its necessity, and should make us think seriously. We have been told that at the beginning of the recent National Mission of Repentance and Hope a convention of clergy, called together by their Bishop for the purpose of trying to discover what were the chief defects and needs in the religious life of the nation, after several days spent in meditation and prayer for enlightenment, came to the unanimous conclusion that the chief reason for the decline of religion in modern times was the loss of the sense of the majesty of God. The instinct which made the prophet hide his face when he heard the " Holy, holy, holy," of the angelic worship has died out, and men cannot love God because they have lost, and cannot relearn, their fear of Him.

We need, then, to remind ourselves, as has been courageously said, that " The primary object of the work of Christ was not to display the *love*, but the *righteousness* of God,"[1] even though we see that righteousness working through love to impress the truth upon men. Whatever may be the fundamental characteristic of God, this is unquestionably the order of religious development in humanity; and as it would have been dangerous to clearly reveal to a polytheistic world the doctrine of the Trinity until the truth of the one God had become firmly established, so it is dangerous in an easeful, selfish, and complacent world to build up the doctrine of God's love until the truth of His holiness has become fixed in men's minds as the foundation of His character upon which all religion rests.

We need Milk for Babes as well as Strong Meat for Men.

There has been a tendency to invert this natural order, and to try to develop " holy fear " upon the

[1] See article on " Reconciliation " by A. Adamson in Hastings' *Dictionary of the Bible*.

4

basis of love. And it is true that the Psalmist teaches, " There is forgiveness with Thee that Thou mayest be feared ";[1] but it is also certain that this does not express the earlier so much as the later spiritual experiences of religion. Devotional literature is naturally written by people who are more advanced in spiritual things than the majority of mankind, and who therefore feel the force of and respond to such teaching; but it does not appeal to beginners nor to the great mass of people in the same way. We must remember that a person who has made some advance in spiritual things is liable to find it just as hard to realize the beginner's standpoint as a full-grown man to see things with a child's mind. A boy does not reverence God because He is loving and forgives, but because He is just and all-holy and condemns sin. It needs a certain nobility of character to respond to the appeal of love. The ordinary, commonplace soul is incapable of feeling its force, and the mean man will even take advantage of it if he can. It is therefore doubtful whether the appeal to God's love does not occupy a proportionately larger place in religious thought than we should find justified by its practical effect if it were possible to take a large view of the whole mass of Christian life. Its appeal is dramatic. Once known, it can never be overlooked nor forgotten. Moreover, it is practically effective particularly in the case of " prodigals " who have been living a manifestly irreligious life, and whose conversion, and the cause of it, is therefore readily recognizable; while the far more numerous cases of the great mass of lives moulded from the beginning by the normal influences of the fear and holiness of God are less conspicuous, and so passed by without notice.

These considerations make one feel that such conclusions as that solemnly arrived at by the convention at Malvern ought not readily to be discounted. When, moreover, we meditate upon the lessons of the war,

[1] Ps. cxxx. 4.

we feel that at the present time the wisdom of God, as revealed by the workings of His providence, is directed to turn men's thoughts towards the requirements of His holiness, as a matter of the first importance which has been suffering from undue neglect, rather than to the long-familiar appeals of His love. The first impression created by the war upon the general mind is not that of God's love. Love may be discovered in it, no doubt, but it is not altogether ingenuous to shut out direct primary motives in order to introduce secondary ones.

The Recognition of the Holiness of God needs Re-enforcement.

For these reasons, although feeling strongly how much one stands to lose by possibly alienating some of the sympathetic response which the appeal to love naturally calls out, and though, perhaps, it necessitates throwing oneself across the present main stream of religious thought, yet it seems clear that one should not shrink from presenting the claims of holiness to be considered as at least *a* fundamental, if not *the* fundamental characteristic of God's being. In any case we need to be reminded of its relative importance and that God laid the basis of Christianity as the religion for man's redemption in the Judaic law and ritual, and founded these upon the requirements of holiness. This method is confirmed by our Saviour's own teaching; we may expect, therefore, that no explanation of the Atonement can be satisfactory which ignores this consideration. We need to go back to this divinely revealed order, and remind ourselves that holiness is the feature of God's character which He pressed first and most earnestly upon mankind in their preparation for Christianity.

In considering the remedy for the present state of things, one further thought suggests itself.

It seems likely that the failure to attach due import-

ance to " holiness " in the divine character is not
unconnected with the failure there has been in the
Church, now becoming more generally recognized, to
give the Holy Spirit His rightful place in our religious
thought and worship. The Persons of the Father and
the Son are presented to us under titles which suggest
definite ideas, owing to the similar human family
relationships with which we are familiar. These relationships naturally present to us Love as the ideal spirit
which should animate them, and for this reason it is
comparatively easy for us to grasp the idea of love being
a guiding principle in the life of God. In this way the
predominance given to the Father and Son in the great
mass of ordinary religious thought tends to give love
a predominating position in our religious conceptions,
and the comparative neglect of the Person and doctrine
of the Holy Spirit has had the effect of depreciating our
sense of the importance of holiness in the being of God,
and consequently also in our moral and spiritual esteem.
The remedy is, not in any way to disparage love, but
to elevate and duly honour all the other great virtues
in our religious conceptions as being equally necessary
to the perfection of the divine character; and, above all,
to restore to the Holy Spirit His due place in religious
thought and worship.

PART II

CHAPTER I

FREEWILL AND PUNISHMENT

WE have seen what God is—viz., holiness. We go on
to see what God does, what holy actions result from His
holiness of character. One obvious result must be
active opposition to evil.

The Inherent Antagonism between Good and Evil.

For when we consider the relations of holiness to evil
it is reasonable to suppose that, as healthful life must
everywhere oppose and tend to destroy disease, so
God's holiness must everywhere oppose and tend to
destroy sin. Or, to present the analogy in its more
personal aspect: As a doctor is morally bound to oppose
and treat disease, generally by imposing disagreeable,
restrictive, or even painful measures upon the patient,
so God is morally bound to oppose sin in men, even
though it involves the imposing of penal suffering. The
object in view in both instances is generally remedial,
but not always. Sometimes the disease is beyond
remedy and the patient doomed to death from the first,
but the medical man still continues to treat him, sometimes even by a painful operation in order to save still
greater pain, or by other methods with a view to pre-
venting the disease spreading to others.

53

In the moral sphere similar analogies might be drawn from the law courts and the school; and in both cases the final, extreme measure taken with an offender is separation from society, either by death in the one case, or expulsion in the other. But in all these cases where pain is imposed, even when remedy is impossible and therefore not in view, it would be obviously absurd to talk of its imposition as revenge; and it is equally unjustifiable in God's dealings with sinners to assume, as has been too often done, that any penal suffering which is not remedial must necessarily be of the nature of vengeance. For it is clear that such penal suffering might be at any rate preventive. But, in addition to all this, God's holiness is of such intensity that its relation to sin is more analogous to that of light to darkness, which, by its very existence, it must destroy as a necessary consequence of its essential nature. In the same way it is the very law of holiness, as God's moral nature, to be injurious and antagonistic to sin.

The Permission of Evil, Freewill, and Sin.

Since this is the moral nature of God, and holiness is fundamentally and essentially hostile to evil, the question arises, " Why, then, since God is almighty, does He allow evil to exist ?" Or to go back still farther, as reason requires, we have presented to us the old difficulty as to the origin of evil.

One explanation of this which appears to satisfy reason may be stated as follows: As being perfect holiness, including perfect love, God must desire the very highest possible moral attainment for man. The highest moral attainment conceivable for man is that he should love God perfectly. But love, to be perfect, must be voluntary—i.e., there must be freedom not to love; and to refuse to love God when that is possible, and He desires it, is moral perversion. Opposition to God's will is the antithesis of love, and when persons take immoral advantage of their liberty in this way they commit sin. So, in this indirect way, the origin and permission of evil, and sin itself, is an indirect corollary of the perfect holiness of God.

Whether this be the true explanation or not, freewill is accepted as a fact of personal existence among the overwhelming number of Christians. Our consciousness of it is too strong to be overcome by the most persuasive or correct logic, and it must necessarily be an important factor in determining God's relations towards men. Its importance is, indeed, so great that its further consideration is essential to our subject.

The Principle of Freewill and our Lord's Methods of Work.

When our Lord came to set up the kingdom of God in the hearts of men, there were at least two methods open to Him. He might have employed the extraordinary force of His personality and the influence of His divine miraculous powers to compel the world to recognize His claims. This is what the mass of the Jews wished Him to do. They clamoured for miraculous " signs," and brought pressure to bear to precipitate His declaration of kingship. And in this they were only acting in accordance with the ordinary instincts of human nature, which likes what it calls a " strong lead " and the " clear-cut decisions of a strong personality." Men like to be told plainly what they should do, for this saves the effort of thought and decision for themselves, and it is easier to follow than to lead.

But in making man in His own image and giving him freewill, these powers of thought, decision, and independent action were the very qualities with which God had endowed men in order that they might develop them by the travail of their souls. God set up two great potential ideals for man: (1) That he should choose Him and love Him of his own freewill. Hence the existence of temptation and the possibility and origin of sin. (2) That this love should be not only perfect in its freedom, but also of the highest possible quality, that man should be able to love Him with all his heart, and mind, and soul, and strength, with a love which should enable him to trust Him to the utmost. Hence the trial of death.

These capacities God had bestowed upon man as His most precious gifts. " What shall a man give in exchange for his soul ?"—*i.e.*, for his will, personality, power of choice. When man fell, these gifts of unspeakable value could not be withdrawn or even have their completeness threatened. So the path of an overwhelming demonstration of His personality and powers was closed to our Lord in His struggle against evil, for that would not have left men really free to reject Him. He shut the door on that way of salvation when He rejected the last two temptations in the wilderness; and it is well to remember this when we are being asked by scholars to throw aside one article of our creed after another on the ground that the evidence for their acceptance is insufficient: that it does not amount to a proof, but only to a possibility. Proof and logical demonstrations do not leave men free. They compel intellectual acceptance; and God made men free, and desires their free choice and their free love. We are to live by faith, not by knowledge. For this reason true religion goes, and must go, beyond reason, though not against it. It must contain mysteries.

The other method of operation left open to our Saviour was to win, instead of compel, acceptance by men. " Not by might, nor by power, but by My spirit, saith the Lord of Hosts ";[1] and the spirit of God is the spirit of love. So Jesus set out to develop a claim of love; He went about doing good, and preaching the good news of God's love to win the hearts of men. But this was not enough. In view of the tremendous forces

[1] Zech. iv. 6.

of temptation, and the fatal bias of man's fallen nature towards sin, it was necessary, in order to give man's freewill a fair and equal chance to choose the right, that the appeal of Christ's love should be of a peculiar and sufficient force. To set up a sufficient claim of this kind it was necessary that He should not only devote His life to men, but also give it for them. Only in this way could His appeal be of sufficient cogency to meet the needs of His own and all future generations. So the Cross was set up as God's magnet, which should not compel, but win; which should not drive, but draw all men unto Him (John xii. 32). No doubt there were other considerations which also influenced Omniscient Wisdom in deciding upon this plan of man's salvation;[1] but it appears that such considerations as these must have had some influence in God's decisions, and they account in some degree for our Saviour's statement: "The Son of Man *must suffer* many things." This brings us back to the point that, human nature being constituted as it is, men can only be won from sin to God by the self-sacrifice of those who act for Him towards them. In the salvation of men suffering is a necessary element, there is a spiritual law of δεῖ παθεῖν.

Freewill and Moral Law.

One necessary consequence of freewill in a world of order, though at first sight it may appear to be a contradiction of it, is the punishment of sin. The two words forming the familiar phrase "law and order" have not come together by chance. The two things they stand for are closely associated by nature. "Order" means the relation of things to one another in a regular arrangement, each having a recognized position; and

---

[1] For instance, there are the great considerations explained in Part I. dealing with the requirements of Divine Holiness, and also those of human need summarized on pp. 147-149. It is by no means meant to imply that the subjective appeal of the Cross is of greater value than its objective achievements. There is room for both, and all have their place in God's plan.

" law " means the flow of cause and effect in regular sequence. The idea of regularity is common to both; and this orderliness or reign of law which the phrase describes is the difference between chaos and rational management, and as such is a prevailing phenomenon throughout creation. It has been used to prove the existence of a personal Creator, and we base upon it the belief that God is a God of order.

God must rule either by law or chance. If He alternates according to some plan, then He is still ruling by law. If He alternates independently of any plan, then He rules no longer by law, but by chance, for the very essence of law is regularity of action. Any break is inconsistent with the principle of law. The operation of secondary laws may indeed be affected by primary laws, as when personal will interposes an umbrella between its owner and the fall of raindrops. But this also is the operation of law, and is " in order." It is a regular sequence of cause and effect under God's providence. God rules by law.

Law and Penal Suffering.

But although this is a fundamental principle of God's nature, He has, as we have already noticed, also bestowed upon man the gift of " freewill," and this contemplates the possibility of the breaking of His moral and spiritual laws by men in a way involving defiance of the whole creative scheme as expressive of the divine character.

Law and the lawgiver are honoured by the observance of law and dishonoured by its breach, and man is the only thing in material creation which can and does defy God's rule and dishonour His laws in this way. As this defiance of law is quite contrary to God's economy, it is impossible either to allow or ignore it, and the question arises, How is the principle of law to be maintained in association with the existence of human freewill ? for to rescind either would be for God to deny or dishonour His own nature. This problem is the main, underlying factor conditioning man's relation to God, and the only possible answer to it is found in the punishment of sin. For punishment, whilst permitting the breach of law where freewill chooses to break it, does so only under protest and at a cost; and this cost in suffering is a recognition of, and pays homage to, the rightful supremacy of the law which has been broken.

Punishment the Corollary of Freewill.

It safeguards its majesty in spite of the defiance of will, and it is the best safeguard conceivable. This controlling law, therefore, has added to the others that the breaking of God's will expressed in His moral and spiritual laws shall be followed by penal suffering and loss. Such suffering confirms the voice of conscience in proclaiming that law ought to reign, and therefore, when a man brings himself to acquiesce in punishment, it is an acknowledgment that the law he has broken ought to have been observed.

Since this is the best way, in view of man's freewill, by which the sovereign right of law can be maintained, it is correct to say that law can only exist by penalty and that punishment is a necessary corollary to freewill. Outside the sphere of personality the rule of punishment is simply part of the law of cause and effect.

Penal suffering inflicted from this motive is " vindicative," and although Dr. Moberly attaches no ethical value to punishment of this kind, yet he is forced to recognize its existence (e.g., in the case of the "tigerman") in the divine economy. And it should be noted that the very fact of its existence is a sufficient proof in itself that this kind of punishment has real moral value, for a loving God would not permit any suffering unless required for an adequate purpose.

In this way suffering and punishment arise as the inevitable result of the clash of freewill with God's holiness in a world of law and order, in spite of, or, indeed, because of, His perfect love; and it seems possible that this punishment may even become a permanent condition—*i.e.*, everlasting punishment.

Everlasting Punishment : Is Hell Remedial ?

This last, however, is questioned. For the view has been taken that even the punishment of hell is remedial, and therefore only age-long. It has been said: " God, having tried all other appeals, at last gives men over to sin; that they may see its awfulness and effect, and therefore turn from it. The punishment of hell is always remedial in its purpose so far as our experience goes." And again: " . . . He [*i.e.*, God] is obliged at last to let them depart from His face—to hell—because this is what they have chosen. But He gives them thus up to a reprobate mind (Rom i. 28) that they may realize at last, as the prodigal son did, how empty and appalling life is without God; and meanwhile His whole heart goes on yearning for them."[1] This last assertion suggests the question whether, if a soul attains " a condition of evil unmixed with good "[2]—*i.e.*, wholly evil—God can love it; whether He can love anything wholly evil; that is, whether God, being holy, can love pure evil. It is at least questionable; but apart from this the writer is clearly contemplating a condition of existence under which the balance of freewill at present obtaining would be upset, and greater pressure would be brought to bear through penal suffering than under present conditions, in order to decide souls to turn from sin to God. Though elsewhere the idea of appealing to men's self-love and fear of punishment is deprecated by this author, as tending to make men worse rather than better,[3] yet this conception of the object of the punishment of hell is really nothing else, and therefore equally immoral or non-moral. It is also difficult to see how, when the presence of the Holy Ghost within a man has

[1] *The Incarnation of God*, p. 307.   [2] *Ibid.*, p. 307.
[3] *Ibid.*, p. 311.

been wholly quenched, so that a soul's condition is one of " unmixed evil," there can be anything left capable of desiring good in the personality. It appears more probable that nothing but furious hatred and rebellion can remain, a " wailing and gnashing of teeth," and a worm that " dieth not."[1]

A Remedial Hell would seem to involve an Inferior Heaven.

But however this might be, what is clearly contemplated is a condition under which by " appalling " suffering greater pressure would be brought to turn souls from evil to God than exists under the present dispensation; and if this be so, then it is clear that the balance of temptations to sin and inducements to holiness which at present obtains, and leaves us with real freedom to choose or neglect God, would be upset, and a special bias given in the right direction.   Under these conditions it is clear that the will would not be so wholly free as it is now, and though a condition might be attained which would save men from eternal separation from God, yet there would be a modification of God's highest hopes for such souls, and the standard of holiness, of perfectly free love of God, to which it is possible for men under the present conditions to attain in heaven, would be closed to them for ever.   It would be " too late."

Universalism Uncertain.

If, in order to maintain the balance of freewill, the increased penal suffering were met by increased force of temptation, there is no reason to suppose, but rather the opposite, that there would be any change in the choice of will already once made, and the process might be continued indefinitely.

But whatever the truth as to everlasting punishment

[1] Mark ix. 48.

or universalism may be, it is this requirement of love itself, for man to attain the very best through freewill, which brings with it its own disappointment in the existence of sin and suffering. Everywhere we are reminded of St. Augustine's profound saying that things exist by their opposites. Ranged against God and goodness we have Satan and evil; against freedom, punishment; against pleasure, suffering; against life in God's presence, the death of separation from Him; against love, hate. Nothing is found in triumphant isolation, and we ask whether this is an everlasting law of existence, but can find no answer.

Penal Suffering as a Law to counterbalance Evil Inclination.

Our reflections upon freewill and punishment have, however, brought to view a possible law of existence which appears to be of considerable importance in helping us to find an explanation for many of the sorrows of life. We have been led to consider the possibility of a balance between the force of temptation on the one hand and the weight of suffering which follows sin on the other. It is unquestionable that these two things exist as facts of experience, and also that their influences upon the decisions of freewill with regard to right and wrong are mutually antagonistic. It does not seem unreasonable, therefore, to suppose that the law of penal suffering for sin is God's provision for the purpose of counteracting the tendency of our fallen nature towards evil and maintaining the balance of freewill. If we can accept this view, such suffering stands revealed as the outcome of God's love as well as the natural reaction of His holiness against evil, and we find the motives of love and retribution in alliance in requiring penal suffering. Moreover, since such a law would be preventive in its nature rather than restorative, it is clear that its enforcement would have to be inviolable in order to produce its required effect, since this is depen-

dent upon the sense of inevitableness. All this makes
in the direction of bringing the laws of God's moral rule
into line with His other laws of nature in the certainty
of their operation.[1]

[1] Bishop Gore's teaching on this point in his recent book, *The Religion
of the Church*, may be noted here. He argues that (1) universalism,
though supported by some early Christian authorities, is flatly, plainly
contrary to the language used by our Lord and in the New Testament
generally. That (2) by excluding universalism we are not absolutely
shut up by biblical language into the almost intolerable belief in
unending conscious torment for the lost. Final moral ruin may involve
such a dissolution of personality as would carry with it a cessation of
personal consciousness. See pp. 91, 92.

CHAPTER II

THE NATURE AND ETHICS OF PUNISHMENT

The Tendency to question the Ethics of Divine Punishment.

THE word " punishment " suggests at once the thought of the dislike which lately has been increasingly shown to bringing it into any connection at all with Christ's atoning sacrifice. Canon Wilson has written that " it is not only permissible, but obligatory for us gradually to eliminate from our thought of the reconciling work of Christ every trace of expiation or penalty except as illustrations such as might be given in parables and metaphors ";[1] and another writer on the Atonement says: " It is most misleading to speak of the retributive wrath of God. That implies that He wants an equivalent in punishment for the sins of sinners ";[2] and again: " God did not require a satisfaction or propitiatory sacrifice for the sins of men to appease His wrath in any sense which is connected with our notion of desiring vengeance or satisfaction for injuries which are done to us."[3]

Reasons for this Tendency : Punishment and Vengeance.

The line of thought which these quotations illustrate is very general, and is due to the feeling that any inflicting of punishment can only be inspired by a desire for retaliation or vengeful retribution. Dr. Moberly, in his work on the Atonement, discusses

---

[1] *The Gospel of the Atonement*, p. 91.
[2] E. L. Strong, *The Incarnation of God*, p. 61.
[3] *The Incarnation of God*, p. 58.

remedial punishment as if it were the only alternative to this.   What might be required in the way of penal suffering by divine love, for instance, on other than remedial grounds, is not considered by him; and his influence has done much to determine the course of recent views upon the Atonement, so that this view has often been assumed to be unquestionable.[1]   As a result a restricted view has been taken of the subject; and on the assumption that infinite love must always love all souls there is a logical tendency towards belief in universalism.

Difficulty in reconciling the Claims of Justice and Love.

This tendency to connect any thought of punishment other than remedial with ideas of retaliation is strengthened by the difficulty found in reconciling the apparently rival claims of justice and love, and partly by our deep sense of the imperfection of human justice.   In human administration every criminal sentenced to punishment has received wrongs from society as well as inflicted them, though, maybe, his judges can take no notice of nor make allowance for the former.   Therefore, only a rough approximation to justice is humanly possible, and for this reason it is suspect and we are disinclined to press its claims.

God's Justice and Man's not Comparable.

But with God this is not so.   His justice is perfect, and as part of His character, and a constituent element in holiness, its requirements have a moral claim to be satisfied.   It is not enough to give it the bad name of " forensic morality," or speak of " legal transactionalism," or " substitutionalism," and then dismiss justice as a thing unworthy of consideration in connection with the Atonement.   True justice is not to be confounded with " legalism," which, as we know, is sometimes

[1] For instance, Strong says plainly that there is no other alternative (pp. 218, 301).

extremely unjust; and in discussing God's dealings with men what we have to do with is not man-made law, but divine justice.

Some False Assumptions : Retribution and Quantitative Punishment.

Another reason why many people object to the word " punishment " in connection with God's rule is that it has been so generally associated not only with ideas of vengeance, as we have already noticed, but also with retribution and " quantitative punishment." As a consequence, when God's punishment of sinners is spoken of, men are apt to feel that such a thing is unworthy of God, and to ask: " Do you, then, believe that God takes pleasure in seeing sinners suffer, and desires to see so much suffering inflicted in punishment for so much sin ?" And the same kind of ideas have become attached to the word " satisfaction " in connection with the Atonement.

But there is no justification for these ideas. The assumption is natural, but mistaken, that all antagonisms are inspired by a spirit of vengeance, and therefore, for example, that justice must wish to avenge itself upon wrong. But a very little thought shows how unfounded such an assumption is. Water does not hate fire, although it extinguishes it; and one person may be opposed to another even in active hostility without any feeling of hatred or vengeance. When the Duke of Wellington was asked by the Captain of a battery to allow a gun to be aimed at Napoleon, who had accidentally come within range, he said: " No; Generals do not fight one another." In the same way a judge is not expected to be actuated by feelings of personal hatred towards the criminal he condemns, and the penalties which God's moral nature requires Him to enforce in dealing with human sin may be supposed to give Him no more pleasure than a humane judge feels in condemning a murderer to death, or a General in ordering a deserter to be shot. It is really no more justifiable to assume that one gives pleasure than the other, but duty, whether divine or human, must be fulfilled. Divine love is not free to neglect the duties of justice.

Again, the idea of quantitative punishment has arisen from the requirements of human law courts; but it does not apply to those of God's holiness, where sin is infinite, and the need is simply to express the fact that the divine nature is opposed to sin. In any particular punishment, no doubt, there is also the further remedial object of inducing penitence in the sinner, and with this aim in view we can conceive the various divine characteristics co-operating, as it were, in accordance with the requirements of each—God's holiness simply requiring that sin should suffer as an expression of His moral character; His purity that the suffering should include separation from Himself; His love demanding that it should be remedial in its character; and His justice requiring reparation in the way to be considered later.

Retributory Punishment not the Only Alternative to Remedial.

If it were otherwise, or if retaliation were indeed the only alternative to remedial punishment, and the only motive inspiring all other penal suffering, the shrinking we have noticed would be more than justified; but as things are this is not so. To take the view that any punishment other than remedial is necessarily a form of vengeance or retributory tit-for-tat, the result of a desire for an " equivalent in punishment," is, to say the least, inadequate. A little reflection reveals other aspects which may include no element of retribution at all, nor anything at all questionable from the moral point of view. Rather, as we think over things, we come to see that the punishment of sinners may be even a necessary expression of holiness.

Punishment is the Operation of Law, but Personal, not Mechanical Law.

What, then, is punishment ? We have seen it as the result of a law instituted to balance the disorder otherwise introduced into the world as a result of God's gift of freewill. But it is not *only* law—at any rate, not of merely mechanical, impersonal sequence. It is more than that, yet the full truth may usefully be approached from that direction.

There are many who shrink from the use of the word " punishment " in connection with God's relations to sinners, but feel strongly the attraction of that mode of viewing existence which sees it as a sequence of orderly events; and these people would generally be willing to accept penal suffering in consequence of sin as part of the universal reign of law. This way of looking at the question would be a help to them, and as a matter of fact punishment may rightly be regarded as an orderly sequence of moral cause and effect determined by the higher laws of personality. If we regard natural law in this way, as operating under the supreme laws of divine personality, then, since good actions are in harmony with God's scheme of things and of life, whilst evil actions are in conflict with them, the natural consequences of good actions will be things that, by adding to it, enrich life—*i.e.*, rewards; and the natural consequences of evil actions things that impoverish life and so cause suffering—*i.e.*, punishments. In this way it is clear that the results of good and bad actions have nothing artificial about them. They are not arbitrary fiats of God's will, but perfectly natural consequences flowing from the fundamental facts of His nature.

As the Natural Operation of Moral and Spiritual Law, Punishment cannot be readily revoked.

In human administration the rewards and punishments dealt out have a considerable degree of artificiality about them, because they inevitably are not the natural outcome of the action concerned. Where God sends an illness, a judge can only impose a fine or imprisonment as the penalty of vice. In the working of Divine Providence punishments are the natural consequences resulting from the operation of divine law, and for God to alter these natural consequences would be for Him to some extent to contradict Himself and reverse His own laws. It would be something in the nature of a miracle. It might be done in response to the requirements of some higher law which absorbs the lower, but only in this way.

Therefore, unless some favourable preventive force be interposed, we may always be sure our sin will find us out. In other words, the penalty of suffering *must* follow sin, unless some preventive cause be interposed. Punishment, viewed from this point, is simply " order " in the moral and spiritual spheres. It is the operation of law in these higher spheres manifesting itself in lower planes of life, and this suggests another obstacle to the free forgiveness of sin. For just in the same way as it is recognized that God does not interfere with the operation of His laws in material nature in order to prevent accidents because that would be contrary to the constitution of His being as a God of order, so also would it be equally contrary to His nature to abrogate the laws of punishment in the moral and spiritual spheres.

It is such considerations as these, enforced by the inevitableness of the penalties following the violation of natural law as indicating the divine mentality, and by our recognition of the fact that, however terrible the immediate consequences may be, yet it is on the whole a benefit to humanity that the inviolability of natural law should be maintained—it is such considerations as these which make us question whether it is true that " it is not only permissible, but even obligatory, for us gradually to eliminate from our thought of the reconciling work of Christ every trace of expiation or penalty, except as illustrations such as might be given in parables and metaphors."[1] We feel that the evidence as a whole points to a different conclusion, and that the punishment of sin is probably as much a necessary consequence of God's justice as salvation is the outcome of His love, and equally deserves our appreciation. Justice and love are equally attributes of His character, and to disparage the former in comparison with the latter, whilst natural to us as tending in our favour and in accord with the spirit of the age, is really indefensible. Each is necessary to the perfection of the divine character.

Instinct supports Punishment as being Just.

The fact that opposition to evil in man is a law of God's being is perhaps the best explanation of the instinct within us that wrong-doing should be punished, which is commonly spoken of, though perhaps not quite correctly, as the " sense of justice "—that ineradicable instinct that a man should get his deserts whether of penalty or reward, which is so strong in the fresh, unspoilt instincts of children. Quite apart from any consideration of moral benefit, a right-minded boy who has done wrong feels that he deserves to suffer, and as a rule this instinct is sufficiently strong to overcome all his natural prejudices in the other direction.

In the case of the penitent thief we have perhaps the best-known instance of the acknowledgment of the righteousness of punishment, which in his case could hardly have been felt as remedial. When, standing on the brink of eternity, he said that the death he was suffering was only the due reward of his deeds, there was in that acknowledgment and in the feeling it arose from something true and right which won for him the immediate sentence of forgiveness. His acknowledgment was the only reparation he could make for his

---

[1] Wilson, *The Gospel of the Atonement*, p. 94.

breaking of the divine law; and, combined with his contrition, it was accepted as completing the reparation of perfect obedience to God's will which his Saviour was offering at his side. Our dues are what we ought to get, and the penitent thief's acknowledgment amounted to no less than an assertion that sin ought to be punished. That this feeling in sinners is not due to any unconscious remedial instincts they may possess is proved by the fact that even where, in any particular case, there can be no chance of amendment being brought about, we feel punishment to be no less right nor just on that account. Its morality does not depend upon its remedial effects, but simply upon its harmony with the whole order of existence as expressing God's moral law.

The relation of punishment to justice and the duty of enforcing it have been well expressed by the author of *Watchman, What of the Night?* He says: " If the justice of God is to be vindicated upon earth, it means that punishment must be inflicted upon evil-doers— because they deserve it. The idea of punishment according to deserts is not popular now. We seem to think only of bringing the evil-doer to a better mind. That is, of course, an end of which we must never lose sight, and we are not completely successful if we fail to gain it. But we must not forget as Christians we have another duty as well. We have not only to bring the evil-doer to a better mind if we can: we have also to see that he is punished as he deserves. There can be no talk of restoration until that has happened. It may often be beyond our power to effect his conversion. It is very seldom beyond our power to punish him adequately, and the distasteful nature of the duty is no excuse for declining it. . . . Forgiveness means restoration after the penalty for the wrong done has been fully borne. Otherwise justice is not satisfied."[1]

We have here expressed by an author whose thought-

[1] Pp. 216, 217.

ful writing has won wide acceptance the deep-seated instinct that sin ought to be punished even by ourselves, sinful as we are, and therefore much more by omniscient and all-holy God. As the prevailing spirit of false humanitarianism dies away, and men come to recover, perhaps under the experience and revelations of German " frightfulness," what the true nature and malignant devilishness of evil really is, it is probable that the moral duty of just punishment will become increasingly evident. In this connection it has been said, " Some kinds of peacemaking are worse than fighting, because they involve a sacrifice of justice ";[1] and we feel in the same way that a peace between God and the sinner bought at a similar price would be equally immoral, and that to postulate it as necessary is to assume a bankruptcy of the divine resources which cannot be justified.

The connection between the great war and the sins of materialism, greed, and selfish ambition is so clear that none can deny that the suffering caused represents the penal consequences of sin. The thunder of the cannon has proclaimed to the world the irrevocable laws that " the wages of sin is death,"[2] and " sin, when it is completed, bringeth forth death."[3] Nor can it be denied that this operation of law has taken place under the providence—that is, with the permission—of God, and that the lesson thus taught is not one of gentleness but of severity.

That is to say, we have to admit that at the present time in the world's history God's wisdom judges that men need to be taught the sternness of His love rather than its gentleness. This reflection affords matter for serious thought, and seems to suggest what ought to be the guiding principle dominating the policy of our religious leaders at the present time. Surely it will be the Church's wisdom at this crisis in our religious

---

[1] *Church Times*, August 2, 1918.   [2] Rom. vi. 23.
[3] Jas. i. 15 (R.V.)

history to accept this guidance, and co-operate with God by doing what we can to concentrate men's thoughts upon the sterner aspects of the Christian religion ! We must preach over again the immutable law of God's holiness, that men may come to value His Gospel.

Definition of Punishment.

What else is punishment besides being the operation of law ? Webster defines it as " Any pain or suffering inflicted on a person for a crime or offence by the authority to which the offender is subject, either by the constitution of God or of civil society." This is in harmony with what we have already noted to the effect that punishment is a personal thing, with a personal origin, and directed against personal breaches of the law. It is not the outcome of merely impersonal forces or laws, or of accidental circumstances. A man who breathes in a microbe while going about his proper occupation, and apart from any carelessness, catches an illness, or suffers some accident as the result of the operation of natural laws, cannot be said to be "punished," except in so far as such suffering is attributed to God as its personal cause and in response to wrong-doing.

Punishment, then, being of the nature of suffering personally inflicted, its morality will depend upon the motive inspiring it. For nothing else but a good object can justify the infliction of pain.

Motives of Punishment.

Among common motives for punishment we may note five chief ones.

(1) Vengeance.

In some cases the motive may be of the nature of vengeance or retaliation, even though it be inflicted by lawful authority. In these instances the motive is, to say the least, non-moral, and probably definitely immoral, for no good purpose is in view. Inflicted by men, it is difficult to see how retaliation can be other than immoral, as being cruel. Of course, even this kind of punishment might do good to the sufferer. No doubt it often does, but this does not in any way excuse the inflicter of it. It only shows that God can bring good out of evil. Infliction of punishment of this kind is, of course, unthinkable in connection with God.

(2) *Reparation or Restitution—the Claim of Justice.*

A second object in punishment may be to obtain reparation or restitution from the offender for injury he has caused to another. It is clearly wrong that the innocent should continue to suffer loss if it can be made good. Mere common justice, therefore, demands compensation for injury, and if any code of law were directed so exclusively to the reclamation of criminals as to employ remedial measures at the cost of failure to obtain restitution for injury done, its methods would represent a failure rather than a triumph of justice. The enforcement of restitution is a prior duty to the reclamation of a wrong-doer. In fact, restitution is part of his reclamation, for he is not reclaimed until he has made what reparation he can. It is not allowable in morality to wink at the sufferings of one in order to obtain benefit for another, or to permit wrong that good may come of it. The duty of justice on this point is quite clear, and any legal code which denied it would be a prostitution of justice.

Yet one constantly finds, even in religious and moral matters of this kind, that one is forced to insist upon the right of justice to be heard. Dr. Moberly, for instance, in considering the question of punishment, restricts himself almost entirely to the effect of punishment upon the culprit, without any attempt to consider the claims his victim has upon justice for reparation. If he had chosen such crimes as theft or libel by which to illustrate his argument instead of murder, where reparation to the victim is clearly impossible, the question of reparation and the consequent penal suffering of the criminal in making it would almost certainly have suggested itself. But, as it is, all this side of justice is entirely overlooked, and moral punishment comes to mean no more than the " restorative treatment of the criminal "; while all other forms of penalty are connected with ideas of vengeance, as if the rightful claims of the injured party to just restitution had been overlooked in the yearning love and interest excited for the sinner. That there is something unbalanced and wrong in this is clear when we remember how decisive is the voice of conscience in insisting upon the duty of making restoration so far as possible to anyone we have injured. The frequent payment of conscience-money is an illustration of this. The decision of Zacchæus to make a fourfold restitution is a striking instance of it, and every instructed Christian is taught that restitution is a necessary part of true repentance. To forget this, and, moreover, to overlook the interests of the many in that of the individual, is an imperfect morality; and what is required of perfect righteousness is that, if the claims of mercy and justice are in conflict, they should somehow be reconciled, rather than that the one should be satisfied at the expense of the other. In any case, with regard to God, His virtues cannot be intermittent: His mercy and justice cannot alternate. He must be just and merciful always, rather than just at one time and merciful at another. In being merciful He must at the same time be just, and in justice He must also be merciful: merciful in punishment as well as just in forgiving. Mercy and truth must meet together,[1] and both be satisfied. That is much better than erasing one or the other from the tablets of divine morality. Clearly, the great problem presented by man's sin cannot be solved by ignoring the claims of justice. That would not be absolute, perfect holiness, and imperfect morality can have no place in God's being.

[1] Ps. lxxxv. 10.

(3) *To Express the Law.*

A third reason for punishment arises from the necessity of expressing the law. The quip that " laws are made to be broken " is, of course, the direct opposite to the sober truth, which is that laws cease to be laws if not observed. They become " exceptions." Moreover, experience proves that it is worse than useless and morally injurious to make rules unless they are kept. That is true even of artificial, man-made law, and as divine law is simply the expression in practice of the divine nature it is still more true of it. It is essential to the consistency and truth of God's character, and the penalties which follow the breaking of it are simply the consequences of God being what He is. Although many people prefer to speak of the " consequences of breaking moral and spiritual laws," this is, as we have seen, really only another name for the divine punishment of sin. For since these laws are simply the expression of God's will, it is not really possible to distinguish between " natural consequences " and " divine punishments."

Under any system of rational government of the universe where holiness is omnipotent it is clear that sin—*i.e.*, personal rebellion against holiness—must involve either suffering or the painless extinction of the sinner as the two only reasonable alternatives. And even in the latter case there would be loss of happiness, which in the case of conscious beings sensible of their loss would in itself be a form of suffering. It is therefore impossible to avoid the conclusion that so long as God is holy, sin must necessarily involve suffering as an inevitable expression and corollary of the divine character.

In his pamphlet on the League of Nations Viscount Grey says that " ' Learn . . . or suffer ' is the rule of life." There is, however, a gap in his statement, and, strictly speaking, he means " Learn, and practice what you learn, or suffer "—that is to say that " obey or

suffer is the rule of life." It is Bacon's discovery that
the way to rule Nature is to obey her, presented from
another point of view. Regarded in this way punishment is no more than part of the law; and as law is
identified with God's will, is " alive in Him," it is a
part of divine consistency. It is perhaps more true to
say of this kind of punishment that it is simply a consequence than that it has any ulterior object. So far
as it has an object, it is simply to fulfil God's nature.

(4) *To Reclaim the Sinner—the Remedial Motive.*

The next object we may notice as a right one in
punishment is the moral and spiritual benefit of the
offender. The ethical character of this " remedial "
punishment is everywhere admitted, and so need not
be discussed here. Some have seemed to regard it as
the only justifiable motive in punishment. Dr. Moberly
has based his theory of the Atonement upon this view,
arguing that all that is necessary for the forgiveness of
sin is penitential sorrow, and that the only justification
for punishment is that it assists in producing it: " All
our punishment (*i.e.*, God's punishment of us) has really
the disciplinary motive and meaning."[1] As this form
of punishment is so generally recognized, it needs no
further comment, and we can pass on to the last kind
of punishment needing notice—vindicative punishment.

(5) *To Support or Vindicate the Law in the Public Eye.*

The object of vindicative punishment is to assert the
majesty of the law—that is, to bring home to men the
realization of the existence and supremacy of law, and
confirm its claim to rule. It does this by proclaiming
through penal suffering the Mosaic teaching, " Be sure
your sin will find you out." As compared with remedial
punishment, it is preventive.

[1] *Atonement and Personality*, pp. 23, 24; *cf.* also the whole chapter
on Punishment.

The Moral Value of Vindicative Punishment.

The moral value of this kind of punishment has been questioned in recent years, and in view of the importance of the subject it deserves careful consideration.

Dr. Temple in the Bishop Paddock Lectures for 1914-15 says: " But how are you, as a matter of fact, to attack the evil will ? The mere infliction of penalty will not of necessity achieve this goal at all. We know it is very seriously debated whether our whole system of punishment in the civilized States of to-day has any really moral effect—at least, upon those who fall under its most severe penalties. Probably most convicts leave prison worse men than they entered. For if a man is below a certain level in moral attainment, pain, far from purifying, only brutalizes and coarsens."[1]

This is very clear, but the effect is weakened when, with regard to children's moral development, he goes on to argue: " Here merely to keep forcibly within bounds the development of certain impulses, which tend to grow out of proportion to the proper economy and harmony of nature, may indirectly have the effect of preserving that harmony, and thus develop genuine virtue in the soul. And again, with those whose characters are relatively formed, the direct restraint, for example, of State action may have positive moral value, inasmuch as it is the expression of the moral judgment of Society."[2] And again: " The fact that certain actions would involve us in State penalty most undoubtedly does keep all of us from indulging in those actions. . . . We should perhaps usually pay for our places in the train even if there were no ticket-inspector; still, the existence of the inspector just clinches the matter. The possibility of the penalty as a matter of fact helps to maintain our general, permanent, and deliberate purpose of honesty . . . helping us to live

[1] *The Church and Nation,* p. 65.   [2] *Ibid.,* p. 66.

up to our purpose, or, in other words . . . increasing our real freedom."[1]

In these instances Dr. Temple appears to argue that force is only morally useful to help the immature characters of children, and those who are on the whole inclined to do right, not to give way to momentary temptation, while it is useless in dealing with hardened sinners. But elsewhere he seems to think it useful in these cases also: " Our Lord's example . . . shows us that the use of force is permissible in dealing with those who are so case-hardened that the appeal of love can never reach them until their present state of mind is broken up. . . . Now, in our Lord's denunciation of the Pharisees, in those words which are thrown burning and smashing into the self-complacent contentments of those upholders of tradition, there is every moral quality of force and violence."[2] So, also, he argues that force may be rightly employed by the Church: " Supposing the use of force as discipline may be of advantage to moral development (and up to a certain point I am sure it may) . . . the Church will be right to do what is best for the character of those for whom it is concerned;"[3] and illustrates his point by the right of a congregation forcibly to remove a convert who has been temporarily excluded from public worship as a penance.

On the whole, then, there does not seem sufficient ground here for upsetting the claim that punishment is of assistance in supporting the law. It seems to come to little more than a doubt whether punishment does any good to confirmed criminals, while the general usefulness of it is allowed.

In Addition to the Remedial Motive, three other of these Motives are definitely Moral in Character.

We have now reviewed some of the chief motives of punishment, which may be classified as retributory,

---

[1] *The Church and Nation*, pp. 74, 75.   [2] *Ibid.*, pp. 17, 18.
[3] *Ibid.*, p. 168.

expressive or resultant, compensative, remedial, and vindicative. Of these five, the last four are even necessary to our conception of God as a righteous ruler of the world, and are not in any way opposed to the requirements of love. Indeed, they are either in full harmony with those requirements—*e.g.*, compensative and expressive punishment—or they represent activities actually required by love for the welfare of mankind, such as the infliction of remedial and vindicative penalties. It is not, therefore, correct to argue as if the only alternative to remedial punishment were that of vengeance.

PART III

THE REQUIREMENTS OF DIVINE HOLINESS AND REASON

CHAPTER I

HOLINESS REQUIRES FULL MORAL EXPRESSION

HAVING now seen that punishment is not necessarily vindictive, nor even non-moral, but may be a positive moral duty, we may go on to consider what Divine Holiness, so far as we can judge, requires in order to make the remission of it and forgiveness a morally righteous thing, remembering always that the two things are distinct, and that the first does not and should not necessarily follow the second. And with regard to the first, since sin, as we have seen, is moral evil in persons, the question we have to consider is, What does Divine Holiness require with regard to sinners for the remission of penalties deserved ?

Holiness requires the Expression of Hostility to Sin.

We answer that in the first place it requires that its inherent hostility to sin should be expressed. In extending forgiveness to sinners, God, as holiness impersonated, must not be untrue to Himself and the moral law of His being. Any act of forgiveness must not be inconsistent with the moral perfection of His character, which requires that He should oppose sin; and therefore any forgiveness must be under such conditions that it in no way restricts the expression of that antagonism. Bearing in mind the clear, recognized difference between forgiveness and remission of penalty, and that the former by no means necessarily involves the latter, this suggests that, though the sinner be forgiven, God will still find it necessary to express His hostility to sin by somehow enforcing the penalty. For God cannot be neutral. Goodness cannot condone evil. In moral matters neutrality is pusillanimity; it is weakness; it is to take up a non-moral attitude; it is to cease to be good on the positive side. So God must take sides, and His holiness must discriminate between right and wrong by showing approval and disapproval in a practical manner. He cannot treat goodness as if it were evil, nor evil as if it were good; and He is therefore under an obligation to express Himself by support or opposition. For no all-powerful ruler can stand by and merely ignore wrong, or see evil done or injuries inflicted which he could prevent, without becoming practically an accomplice in the wrong. Just as a medical man must oppose disease, the power of life struggle against death, light dispel darkness, so also must right attack wrong and God oppose sin. God must react against sin when man's evil will brings it into His presence.

The Obligation to Oppose Wrong is binding in Proportion to its Difficulty and the Greatness of the Evil.

The great war showed the law of hostility between right and wrong to have a wide range, applying to national as well as individual life, and covering every side of it, material, moral, and spiritual. It showed also, as witness the great response made to the call for voluntary service, both civil and military, that it has moral binding force in proportion to the greatness of the evil threatened—*i.e.*, that there is a moral obligation resting upon everyone to prevent or cure evil so far as lies within his power. To fail to make the necessary effort is a moral neglect; to make it and fail of success proves lack of power. If the effort involves self-sacrifice, the moral claim is in some sort all the more binding, for the duty is the more likely to be omitted by others, and the evil remains unremedied. In view of the further consideration that right is not supreme if evil finally triumphs, it seems clear that Almighty God could not stand by and let sin, the greatest of all evils, conquer humanity. And if this could only be prevented by the sacrifice of Himself, He was all the more morally bound to pay the necessary price, since He alone could do so. Regarded from this point of view, the crucifixion was not the result of God's arbitrary decision to punish someone for sin, but His inevitable response to the law of His own holiness which makes it impossible for Him to tolerate evil. Just as it was morally justifiable for England, and, more than that, her bounden duty, from which she could not shrink without moral culpability, to take upon herself the load of suffering involved in the war, and to call upon her sons voluntarily to suffer and die in order to prevent the triumph of German immorality in the world, so also was God morally justified, and even bound, by the operation of the moral laws He had Himself ordained to accept the voluntary sacrifice of His Son, and, suffering with Him, send Him into the world to prevent the triumph of evil by methods we shall consider later through His agony upon the cross.

No one can seriously question the moral obligation of God to oppose sin. " God must hate and be opposed to sin altogether, because He is perfect love, and sin is its opposite," so that God hates it " with the whole force of His being,"[1] and consistency demands that He should oppose it in whatever form it is met with.

Sinners necessarily involved in the Operation of the Moral Law against Evil.

This is generally conceded. It is only when sinners are included in the sphere of the operation of the moral

[1] *The Incarnation of God*, p. 309.

law, and God's anger against sinners is spoken of, that
men begin to question the morality of the conception.

Yet when God's holiness moves Him to react against
sin, that must also affect His attitude to the sinner.
For the sin is part of the sinner, of his life and character,
as holiness is part of God's life and character. Sin does
not exist apart from personality, any more than holiness
does. Unattached, it is only evil, an impersonal thing.
But when a person sins he associates himself with evil.
The very core and essence of personality is the will, and
when we sin, though there may be hesitations, yet the
will as a whole has embraced sin, and so has practically
associated itself with evil and passed into the sphere of
things hostile to God. The saying " God hates the sin,
but loves the sinner," does not represent the whole
truth. You cannot be angry with sin and be free
altogether from anger with the sinner. The Prophet
Hosea likens the sin of Israel to a woman who has formed
a union with another than her husband. So with us.
Sin is the attaching of oneself in union to evil, when
God has the first and only true claim upon us. And
such " attachment " cannot rightly be overlooked. It
has been said with reference to God's almightiness that
He Himself cannot make what has happened not to
have happened. " Because it is part of the character
of the very self, and the self remains, therefore the past
sin remains, for me and in me, still. . . . How can I,
if I have lied, be not a liar ? . . . How can I, if I have
sinned, be not a sinner ?"[1]

Divine Holiness cannot ignore Sin.

It follows that God cannot ignore the sins we have
committed. Any conceivable degree of penitence or
subsequent Christian holiness cannot remove the fact
of past sins from our lives. What a man has been is
part of what a man is. Though he be now a saint, he

[1] Moberly, *Atonement and Personality*, pp. 34, 36.

is still a saint who has sinned. The blot is still there. Our sins are, and ever will be, an integral part of our personal life and history. The past in that respect is an everlasting present, and God's holiness cannot ignore, nor endure, nor receive it undealt with into His presence. That would be a less worthy way for God to take than to accept and remedy the fact of sin. A form of holiness which ignored or slurred over sin would obviously be imperfect. Nor can God impute to us a purity from sin which is not there. A way must be found, then, which will satisfy the demands of His character—that is, satisfaction for sin must be provided. Righteousness and truth must meet together; justice and sincerity with regard to sin be harmonized in mercy.

God's Nature as Infinite requires Full Moral Expression.

The nature of God as " infinite " requires this. It is agreed by theologians that this term as applied to the divine nature does not refer to dimensions of time and space so much as to the perfection and completeness of His qualities. It expresses that His love is perfect, His holiness complete in every virtue, and so on.

It follows, therefore, from the " infinity " of His nature that God must perfectly express Himself and completely fulfil the laws of His being. Consequently, with regard to things which come within the range of His love, His love must be perfectly and completely expressed towards them. And again with regard to evil, which He must and does hate, His antagonism towards it must be completed by full expression. This fulfilment of the ethical law of His timeless being need not be immediate, but it must be ultimately attained, for otherwise God is not infinite, perfect, nor complete in His moral expression—i.e., in His actual ethical life and action—but limited.

God's Antagonism to Sin in its Full Expression requires Punishment.

This law of God's moral and spiritual nature must apply to sin, and to sins in men as well as to other evils. His antagonism towards them must be fully expressed. His love requires that it should not be immediately expressed in its fulness, for that would be our destruction; but the harmony of God's nature requires that a way must be provided by which ultimately, in co-operation with His love and other qualities, God's antagonism to the sins of men shall be fully expressed. The result of this expression must apparently be the endurance of penal suffering by the sinner; for, as far as our actual experience goes, that is the manner in which God's holiness properly expresses its natural antagonism to sin, and we can conceive of no other possible method. This penal suffering may be vindicative, as a protest against moral passivity and supineness, and to support the appeal of the moral law in men's consciences against the spirit of *laissez-faire* ; or preventive, in opposition to the enticements of sin; or remedial, to encourage penitence; but whichever of these it may be, all of them, as we have seen, are positively moral in their aim and nature, and in full harmony with the requirements of love.

Our Experience of God's Antagonism to Sin in Our Own Lives as Incomplete suggests Further Provision for Full Expression.

Some of this expression of God's attitude towards sinners is experienced by us in the disciplines of life. Sin commonly brings suffering, but not always; and when it does, those who are holiest and in closest harmony with the mind of God are those who feel most strongly that the suffering they endure is far from being a full expression of God's hatred of their sins.

The full expression of it must therefore be sought elsewhere than in our own experience. There is reason to think, as we shall see later, that this full expression was experienced by our Lord upon the cross, and endured by Him without any contradiction of the requirements of justice; and that by an adequate identification with Him every Christian may be brought into connection with His experience of the full expression of God's holiness with regard to sin. It is conceivable that in this way the supreme wisdom and love of God have made provision for the vindication of the law of His holiness by the real inclusion of Christians in the punishment of sin without violating the requirements of His love. It remains for us to see whether this conception of the Atonement can be reasonably applied.

CHAPTER II

Divine Measures against Sin are both Preventive and Remedial.

UNTIL this reconciliation can be brought about, the opposition of God's holiness to evil in sinners will apparently take two forms. There will be (1) preventive measures to save men from contamination by sin; and (2) in those instances where contamination has already taken place—*i.e.*, with regard to actual sins—He will take such means as are possible for the restoration of the sinner by withdrawing him from his identification with sin. That is to say, He will take measures to warn men from committing sin, and He will encourage penitence, which is, in its essence, the breaking of the will as the centre of personality from contentment with the sins to which it has consented.

Measures against Sin involve Penal Suffering.

Such measures in practical form seem to necessitate the infliction of suffering as the consequence of sin, for it is difficult to see what other adequate form they could take. Teaching of a minatory character might be given for this purpose, but consistency would demand that the warnings given should be actually enforced if unheeded. Teaching on the beauty of holiness might also be given, as, indeed, it has been to attract men to holiness. But history and experience prove this to be inadequate by itself; and we know, as a matter of

fact, that if our wills are to be really free, if we are to
have a fair chance to choose the good and resist the
evil, the enticements of the latter, and our inborn
preference for it, must be counterbalanced by our natural
shrinking from pain—the fear of punishment.

Divine Preventive and Remedial Measures a Duty of Love.

Thus God owes it, not only to Himself, but also as
a duty of love to mankind, to enforce observance of His
laws by penal suffering if need be. Apart from all
selfish considerations, or undue sense of his own importance, the head of a household or business or the
teacher of a school, knows that it is his duty not to let
his rules be defied, because it is bad for those under
him to be allowed to neglect and so come to despise
both himself and his rules. In the case of God this is,
of course, incomparably more true, because He and
His laws stand for absolute right. Moreover, they
contain no folly nor weakness to justify criticism, and
therefore to despise them is to despise right and to
make an approach towards evil.

No One but God can enforce these Beneficiary Laws.

In addition to this, while a man in any official position
of authority may feel that if he gives way someone else
will fill his place, and possibly fill it better, and to the
increased advantage of those under him, it is not so
with God. No other being can fill His place, nor
exercise equal beneficence towards mankind. For their
sakes, therefore, as well as for His own, He must rule
and vindicate His laws. A king might say to a criminal
with perfect justice: " So far as your crime is directed
against me through my laws I could forgive you. I am
beyond your reach. You can do me no personal harm
and your punishment can give me no pleasure—indeed,
only pain. But inasmuch as your crime does injury
to the kingdom, I cannot overlook it. The laws were
drawn up because they were necessary to the highest

interests of my subjects, and therefore to allow them to be broken would be to neglect their welfare, and that I cannot rightly do." In the same way God cannot rightly allow the moral laws of His kingdom to be defied without the protest of punishment. Otherwise —an impossible alternative—God fails as the ruler of the world.

If divine, infinite Love were passively to accept Evil's rejection of Himself in the ultimate positive and active degree, that would be to accept the triumph of evil over good, and Almighty Holiness obviously cannot acquiesce in that. He must compel recognition of His supremacy, and how else can this be done than by either the prevention or the punishment of disobedience to His will ? Prevention would be to stultify His own creation by depriving man of freewill, and punishment is left as the only alternative by which God can oppose evil.

Dr. Dale on God as the Vindicator of the Eternal Law of Righteousness.

The thought that sin must be dealt with by God is one of the main features in Dr. Dale's great book on the Atonement, and with regard to God's relations to the eternal law of righteousness for which he contends, he argues that " . . . falsehood, cruelty and injustice . . . would be evil though no Divine Authority had forbidden them; and . . . the opposite virtues would be good though no Divine Authority had commanded them. If . . . righteousness is right because He commands it, and if sin is evil only because He forbids it, how is it possible for us to love and reverence God because of His moral excellence ? . . . God can have no moral perfections if the distinction between good and evil is the creation of the Divine Will."[1] He next argues that God, in His official capacity as ruler of the world, was bound to enforce the law of righteousness which co-

[1] Pp. 368, 369.

exists with and is alive in Him, or in some other way adequately express His hostility to sin, and this was done by His Son's death.

Vindication of the Law is a Duty God owes to Himself.

Dr. Dale's conception of a law seemingly apart from God Himself does not commend itself to some persons, but his expression that the eternal law of righteousness is " alive in " God does much to bring his teaching into line with the view that " the law He upholds is that of His own life, and therefore of ours, for our life is but our finite share in His."[1] This explains why God cannot overlook sin, since to do so would be unfaithful both to Himself and also to the law of His children's life. And being eternally changeless, the broken law must be vindicated, not ignored.

In support of this view we may note that Archbishop Lang, in discussing the cause of the lack of a sense of sin so noticeable in recent religious life, says: " What we need . . . is the recovery of a truer conception of God in His relations to human life. First of all we must learn to look upon God as *Law*. . . . This moral law is not something which God Himself can set aside with a sort of large-hearted generosity. It is part of Himself." And he adds a little later that to neglect the warnings of conscience " must involve some real and terrible retribution, because it is part of the inviolable law of the universe."[2]

It is this law of holiness as the law of God's own life which causes estrangement between God and the sinner, and is the obstacle between them presupposed in all that we read in the Bible about propitiation, redemption, atonement, and reconciliation. " Because God is holy and loving He cannot be indifferent to sin."[3]

If we accept this view it follows that any true theory

[1] *Cf.* Article on " Reconciliation " in Hastings' *Dictionary of the Bible*, iv., p. 205.

[2] *The Parables of Jesus*, pp. 225, 226.

[3] *Cf.* article on " Atonement " in Hastings' *Dictionary of the Bible*, i., p. 198.

of Atonement must fit in with the requirements of God's holiness as a fundamental factor in the problem; and it is obvious that from its very nature holiness must be hostile to, and indeed destructive of, the sins which are part of the sinner's life.

Punishment of Sin in support of Morality is required also as a Public Need.

But, as we have already noted, God's holiness requires the vindication of His laws for the sake of mankind as well as for Himself.

It is generally recognized that, in the administration of law, that system is most successful in restraining crime and encouraging virtue which best provides for the unerring and inevitable punishment of wrong-doing. It has been found that a sense of the inevitableness of punishment is a much more effective deterrent than severity, and that the more clearly this truth of the inevitableness of sin's punishment is realized, the better the law is kept. It is not only that when the consequences of wrong-doing are felt to follow almost automatically such administration of the law is obeyed from fear, but also because a higher opinion of the dignity of the law is formed under these conditions.

Punishment, therefore, clearly has a definite moral effect, and consequently it must be ethically advantageous for men to feel God's indignation against sin as well as His desire for their moral and spiritual recovery.[1]

[1] That this conception of public morality needing the support of the punishment of sin is true and the need deep-seated is confirmed by one of the ideas connected with the Jewish sin-offerings—viz., that they vindicated the holiness of the community in which Jehovah dwelt (cf. Hastings' *Dictionary of the Bible*, article " Propitiation," iv., p. 130). That is to say, the Jews felt the need of asserting and showing that, in spite of the sin for which the sacrifice was required, the community of Jehovah was based upon holiness. In modern life the only way to vindicate God's laws is to obey them, or punish disobedience by penalty. This, roughly speaking, the law does. The punishment of crime may be regarded as a sacrifice offered by the community, with the criminal as the victim, to vindicate the law of holiness and clear itself by its support of the law.

If they do not realize it, sinfulness comes in time to appear to them only as a moral and spiritual condition somewhat less estimable than the holiness God desires men to achieve—as a negative thing, a lack of ideal virtue, rather than a positive evil, as ignorance compared with knowledge. But, as things are, God is seen, by His punishment of it, not only to desire our recovery and growth in holiness, but also to hate sin with unspeakable shrinking and indignant abhorrence.

The Punishment of Sin required as an Individual Need.

For these reasons holiness requires the support and enforcement of God's laws by punishment if need be as a matter of the first importance in encouraging us to adequate effort in the struggle against sin. For in spite of any clever arguments to the contrary, we know, as a matter of experience, that we have a tendency in that direction. " To err is human," we say, and this remains true in spite of the very general belief that sin is sure to find us out in the long-run, and spoils our life. It may be true that the criminal always counts on escaping the punishment of the law, but it is equally true that he has a deep-seated instinct, at any rate at first, and until he has become hardened, that in the end he will have to pay for his sins. Sin is really a desperate sort of gamble, in which, under the stress of temptation, the sinner persuades himself, partly in conscious opposition to deeper knowledge, that the present indulgence is worth the future penalty. If evil has this power even under present circumstances, it is clear that the scales would be altogether too heavily weighted against our moral and spiritual nature if, instead of this present very general conviction, there was a feeling abroad that men could sin without any certain penal consequences either now or hereafter. If under present circumstances freewill has only an even chance, and is equally able to decide for right or wrong, then under those other conditions we should not have a fair chance; the scales would be weighted against us. Divine justice to humanity makes it necessary that sin should carry with it penal consequences. It is easy to speak disparagingly of the usefulness of the fear of punishment as a deterrent, or of the quality of virtue based upon it; but after all, if the matter be coolly and carefully considered, there is probably no greater force in existence for the maintenance of law and order and the formation of character. And what is true of the law of the land is equally true of the moral and divine law. The point to notice is, that in either case the sinner's welfare is the principal consideration inspiring the infliction of penalty, and the motive is love, one of the most compelling influences which determine divine action. Vindicative law is therefore the exact opposite to vindictive punishment. It has in it no element of revenge.

CHAPTER III

THE REQUIREMENT OF DIVINE HOLINESS, AS PURITY AND LOVE, FOR SEPARATION FROM EVIL

THE second thing required by God's holiness as purity is separation from sin or the purification of its guilt. This motive may work in two opposite directions. So long as there is any hope of success, purity, in co-operation with and inspired by love, will work for the separation of the sinner from the contamination of sin by reclamation; but when the sinner's will has become so fixed on sin that evil has become his good, purity then can only withdraw itself, and require for others also separation from him.

To take the latter of the alternatives first, one would like to think that there are none who are hopelessly bad and need to be despaired of; yet our Saviour's teaching and denunciations suggest the opposite conclusion, and it seems to be borne out by the records of history. In any case one cannot doubt that there are men and women whose presence is a moral danger to the public. It is not easy to judge when a person is beyond reclamation, and no doubt human justice has sometimes hounded to ruin or driven to despair men and women who might not have been beyond recovery. But divine wisdom makes no mistakes and can decide infallibly what souls require to be separated, so that into heaven there shall enter nothing that maketh abomination nor uttereth a lie, to mar its perfect peace and happiness.

The Bible reveals that God's Holiness requires Separation from Sinners.

In the Bible this requirement of holiness is plainly laid down as the consequence of sin. In its opening chapters we have the expulsion of Adam and Eve from the garden where God walked, as His immediate sentence upon their sin; and in its last pages we have St. John's statement that there shall in no wise enter into heaven anything that defileth (Rev. xxi. 27, xxii. 15). Indeed, it is not too much to say that, together with the doctrine of the unity of God, the truth of His holiness and separation from sinners was the chief end to which the Mosaic law was directed. All that was unclean was, by that very fact, divorced from His presence, while the sinner was " cut off " from the congregation and temple of Jehovah, and from the ordinary religious observances, until he had been purified and atonement made by ritual observances, washings, and sin-offerings. It is true that at first the conceptions of uncleanness and holiness were connected only with physical and material ideas, but this was only a concession to the imperfect moral conceptions of the people, and in order that the teaching might be more generally and deeply apprehended by all. Nothing so much touched the daily life of the Jew as the laws of cleanness and purification, nor his religious life as the atoning sacrifices; and the whole system led up to an ethical and spiritual appreciation of the reiterated command, " Be ye holy, for I the Lord your God am holy," and to the realization that " without the shedding of blood there is no remission of sin," which otherwise cuts off the sinner from God's favour.

This Truth was taught by the Prophets also.

This, combined with the certainty of God's punishment of sin, was also the chief ethical teaching of the prophets. It is perhaps most clearly stated by Isaiah, who continually describes God as the " Holy One of

Israel," and declares: " Your iniquities have separated
between you and your God " (Isa. lix. 2). His vision
of God " high and lifted up," worshipped with the
seraphic *Trisagion*, " Holy ! Holy ! Holy !" and forcing
upon him the realization " I am a man of unclean lips,"
is characteristic of the prophetic attitude forcibly
summarized by Habakkuk's statement that " God is of
too pure eyes to behold evil." So it has been said:
" Holiness (in the Old Testament) is the perfect purity of
God, which in and for itself excludes all fellowship with
the world, and can only establish a relation of free
electing love whereby it asserts itself in the sanctification of God's people, their cleansing and redemption
. . . manifesting itself in atonement and redemption
and correspondingly in judgment " (Cremer, *Bib. Theol.
Lex.*, *s.v.*, quoted in article on " Holiness " in Hastings'
Dictionary of the Bible).

Our Lord and the Apostles in the New Testament.

All this teaching upon God being " separate from
sinners " is confirmed in the New Testament by our
Lord's statement as to the " great gulf " fixed betwixt
Dives and Lazarus in Abraham's bosom (Luke xvii. 26);
His sentence upon those who make empty professions;
" Depart from Me, ye that work iniquity " (Matt. vii.
23; see also Luke xiii. 27); and His use of the expression
" outer darkness " to describe the state of sinners as
divorced from the light of God's presence. We also
have the teaching of the Epistles and St. John's description of the inviolate purity of Jerusalem above—the
" Holy City " into which nothing sinful can enter.

This doctrine of separation is required by God's love
as much as by His justice, since the Bible shows that
His love desires the union of all the sanctified with
Himself, both for His own and their happiness; and if
sinners were not separated from Him, those He loves
would be brought into eternal contact with sin. We
are justified, therefore, in believing Scripture to teach

us that God's holiness cannot tolerate the presence of the sinner, or perhaps we should rather say acquiesce in it as a permanent condition of His existence. This divorce is in no sense an artificial nor arbitrary sentence, but the natural, inevitable consequence of the divine character.

Science supports this Teaching.

This conclusion, based upon the teaching of the Bible, is supported by science, which shows that evolution may lead along paths which lead farther and farther from the main stream of development, and in the end prove to be cul-de-sacs which cut off the creature from the true current of life, and inevitably end in extinction.

An Alternative Separation desired by Love is Atonement obtained through Purification of the Sinner.

It appears, therefore, that either there must be divorce of the sinner from God's presence, or some way found of satisfying the requirements of God's holiness with regard to him. It is this latter alternative which God's love led Him to choose, and which our Lord's Atonement provides.

In this alternative of the Atonement we find, as the word itself denotes, God's purity operating in the opposite direction to separation: working for union, and working in full harmony with love for the purification of the sinner by a reclamation which would make separation unnecessary; and aiming at it, not only to save others from his contaminating influence, but also for his own gain by purification. The inspiring motive in this work is obviously that of love seeking for the restoration of the sinner because it is in itself so desirable a thing for him. Divine holiness longs for men to love what God loves, and hate what God hates; longs to win the sinner from the perverted views and disablement of sin.

CHAPTER IV

THE REQUIREMENT OF DIVINE HOLINESS, AS LOVE AND JUSTICE, FOR REPARATION

AT this point love appears as a connecting-link between purity and justice, enabling them to combine in claiming reparation.

For, as we have seen, it is the inspiring motive which determines purity to seek for the reclamation of the sinner rather than for his separation; and this, so long as a man possesses freewill, can only be brought about by his repentance—that is, by that change of outlook upon life which leads a man to determine to serve the God he has neglected, and to make reparation, so far as that is possible, for the insults, neglect, and disobedience of the past.

Love supports, also, the claim set up for reparation by justice. We are apt to think of the duty of reparation as being based mainly upon the claims of justice, and certainly this is the first view which presents itself: and a correct view too, though not the only one.

A Complete Morality demands Reparation.

Dr. Moberly's failure to bear in mind this claim of morality led him to base his theory upon penitence only, and consequently to present us with a conception and picture of true sorrow for sin which is of immense value, but also with a theory of the Atonement less complete and satisfying than it otherwise would have been. If he had kept in view this other side of the question his conception of the necessary scope of a complete theory must have been enlarged, and it would have led him to provide not only for the restoration of the sinner, but also for restoration of the injury caused by his sins; and when it is remembered that the greatest injury done by sin is to God Himself, it is at once clear how greatly such an omission must affect any theory of the Atonement.[1] If this consideration had been kept in view, he might have found it possible to include some form of the doctrine of " satisfaction " in a modified, personal rather than a " quantitative " sense, which would have enabled him to accept rather than question Anselm's teaching that " everyone who sins ought to render back to God the honour he has taken away, and this is the satisfaction which every sinner ought to make to God."[2] Conscience confirms that " ought," and if Dr. Moberly had seen his way to a fuller agreement with it, it would be easier to bring his theory into harmony with Hooker's view that " so inevitable is the punishment of sin, that it is a kind of restraint unto God Himself to punish—yea, to punish them whose sin He hath pardoned and received into favour. . . . It cannot, therefore, be doubted of but there is pain due for sin after sin be remitted."[3] Such a view as this can find no place in the purely " penitential " theory; but it is in accord with the deeper instincts of conscience and with human experience, and must be provided for in any satisfying theory of the Atonement. And this is only another way of saying that the claims of justice must not be overlooked. The revulsion against all idea of " satisfaction " has certainly gone too far, and it is necessary to remind ourselves that God has duties which He owes to Himself and to others in addition to the exercise of His love in forgiveness, which, by itself, might degenerate into weak indulgence.

[1] *Atonement and Personality*, p. 20.   [2] *Cur Deus Homo*, i. 11.
[3] Hooker's *Sermon on Pride*, part v.

Death does not cancel the Claim of Justice for Reparation.

With regard to the claims of justice for reparation for past sins, it has been argued: " But what need is there for it ?   Why should the guilt of sin be regarded as eternal, when these bodies with which we sin and the injury we inflict upon others are temporal ? Why should not the sin die out with our bodies and the injury and suffering our sins have caused ?"   Or again: " If the seat of sin is the will, and the will is changed by penitence, so that the evil desire has ceased to exist, why should anything more be required by the holiness of God ?"

This reasoning, however, is based upon imperfect premises. In the first place, it is not only with the body that we sin. The will, as well as the body, is involved in any sinful act, and the will, as the centre of the personality, lives on after death. Sometimes the sin is confined to the will alone. The moral and sinful attitude of opposition to God's will taken up by the personality when an act of sin is decided upon is in itself a sin. Even if the bodily action is never performed, yet such a decision is in itself an act of will; and, though the will may change, that act will remain a fact in the history of the soul as eternal as the soul itself. The dissolution of the body by death in no way affects the existence of the moral and spiritual acts of the soul. Moreover, in addition to all this, we do not know enough of the resurrection body to justify us in assuming that it will contain no element at all of our present sinful bodies.

Again, with regard to the injured party, so far as regards sins committed against men, even though we were to agree that the injury inflicted by sin is more than compensated to the sufferer by ulterior and far greater benefits arranged by Divine Providence—even though we allow this, the claims of justice for reparation

are not affected.   For sin is far more an injury to God
than to any human victim—" Against Thee only have
I sinned."

Nor can Penitence cancel such Claims.

Nor can the evil past be undone by mere penitence.
It remains an eternal fact for which justice requires
reparation, even though the injured party may not
demand it.

It is here that some persons feel most inclined to
question Dr. Moberly's teaching when he argues that
in order to make forgiveness possible all that is required
is for God to have regard to the present moral and
spiritual condition of the penitent sinner, and that if
this is satisfactory all the past may be overlooked, and
there is no need for reparation.   He argues that penitence is a real undoing of the past, " a real killing out,
eliminating of the past from the present me."[1]   " The
past act has no place . . . in the present self,"[2] so that
if a man has ceased in his present character to be the
liar, or thief that he was, he has supplied all that is
necessary to cancel all claims against him by justice.
In this way Dr. Moberly avoids the necessity in his
theory of the Atonement of making any provision for
satisfaction due to God for the injury of sin, though no
doubt the duty of restitution to men for wrongs done
to them would be included in his conception of a true
penitence.   The idea of any reparation being justly due
to God, however, does not enter into his scheme of
Atonement, and to many minds this does not seem to
be so high a moral conception as that of God providing,
in addition to a perfect contrition, for the satisfaction
of justice, and the undoing or healing up of the wounds
in the body of moral righteousness.

But even though the claims of righteousness to a just
reparation are in this way avoided, yet, as we shall see,

---

[1] *Atonement and Personality*, p. 41.   [2] *Ibid.*, p. 38.

the exigeant requirements of love still call for satisfaction, and we are brought to consider the demands of
love that reparation should be made for sin.

Love supplies a Sufficient Basis for a Satisfying Theory of the Atonement.

There is no doubt that many minds, and they of the
best quality, are, if anything, repelled by considerations
which base the Atonement upon claims of justice or
holiness; and, on the other hand, feel the full force, in
a special degree, of the appeal of love. For this reason
it is all the more satisfactory to find that the claims of
love alone afford a quite sufficient foundation upon
which to base the morality of the Atonement. Almost
the whole of what has been written up to the present
point might be ignored without seriously affecting the
argument based upon the claims of love which is to
follow, and such a plan would appeal more strongly to
some minds than the wider scheme which has been
chosen; but the latter has been adopted as meeting
wider needs, and also as giving a fuller if less attractive
statement of religious truth. The instinct of justice
lies deeply embedded in human nature, and if its claims
were passed over in silence there would remain an
uneasy feeling in many minds that some difficulties had
not been faced; and still required explanation. What
men need to feel in religious matters is that the whole
truth has been dealt with, and nothing shirked. Difficulties must be either explained or frankly acknowledged
to be insolvable, but not ignored.

Religion connects Love and Suffering.

The apparent paradox that it is God's *love* which
demands the punishment of sin has received support
from many careful thinkers. It has been said: " Christ
came to a people who had been taught to associate the
best blessings God had to give with death rather than

life . . .; forgiveness and fellowship with God were only obtained through death " (*i.e.*, of victims in the Jewish daily sacrifices for sin).[1] And it is very striking that in His early training of mankind, and in so impressive and persistent a manner, God should have connected His greatest blessings with suffering.

Love demands that the Wrong-doer should make Restitution.

Yet, when we remember that it is characteristic of all true love to desire the very best and highest standards for those it loves, so that it is " exacting " rather than easily satisfied, we can understand why this is so. For it follows that love *must* wish those it loves to be just, and this involves the desire that they should not only wish to make, but actually succeed in making, adequate restitution for wrongs inflicted, and this must necessarily involve some suffering. That we owe reparation for our sins to God is taught by our Lord Himself in the parable of The Unmerciful Servant, and in the petition, " Forgive us our debts " (Matt. vi. 12); yet so far as restitution is concerned, we are apt to feel this is not only impossible, but even that the attempt is somehow incongruous and unfitting. This latter feeling is due to the fact that we are naturally inclined, under our present circumstances of life, to connect the thought of compensation with materialistic conceptions, whilst any reparation to God of this character is, of course, quite unthinkable. Hence the apparent incongruity. Perhaps, therefore, it needs to be emphasized that we quite clearly recognize there can be no question of anything

---

[1] Bishop Walpole of Edinburgh in *The Guardian*, June 25, 1918. The force of this statement is in no way weakened by the fact that in the Jewish ritual the blood of the victim signified life rather than death, for the lesson is still the same—viz., that the sacrifice of the personality required by God as atonement for sin is of such a kind and degree as to necessarily involve physical death. Otherwise it is not adequate, for it is not complete. There is no complete surrender without the surrender of the life.

approaching *quantitative* compensation to God for sin; and that this applies not only with regard to material but also to moral and spiritual compensation. There can be no such thing as the offering of so much obedience or holiness to make up for so much sin. Every sin is infinite. Moral and spiritual things cannot be weighed or measured. All are agreed upon that.

But when we have succeeded in putting aside all quantitative conceptions, the thought of offering moral and spiritual reparation for the wrong done to God does not in itself appear distasteful. Indeed, so far as we can do so, it is clearly seen to be our undoubted duty. The only difficulty is the question of its possibility. We see that what is required, or rather desired, by God's love is that the sinner should be placed *as a whole* in a certain moral and spiritual attitude with regard to Him, should be endued with a certain right character, putting him in a proper relation towards Himself.

Such a thing as this is obviously desirable; and if a thing is rightly desirable, it ought to be possible. And, as a matter of fact, further thought shows that perfect love, far from resenting such reparation, must desire that the object of its love should be able to make it. If even in material matters love desires the ill-doer to make the reparation justice demands, resulting, as it must, in material loss to the compensator, much more must love desire it in matters of spiritual indebtedness, where the wrong is greater, and when such reparation can only result in placing the sinner upon a higher moral and spiritual plane than he occupied before, so that the gain is on both sides. Love *must* wish sinful man to attain his highest possible development; and that is impossible unless he not only desires, but actually achieves, the offering of a true reparation for his sins— *i.e.*, the offering of a perfect obedience at the greatest possible cost and under the most difficult circumstances. This is what God, as supreme, perfect love, must desire man to achieve; and it was attained by the Son of Man upon the Cross, where we see divine love and the consequences of sin brought into direct connection with one another. Love no less than justice demands that reparation for sin should be made, and of the two the demands of love are the more imperious. Justice may perhaps be able to forgo its claims and penalties, but from its very nature love must desire the highest and best at whatever cost of suffering. In the eyes of true love no suffering is an evil compared to that of guilt not atoned for.

The Demand of Love for Reparation acts in Both Directions : (1) From God to Man.

But it is not only the love of God which makes this demand. The love which urges that the sinner should suffer comes from both sides—from the love of the penitent for God as well as of God for the sinner. It is God, however, who initiates the exchanges of love: " we love Him because He first loved us."

A wrong-doer is, as we have seen, under moral obligation to make compensation. It is right that he should; and therefore the injured party, if really loving and wise, will wish to see him not only desiring to make good the injury, but actually doing so; not only trying, but completely succeeding in making full satisfaction. For it is only by sincere effort to make full compensation an actual fact that moral righteousness can be satisfied, and it is only by the complete success of the effort that the stain of wrong can be most nearly removed.

To attain this " intention " alone is clearly not enough. A man is in an unhappy position who, having committed some fault, finds he has done an irreparable injury to his brother. Still more unhappy is the fate of him who stands in this position towards God, to Whom he owes all, and Who loves him with an infinite love. Therefore, a penitent sinner must wish to make reparation to God, and God, as all-holy and loving, *must* desire men to be able to make full compensation

to Him for their sins. Otherwise man's victory over
sin will be incomplete, and he must suffer an eternal
moral and spiritual humiliation and a failure in achievement which perfect love could not willingly permit.
Since "Love is goodness in earnest to make others
good,"[1] God's very love for man compels Him to demand
and to find a way for full reparation for the injury done
Him by man's sin.

In this matter of full reparation it appears necessary,
therefore, that God's love should discover some method
by which it may not only be possible for men to attain
such a state of purity in some future condition as will
enable them to be received into God's near presence,
but also to make full reparation for their past sins.
Some recent writers on the Atonement present the
former condition alone as the utmost mankind can hope
for.[2] This, however, does not appear to be sufficient,
for the reason that we should, under these conditions,
enter God's presence owing a heavy debt of sin. Perfect
love could not rest satisfied with this, and must therefore desire to provide for the liquidation of our past
debts, as well as for our future holiness. Just as a
father would wish his child to be able to pay old debts
as well as meet future obligations, so God must wish
and plan that men, for their own sakes, may be able to
make full reparation for all their unrighteous deeds.
It is a greater conception to think of God as providing
restitution for past evil as well as for present repentance
and the future holiness of man, than to believe that
He has not cared or has been unable to provide the
former.

What God's Love desires His Power will provide.

This seems clear, and what we can conceive of God
doing cannot be too great for Him to accomplish; so

---

[1] Adamson, article on " Reconciliation " in Hastings' *Dictionary of
the Bible*, iv., p. 206.

[2] *Cf. Some Aspects of the Atonement*, by Canon L. Ragg, pp. 116, 117.

that this trust in His love and power supplies good ground for the belief that He not only desires the sinner to be able to rise to the height of making due reparation to Himself, but has also provided a way for him to do so.

It is here that those theories of the Atonement which only provide for penitential sorrow and future holiness seem to be most lacking. Nothing is too great for God, and surely there is nothing incredible or blameworthy in the belief that His love has provided a way for man to make restitution for sin, as well as to offer a perfect penitence and attain true holiness.

God's Love provides for the Remission of Past Sins as well as for Future Sanctification.

There can be nothing wrong nor unworthy in the conception that our Lord's death is a propitiation, not only because it wins us by true penitence to avoid future sin, but also because it remits—*i.e.*, puts away, sends back, and in some sense " undoes "—our sins by making reparation for them. We have, indeed, our Saviour's own words for this on one of the most solemn possible occasions: " This is My blood which is shed for you for the remission of sins." (Note, not " of sinfulness:" Matt. xxvi. 28.) And a thing cannot be remitted until it has first come into existence. The Atonement, then, deals with past sins as well as providing for our present and future moral and spiritual condition.

There seems to be nothing gained by limiting the achievements of God's love to the provision of penitential sorrow without reparation to Himself.

(2) *From Man to God.*

When we come to consider why man's love for God should lead him to wish to suffer for his sins, the reason is, " Because the willing acceptance of suffering is the only possible proof of the sincerity of his sorrow." What other proof could be given ? In the nature of things the test must be something unpleasant, and if so, then it must be of the nature of penal suffering.   It may be said: " Who wants any proof of sincerity ?   God reads the heart, and needs none.   He knows the truth." This may be so, but still the fact remains that in many cases, and they among the best, the true penitent wishes to offer this proof.   A parent may not need to receive a birthday-present as a proof of love, but an affectionate child will wish to give one all the same; and the parent will welcome this fruit of an affection not limited by bare necessity, but prodigal in its ex-pression, and he will welcome it although it costs his child some self-sacrifice.   On both sides this is as love should be.   The rights of a matter are sometimes more truly decided by love than by justice.

CHAPTER V

THE REPARATION WHICH HOLINESS REQUIRES

SINCE the holiness of God thus requires reparation for sin, and requires it even more as an act of love than of justice, we can next consider what the proper reparation for sin against God is.

The Reparation due to God for Sin is Self-sacrificing Obedience.

The nature of the reparation required is suggested by consideration of the nature of sin, and for this purpose we may take St. John's definition of it as " the transgression of the law "—*i.e.*, the law of righteousness, which is equivalent to God's will in its bearing upon each detail of our lives. Whenever we sin we set up the will of self in opposition to the will of God: we prefer self to God. The reparation, therefore, which is due will clearly be a reversal of this. It may include more, but at any rate it will include this.

Adequate Reparation involves Death.

In the Jewish sacrificial system the blood especially was considered to have propitiating powers, because " it is the life " (Lev. xvii. 11)—*i.e.*, the soul, personality, will. The pouring out of this represented complete sacrifice of self to God in death. It is probably the instinctive recognition of this truth which causes simple-minded people to be so anxious, from the religious point of view, for dying persons " to give in." The expression sounds uncouth to cultivated ears, and the idea is no doubt often accompanied by very crude con-

110

ceptions of Christianity, but nevertheless it represents a fundamentally sound view. To them it means: " Make your complete submission to God's will that you should die. Resist Him no longer." " Not suffering merely, but the suffering of death, is the satisfaction demanded for sin. . . . Although there is nothing pleasing to God in death itself . . . yet there is something satisfying and compensating to the law of righteousness (which has been broken) in such a death, and therefore something propitiating in it."[1] Again: " . . . death itself (as opposed to the ' willingness ' of it) had a value all its own if we may trust the impression left us by the Old Testament and the New Testament alike."[2]

We note it was not only " willingness " to submit, but the actual achievement of death which was necessary. As the disobedience of self-pleasing is not only in intention, but also in fact, so the obedience of God-pleasing must be also actual. Another reason is apparent in the fact that death makes the supreme demand upon our submission to God's will; it is the most terrible experience God can ask mankind in general to endure. Hence its significance in any scheme of reparation to God for human self-will manifested in sin. It is the satisfaction justice must naturally demand, and therefore God asks it of us all.[3] In the summons to death, God, as it were, says to the soul: " As you have rebelled against Me in self-pleasing, so now, if you are penitent, submit to Me in this supreme sacrifice. It is what you owe Me: what you owe My love as well as My justice."

The thing, then, that is required of us as the reparation due to God for sin is the practical and final preference of God's will to our own in some supreme act of perfect obedience.

[1] J. B. Oldroyd, *The Doctrine of the Atonement*, pp. 73, 74.
[2] Ragg, *Some Aspects of the Atonement*.
[3] See Gen. ii. 17; Ezek. xviii. 4; Rom. vi. 21, 23; Jas. i. 15.

Man's Incapacity to make Adequate Reparation.

We find ourselves, therefore, in this position, that we are morally bound to make the compensation righteousness demands, but are incapable of it because our fallen, finite nature is both incapable of submitting itself in perfect obedience to God's, and also of making reparation for the injury and suffering our sins cause Him.   For we must never forget that it is not only a question of God's justice inflicting suffering for the reasons we have seen, but still more of His love asking, first, for a desire on our part to make reparation; and, secondly, for this desire to be realized and consummated in actual experience.   A father does not only wish his son to be noble in intention, but also in actual achievement.   And we have seen that this can only be attained in the perfect obedience of a perfect death.[1]

So far as the claims of God's justice alone against a sinner are concerned, it appears that they might be forgone, and the guilt freely forgiven.   But, on the other hand, justice will still demand of the sinner that he should *desire* to make restitution; and these claims of justice, having their source in the sinner's own sense of right, will be reinforced by the requirements of love on both sides.   So that, so far as reparation is concerned, it is required on the divine side mainly by considerations of love (though the requirements of rectoral government and the public conscience must not be forgotten), and on man's side by common justice as well as by love.

Spiritual Experience confirms the Need of Reparation.

In support of this view, that reparation is a necessary condition to God's forgiveness, we note as a fact of

---

[1] For the teaching of the Jewish law on this point see p. 104, note 1. The sacrifice made in death is really the perfect sacrifice of the life: the devotion of the life completely to God.

spiritual experience that until a sinner is ready, if need be, to suffer, in order to make such restitution to God as is possible, he cannot realize God's forgiveness. Of course, nothing he can do is in itself adequate; but until he is at least willing to do what he can it is impossible for him to feel forgiven. Justice demands that at least there should be the desire to compensate, and therefore until this is attained there is felt to be a moral obstacle to forgiveness. The want of such a will is the cause of a great deal of the unsatisfied feeling and want of happiness in many religiously minded people.

But the moral obligation to make reparation cannot really be denied, although at the present time many seem inclined to question it in connection with our relations to God. In the relations of man to man no one does so. All agree, for instance, that, if the German accusations against Belgian neutrality were baseless, the moral claim for reparation for her injuries is irresistible. And in our own private relations to one another we all recognize that wrongs ought so far as possible to be righted and reparation made, and that willingness to make restitution is an essential element in any true repentance, without which no claim to forgiveness can be set up. Between ourselves the claims of justice for reparation are unquestioned.

The Bishop of Edinburgh has expressed it very clearly in an article on the Atonement in which he says: " Forgiveness is not simply remission of penalty, but admission into full fellowship. . . . Such forgiveness could only be received by one who has so repented of his sin as to be ready to give all, if by doing so he could expiate his sin. In other words, repentance and sacrifice are identical . . . and no larger sacrifice can be made than when a man acknowledges that all the punishment which sin has brought is richly deserved, and that he is ready to accept any and every discipline if only he may enjoy again the fellowship which he has forfeited; in other words, he is ready to give his life, if that should

8

be asked." And so he adds later: " Repentance, as we
have seen, when carried to the uttermost, means death.
It begins with confession of sin, but it ends with the
endurance of sin's penalty."[1]

The Penal Consequences of Sin needing Remission are of Two Kinds.

In connection with what the Bishop says about
forgiveness and remission of penalty we may notice that
on closer analysis the penal consequences of sin fall into
two great classes, and it is helpful in studying the
question of forgiveness if this is clearly grasped.

First there is the primary, unvarying result of the
rupture of the spiritual relations between the sinner and
God. This divorce is typified by the expulsion of
Adam and Eve from the Garden of Eden, where God
had walked and talked with them; and it is so pre-
eminently the most important result that it has been
treated as if it were the only one. This consequence of
sin is, as it were, self-acting. It automatically, invariably, and inevitably follows the commission of sin, yet,
because it is purely spiritual in its nature, it can easily
pass unrecognized. We also note that the remission of
this penalty follows equally automatically upon repentance and confession. David's " I have sinned " is
instantly followed by Nathan's " The Lord hath also
put away thy sin." " If we confess our sins, God is
faithful and just to forgive us our sins." So forgiveness
may be viewed as only another name for the remission
of this primary consequence of sin, and the renewal of
the spiritual relations between God and the soul—
which sin breaks.

But beyond this primary consequence there are also
secondary penal consequences. These are variable in
their nature, and often physical and mental as well as
spiritual. Just as the primary effects of many internal
diseases can only be discerned and traced by specialists,

[1] See article in the *Guardian* for June 25, 1914, p, 809.

while the surface, secondary results or symptoms, though of far less real importance, are discernible even to a superficial observer, so also with sin. While the fatal interruption with the source of spiritual life is liable to be overlooked, the secondary consequences such as disease, unhappiness, or misfortune, are often so noticeable and so readily traced that there is a tendency to think of them as the primary punishments of sin, and to consider that forgiveness involves their removal. This is one of the greatest and most common mistakes in connection with the question of divine, personal forgiveness.

Forgiveness does not necessarily involve the Remission of Secondary Penalties.

For it is obvious that such secondary consequences might be, and often must be, continued by a wise and loving God for disciplinary reasons. We are so constituted that otherwise the great part of mankind would find it impossible to take a sufficiently serious view of sin. So, though God at once forgave David and received him back into communion on his repentance, yet the child, the fruit of the sin, for whom he pleaded, died. In the same way a mother who has sent her boy upstairs as a punishment for an outbreak of temper, on his repentance and confession may forgive and kiss him as a sign of reconciliation, but at the same time tell him he must stay where he is to impress him with the seriousness of his fault. The two things, forgiveness and the continuance of these secondary consequences of sin, are perfectly compatible with one another. The continuance of the latter is simply a question of discipline, and they are not necessarily involved in the question of forgiveness at all.

We notice, further, that, as they are often the ordinary consequences which follow from the breaking of what we commonly call natural law, it would require something in the nature of a miracle to abrogate them. Yet it is a mistake to assert that forgiveness cannot include even this, but only that it must not be counted upon as a result naturally following penitence. It is possible, or even probable, that God often remits the natural consequences of sin when they have achieved their disciplinary purpose without any miraculous intervention being suspected.

It follows from the above that what we have to consider in the Atonement is the remission of the primary consequence of sin, and not its secondary penalties.

CHAPTER VI

THE REQUIREMENTS OF REASON WITH REGARD TO SIN

Reason demands the Operation of Law.

WE have so far based our argument upon the nature of God's moral character as holy and the inherent antagonism between good and evil, and we have assumed the inviolability of law—that " God is mighty enough to make laws, and too mighty to break them." It is perhaps necessary for the stability of our argument to say something in proof of this assumption.

Although there is a connection, as we shall see, between reason and morality in their demand for the inviolability of law, it appears to be based in the first instance upon reason.

We have already noticed that " order " is the arrangement of things in relation to one another in accordance with some regular plan in which each has a recognized position, and is usually the result of " orders " given by someone in authority having a definite object in view.

These " orders " practically become " laws " when sufficiently persistent and widespread in their application. The very word " law " implies inviolability: a more developed and lasting " order." The idea behind them both is the regular and rational sequence of things with reference to some definite object, and as such necessarily implies a directing personality. The want of order implies the want of reasoning control, and is unthinkable under any rational scheme of existence.

Looked at from the opposite point of view, it is equally true to say that law is as necessarily demanded by

117

reason as morality is by holiness. Chaos and confusion are as much the enemies of the former as evil and sin are of the latter. Reason postulates that all effects require adequate causes to produce them, and also that there should be a due or proportionate relation between all causes and effects. Just as in arithmetic reason demands that $2+2-1$ in all their powers should always produce a certain proportionate result, so does it demand that certain causes, with the addition or opposition of certain other causes, should invariably produce a certain definite result. In the realm of physical science the laws of the indestructibility of matter and the conservation of energy are only the law of cause and effect in another form. There is no room for chance under the present system, or it would not be a system.[1] " Chance is unthinkable. Our causal instinct excludes it."[2] In other words, the denial of order is equivalent to the contradiction of reason, which therefore demands that the reign or operation of law should be recognized as obtaining throughout existence. Without this it is not too much to say that reason itself is inconceivable. The denial of order is equivalent to the contradiction of reason.

As Supreme Reason God must require and enforce Law.

It follows that, since creation is the expression of God's nature, and is found to be based upon law, that law—i.e., the operation of cause and effect—has a real relationship to God's nature, and forms an essential feature in His being. God is rational, and the ultimate source of all reason. " Anarchy is the farthest remove from the mind of God."[3]

As God has also almighty power, His nature as supreme reason requires Him to enforce law. For since reason is an essential part of His personality, law is as necessary to God in His rational being as holiness

---

[1] *Cf.* Illingworth, *Personality, Human and Divine*, Lecture IV.
[2] *Ibid.*
[3] Malden, *Watchman, What of the Night?* p. 222.

is to His moral being. Just as His moral nature is holiness, so is His rational nature order—law; and as His holiness compels Him to oppose evil, so does His reason compel Him to oppose lawlessness. He cannot break His own laws, nor ignore lawlessness in others, or condone it in Himself, any more than He can commit evil or wink at sin. To do so would be a denial of His own nature.

Morality supports Reason in requiring the Inviolability of Law.

But the recognition and enforcement of law and order is not only an obligation of reason: it is also an obligation of morality. It is demanded by the duty of consistency to the prevailing order and general underlying principle of existence. Order rules in the sphere of morality as well as in the material world. There are moral laws as well as laws of nature, and it would therefore be as unreasonable, as contrary to God's nature, to break the former as the latter. The laws of God's justice, love, truth, etc., are as inviolable as those of heat, light, and chemical action.

Exceptions would be inconsistencies. For this reason the maintenance of law is a duty of holiness as well as of reason; and at this point, therefore, truth stands as the connecting-link between God's moral and rational natures, since it teaches the proper attitude of personality towards both morality and reason. For the " true " man is true to both natures. He is true, as reason demands, to the facts of existence, and also he acts consistently with the instincts of morality. In the end both the facts of life and the laws of morality demand from men that obedience which is the acceptance in practical life of the consequences of preceding causes. This obedience is the same thing in the sphere of personality as the reign of law in impersonal nature, so that morality confirms reason in demanding of men submission to law.

God's Penal Laws against Sin must be "fulfilled" rather than ignored in the Provisions of Christ's Atonement.

It follows that God also, as " the Truth," is required by morality as well as reason to be loyal to His own laws, whether in the world of nature or of spirit.

In full harmony with this we may claim that when our Lord said that He was not " come to destroy the law, but to fulfil " it, He was enunciating a principle of the divine economy which is of general application— viz., that God completes Himself and His work, not by cancelling any seemingly contradictory elements, but by reconciling them through their " fulfilment " in the exact sense of the word.

This is possible because the apparent contradictions are superficial, whilst the underlying harmony of God's nature is fundamental, being based upon His essential unity. It is illustrated not only by the development of the Mosaic prohibitions, to which our Lord was especially referring at the time, into the corresponding Christian precepts, as " Thou shalt not kill " into " Love one another "; but also by the development of the whole Mosaic covenant into the Christian religion— an evolution the naturalness of which the Jews still fail to understand. In close connection with this we have another instance in the development of the doctrine of the unity of God into the Christian doctrine of the Trinity—an apparent self-contradiction which, again, many acute minds still feel to be absolutely unreasonable, but which philosophy is tending to solve by the discovery that the most perfect personal unity is that of plurality. The mystery of the two natures in the one Christ is also moving towards solution in the same manner, and men are coming to see that in the Holy Trinity the very perfection of the Godhead required that the Second Person should become man, and that the perfection of the humanity of Jesus made possible His divinity. In the relations of faith and superstition towards one another and to reason, we find the same principle illustrated. For while superstition contradicts reason, faith surpasses it, not by opposition but by o'erleaping it. Faith is the " fulfilment " of reason, the goal towards which reason is travelling, the filling up of her cup to overflowing. There is no change, no shadow of turning in the things of God; and all seeming contraries are harmonized, not by their abrogation, but by their " fulfilment "—*i.e.*, their complete development.

So, also, in this other mystery of the Atonement we may be sure that the unity between God and the sinner which it bespeaks is not attained by breaking, or even ignoring, the moral laws of love, justice, and purity, with the reparations and penalties for sin which they call for as its proper consequences, but by some surpassing fulfilment of them which entirely satisfies all the requirements of a perfected holiness.

Because " God is law "—because this is part of the reason and righteousness of His character—He cannot lawlessly remit the consequences of sin imposed by His own moral and spiritual laws. Forgiveness cannot be independent of law, nor arbitrary. It is never free.[1] It is controlled and limited by inviolable law, and for this reason it cannot be easily won nor granted. It is not simply the outcome of God's love being wishful to forgive. There are difficulties in the way which require more than mere contrition to overcome them. The moral law forbids such lawless benevolence, and requires satisfaction. It demands that the proper legal penalties should be endured and the necessary conditions satisfied. The remission of sins is not the same thing as the remission of their penal consequences. The first, no doubt, is possible where true penitence opens a way for the grace of God to prevail over sin, but there is a real sense in which it is true to say that the remission of the penalty of sin is never possible; the penalty must be

[1] See p. 134.

always endured. We must all be crucified with Christ, and in Him bear the consequences of sin required by divine law; and He must bear the sins of the whole world.

The Father does not, as it were, say: " Here is a man who has sinned, but I will save him from the consequences of his sin by breaking the law of sin and death "; but He does something much better. He says rather: " Here is a man who has sinned, but with the help of My Son and Holy Spirit I will make it possible for him to be saved by enabling him to satisfy the law."

When this is generally realized there will be more seriousness, more fear of sin, and more respect for religion in the world.

CHAPTER VII

SCIENCE AND THE CONSEQUENCES OF SIN

Science suggests the Permanent Nature of the Consequences of Sin.

IN support of these arguments, based on reason and Christian ethics, in favour of the inviolability of moral and spiritual law, there are certain considerations supplied by science.

One fact is that the consequences of all action are eternal. " The effects of a single act of freewill extend through the whole of space, and will last as long as the present order continues. Thus the voluntary motion of a man's hand not only affects the motion of the earth by a calculable amount, but also the motions of the sun and of the remotest stars, and the motions of all these bodies will differ for the rest of time from the motions they would have had if the man had not moved his hand."[1]

Since this is true of all action in the material world, one cannot reasonably doubt that, in the much more sensitive world of personality, the same truth holds good; and if so, then it follows that the effects of each sin upon personality are infinite. Granted that personality is everlasting, then, in God's omniscience, each sin is everlastingly working against Him in the souls He loves, and needing some counteraction to maintain the balance of His creation, or, as we might say, " cover it." All-holy justice is ever demanding that a sin's

---

[1] Dr. G. F. C. Searle, *The Modern Conception of the Universe* ; quoted by Dr. McNeile in *Self-Training in Prayer*, p. 27.

ceaseless activities should be ceaselessly atoned for by some adequate and eternal action.

It seems, then, that God must provide some antidote of holiness which shall continue everlastingly to meet the everlasting discords of our sins in the moral and spiritual sphere. There must be some fresh element brought into God's creation which, like the third note in a chord of music, shall mediate to bring harmony to the discord between sin and Divine Holiness.

The Immutability of Law.

To deny that sin calls for punishment from God is to deny the fundamental conception of law in creation, taught, not only by theology, which declares that " the wages of sin is death,"[1] and " Sin, when it is completed bringeth forth death,"[2] but also by science, which asserts that the laws of Nature cannot be broken with impunity—teaching confirmed by human experience, which has found it necessary to found social order upon punishment.[3] In other words, God's law, written in Nature, is that the consequence of law-breaking is suffering—a step towards death. The very word " law " implies this, for law can only exist by means of penalty to enforce it. It is a mistake to assume that God's rule is based upon love. In the ultimate analysis Satan submits because he must—because God is almighty. The same is true also of all the forces of evil. Fundamentally God reigns, not by His love, but by His almightiness. Science teaches us that natural law means nothing more than " natural sequence "— i.e., that certain consequences follow certain causes, motions, or forces, such as, in personal matters, and in the moral or spiritual sphere, men call good or bad actions. Anything which does not follow this sequence is crushed out of existence by pressure of surrounding circumstance.

---

[1] Rom. vi. 23.　　　　　　　　　　　　[2] Jas. i. 15.

[3] *Cf.* President Wilson's statement upon the necessity of basing any hope of peace upon force.

The Law of Punishment.

Under God's reign of law, bad consequences always follow bad actions, so that unless some favourable preventive force be interposed we may be sure our sin will find us out (Num. xxxii. 23). In other words, the penalty of suffering must follow sin unless atonement be made. Punishment, viewed from this point of view, is not " revenge," but simply " order " in the moral and spiritual spheres, and this suggests another obstacle to the free forgiveness of sin. For just in the same way as it is recognized that God cannot interfere with the regular operation of natural laws in order to prevent accidents, because that would be contrary to the constitution of His being, so also would it be equally contrary to His nature to abrogate the laws of punishment in the moral and spiritual sphere.

The teaching of science on this point has recently been stated as follows:[1]—

" It is through ideals that men progress, even though the ideal may be only a better-shaped arrowhead."

" The ideal is . . . the conscious recognition of the vital impulse which has conditioned all the progress of the unconscious beings, and still conditions the progress of conscious man. . . . If he sets himself against the upward impulse . . . he is voluntarily opposing the only thing in nature that is capable of progress; he is enlisting his will on the side of the downward forces that rule matter; it is not too much to say he has set his signature to a treaty with death; and this, I believe, is the fundamental essence of sin " (p. 68).

" The vital impulse urges the race to develop, but it can only act in virtue of the power of development inherent in each individual . . . individuals recognize themselves as bearers of the power of development, not only for the race, but for themselves " (p. 136).

[1] See *Evolution and the Need of Atonement,* by S. A. McDowall. The order of these quotations is not that of the author.

" Experience teaches that to bend the will towards progress is right, while to bend it towards retrogression or to leave it dormant is wrong, because it entails destruction " (p. 74). So that the nature of sin is " the voluntary renunciation of struggle and discomfort " (p. 175), and the " conscious opposition to the vital impulse " (p. 122). " A man does not sin with this full understanding of what he is doing; but in so far as there is the slightest idea of ' better ' or ' worse ' as applied to action, there is recognition of the existence of two tendencies in life, and to choose the wrong path must lead to the suspension of extinction of the vital impulse as surely as it did in the lower stages of creation . . . compromise with katabolism, acceptance of equilibrium, inert disregard of the divine unrest, means death in the long-run. Among the unconscious creatures the race that, as a whole, chooses the wrong path is doomed. And this is equally true of races of men " (pp. 123, 124).

" For the race there are . . . mainly consequences, but for the individual punishments. For just in so far as he recognizes an ideal of any kind . . . he concedes that life is moving towards a goal; just in so far as he spurns that ideal, so far he is voluntarily opposing the progress of life, so far he is opposing the will of Him who gave that life, so far he is liable to the inevitable punishment of separation from God—a separation that must be absolute and complete, however small the sin, since between the Perfect and that which *can never become* perfect an impassable gulf is fixed " (p. 137).

It is probably in this direction of the inevitableness of penal suffering resulting from the immutability and inexorable operation of law that we shall have to look in order to find an adequate basis upon which to build up that sense of the danger of sin from which the great religious movements of the past have sprung, and without which there is reason to think no great improvement can take place at the present time. For the idea

of "service" which has developed and become so
noticeable during the war, especially among our troops,
valuable as it is as a motive for moral and religious
action, cannot be counted upon to take the place of that
conviction of the danger of sin and consequent need of
salvation which has inspired religious movements in the
past.

For the instinct of service is a secondary motive
originating in, and dependent upon, the consciousness
of the need of others. It is this prior condition which
calls it into being and action, and it cannot exist without this foundation to rest upon. The soldiers at the
front see with their own eyes, and generally have
experienced in their own persons, the discomfort,
exhaustion, weakness, and pain which call for the
cheerful and unselfish service of others, and for this
reason are sensitive to its appeal, and ready to respond
when the need arises. Such service is the natural
response to human need.

But the appeal for religious service as a motive to
live the religious life would be issued, as things are at
present, under very different circumstances. For in
this case there is no feeling that others stand in danger
and need to which the appeal could be addressed, and
therefore philanthropical and religious work are not
analogous in the appeal they make for service. So
when the Archbishops' Committee, in its Report on the
Evangelistic Work of the Church, laments the lack of
the missionary spirit and zeal in this work, and proposes
to evoke it by appealing to the spirit of service, we ask:
" But can it be evoked in this way ? Can men be
zealous about saving others so long as they fail to
realize that there is any real danger, and therefore any
real need for them to be saved ?" It seems clear that
the need for saving them must first be realized, and
so long as men do not believe that " the wages of sin
is death "—that sinners are in danger—there cannot
be zeal for evangelization. And at the present time that

is the position.   There is no general belief prevailing as
to either the danger or the need; and therefore, if we
depend upon the instinct for service to provide the
inspiration for a revival of spiritual life in this country,
apart from any deep sense of the need of salvation, we
are probably preparing for ourselves a great disappointment.   It is the creation of belief in this need which is
the real task Christianity has to face.   It is not enough
merely to recognize " the profound difficulty of finding
a motive for repentance and amendment that will
appeal to this generation."[1]   If this motive is a necessary part of spiritual experience, we must go farther
than this, and since salvation is always " the heart of
the Gospel," it is impossible to escape the conclusion
that some adequate motive must be found for creating
a desire to escape from the power and guilt of sin—for
producing a fear of it; and earnest search should be
instituted for its discovery.   It is to be feared that the
desire to serve will not be found sufficient unless it be
a desire to serve by saving; but, on the other hand,
there is reason to think that the old fear of sin and
reverence for God's holiness might be revived by
teaching on the immutable operation of moral law.
And this would, moreover, be in line with modern
scientific thought.

[1] The Report on the Evangelistic Work of the Church, p. 13.

CHAPTER VIII

THE BIBLE AND PENAL SUFFERING

The Old Testament teaches the Penalty of Sin before the New Testament reveals its Remedy.

WE turn from what the experience of life and science teach us to God's revealed teaching in the Bible, and there we find ground for the same belief that Divine Holiness requires penalty for sin.

We have already seen it teaches that the penalty is separation from God, and all that we have seen on that point is in itself evidence that sin calls in the first place for punishment by separation, rather than for restoration. But in view of recent tendencies it may be useful to note how the Bible teaching confirms the view that sin appeals first to God's wrath rather than to His restorative love—how it demands punishment rather than remedy—so that it may be said: " The Hebrew Scriptures, penetrated through and through by the idea of a divine retribution, have a large doctrine of judgment . . . a world judgment."[1]

The Teaching of the Judaic Law.

The idea that sin demands divine punishment underlies the whole Jewish ritual and sacrificial system, of which the general significance has been summarized in the dictum that without shedding of blood there can be no remission of sins (Heb. ix. 22). By the daily sacrifices, by the Temple ritual, by the rites of circumcision and purification, by the sacrifices connected with

[1] Hastings' *Dictionary of the Bible*, article " Eschatology," vol. i., p. 751.

special circumstances and festivities, and especially by the festival of the Passover and the Day of Atonement, it was impressed upon the Jew that death as death is a primary essential in the atonement of sin.[1]   And in this the Old Covenant was prophetic of the New.   It only prepared the way for the acceptance of this truth in a deeper and more spiritual sense.   It is not too much to say that, if this be not so, then the whole teaching of the Jewish system is emptied of its primary significance, and the fundamental views of Christendom for 1900 years have been mistaken.   If the sacrificial system did not point to our Lord as the Victim, the spotless Lamb of God bearing the penalty of man's sin, but only foreshadowed Him as the Priest offering our penitence, then it was wholly misunderstood by the people it was meant to teach; it was misinterpreted by the prophets; it did not prepare men for the truth, but misled them; and God's institution failed in its object. In this case the Holy Spirit has not led the Church into all truth, and her error has been one not only of shortcoming, but of positive misdirection.

The Evidence of the Jewish Wars of Extermination.

In addition to the teaching of the law and prophets, we also have the evidence of history on this point in the wars of extermination waged under divine direction against the Canaanites.   It cannot be questioned that they are represented as wars of retribution upon national sin; and if it be objected that it is not reasonable to produce this argument at the present stage of Old Testament criticism, but that they must be viewed rather as the natural outcome of primitive savagery in

---

1 " The *Kappara* is specially the function of the blood (see Lev. xvii. 11; and *cf.* in the ritual of the sin-offering Exod. xxx. 10; Lev. iv. 30. (23), viii. 15, xvi. 15 *f.*, 18 *f.*, 27; Ezek. xliii. 20, xlv. 19 *f.*) on account, as is expressly said in Lev. xvii. 11, of its being the seat of the soul or life, the most precious and also the purest and most immaterial gift that can be offered to God " (Hastings' *Dictionary of the Bible*, article " Propitiation ").

a nation trying to make a place for itself among hostile peoples, yet it cannot be questioned but that these wars took place under divine providence, and, as historical events, reveal God's methods of dealing with men. As such we learn from them that under the moral conditions of the times they represented an ethical advance upon fraternization. To be at war was morally better than to make treaties of peace with these people; and, so far as we can judge, the extermination which overtook them, and which is represented to us as a punishment for their sins, was advantageous, and perhaps even necessary, to the moral and spiritual advance of the world. Judaism, both in its history and religion, is not hostile to Christianity, but complementary, and represents certain features in the unchanging character of God. Our Saviour did not come to destroy the law, but to fulfil it.

Teaching of the New Testament.

But it is not only the great, general lines of teaching in the Old Testament which present the view of God's retributory attitude towards sin. When we come to the New Testament, all the teaching about Christ being our sacrifice and our ransom suggests the idea that He paid the price of human sin by suffering the penalty demanded by Divine Holiness. The history of the Atonement itself, from the beginning up to recent times— when an effort is being made to explain this view away —proves that it is the original and powerful idea conveyed by this teaching; and some of the evidence to be adduced in favour of the view that, in the first instance, sin calls for divine retribution, and not only penitence, is of the most authoritative nature.

Our Lord's Teaching in the Parables.

Much of our Lord's own teaching in His parables and elsewhere involves the idea of God's holiness demanding punishment for sin as its first requirement, and even that it is due as just retribution rather than as a remedial measure.

At the end of this book a more detailed account of His teaching will be found,[1] but it will be useful to summarize it here. He describes God as an angry King who in His wrath slays the rebellious; He speaks of eternal fire; of outer darkness; of the destruction of sinners; of sins which shall never be forgiven; of the judgment of hell, and He appeals to the fear of it; of vain appeals for mercy; of days of vengeance. Indeed, if one reads them carefully, one cannot help noticing that there is much more about God's wrath and even vengeance upon sinners in our Lord's parables and other teaching than about restorative discipline. The Parables of Mercy—the Prodigal Son, the Lost Sheep, and Lost Piece of Money—fill a very large place in the public conception of our Lord's teaching, but it is out of all proportion to the space it occupies when compared with that filled by His teaching upon God's punishment of sinners. It is only in accordance with the tone of their Master's teaching when St. Paul speaks of the " indignation " of God, " to whom vengeance belongeth," and who " visiteth with wrath "; when the author of the Epistle to the Hebrews writes: " It is a fearful thing to fall into the hands of the living God," the fierceness of whose consuming fire shall devour the adversaries; and when even the Apostle of Love writes of " the wrath of the Lamb " and " the fierceness of the wrath of Almighty God."

Summary of Bible Teaching.

No doubt much might be said to weaken the force of some of these passages, and probably they do not so much supply a definite basis upon which a logical demonstration might be built up as merely indicate a divine attitude towards sin from which retributory action would most naturally proceed; but after making

[1] See Appendix A.

all due allowance for this, the broad significance of this teaching is clear. It can hardly be questioned, and has been too much ignored by those who claim that penitence is all that God's holiness requires, without anything being required in the way of reparation or any other satisfaction being made. When one notices the considerable place taken by penal suffering, even in the form of retributory punishment, in the revealed attitude of God towards sinners, especially in our Lord's teaching, one cannot help feeling that the denial that it can have any real place in God's dealings with man, and the disparagement of it in much modern teaching on the Atonement, is not in real harmony with the full truth of things.

Bible Teaching does not justify the Popular Idea of "Free Forgiveness."

Yet there is no doubt there is a feeling abroad in some quarters that it would be unworthy of God, and somehow inconsistent with the highest morality, with His perfect holiness, for Him to require reparation for our sins. This is due, no doubt, partly to the sense of our entire inability to make any adequate compensation for them, causing belief to jump with desire, although, as a matter of pure morality and justice, there is no doubt we ought to make such reparation as we can. Moreover, it is reasonable to suppose that, since it is better for a man to make reparation for the wrongs he has inflicted than not to do so, God's love will have provided a way by which we can rise to this higher plane of moral existence. When it is made clear that this is so, that God's love has refused to leave us in the unhappy position of having done Him irreparable and eternal injury, but has made reparation possible, men will willingly admit their moral obligation to do so.

Another reason for this prevalent feeling that no reparation is due to God is the mistaken way in which

ideas of vengeance have become intermingled with our
conceptions of justice.

But a still more common reason is the frequent use
of the words " free forgiveness " in connection with
God's attitude to sinners, which has probably arisen
from the expression " He frankly forgave them both "
in our Lord's Parable of the Two Debtors (Luke vii. 42,
A.V.).[1]

" Free forgiveness " is one of those alliterative
phrases which captures the religious imagination with
its pleasant suggestions of generous love. And, like
many other ear-catching and popular phrases, its effect
is profoundly misleading. Indeed, one may venture
to say that in God's relations to sinners no such thing
as " free forgiveness " is known, and that from the
moral point of view it ought not to be. No such thing
is known, for all forgiveness is conditional, and the
satisfying of the conditions which are required is the
price men have to pay for it. Secondly, no such thing
as " free forgiveness " ought to exist, because the
necessary conditions are those required by morality,
and therefore ought to be paid. Forgiveness where
there is no true penitence is either a blunder or an
immorality. God has provided for us something much
better than " free forgiveness "—viz., justification, a
justified forgiveness.

The Conditions for Forgiveness as taught in Some of our Lord's Parables.

What, then, are the requisite conditions ? We have
already spoken of them, and need not go beyond the
familiar teaching of the Church. The thing required is
true repentance in its threefold aspects of contrition,
confession, and restitution. It is clear that in pure

[1] St. Paul's expression " the free gift " (Rom. v. 15, 16) does not
refer to forgiveness, but to the gift of righteousness (see verse 17)—
i.e., to God's whole plan of salvation, by which it is possible for sinners
to be cleansed from sin and clothed with holiness. Hence Alford says
that " the free gift " is justification.

morality these are as much—indeed, more—due to an injured God, than to a fellow-sinner.

In the Parable of the Unmerciful Servant, from which the phrase probably arose, the plan of the story assumes that in the first instance the King mistakenly supposed a state of mind in the debtor which would justify forgiveness. The man did not deny his indebtedness, and in great distress fell on his knees and besought mercy for himself and his family. The King, therefore, was justified in remitting the penalty, since the offender's words and actions seemed to satisfy all the necessary conditions. Contrition is represented by his distress of mind, confession of penalty deserved by his acknowledgment of the debt, and prayer for mercy on his knees; and the spirit of reparation by his apparent willingness and promise to pay all when he could. This attitude of his whole personality justified the King's action, by supplying the conditions under which forgiveness became morally possible. If the debtor had denied or excused his debt, or denied the moral right of the King to require payment, or had ignored his claim, or defied him, can we believe that forgiveness would have been forthcoming? It would not have been right to grant it; and if we want to know whether or no our Lord teaches in this parable that forgiveness is free, we have only to look to the end of it. For when the King found out the debtor's true state of mind, and that the moral conditions which justify forgiveness were lacking; that the man had so little sense of his true position, and consequently so little real appreciation of the value of forgiveness as his subsequent actions revealed, then his forgiveness was completely revoked, since the conditions upon which it had been granted did not exist, the price of it had not really been paid.[1] There is certainly no free forgiveness in the sentence delivering him " to the

[1] See Trench on the Parables, who points out that the servant was condemned, not for his fresh offence, but for his old debt (pp. 162-164, 14th edition).

tormentors till he should pay all the debt that was due."
The fact is, as the context shows, that this parable was
intended as a warning against the spirit of unmerciful-
ness rather than a lesson upon the principles of forgiveness, which, although they are deducible from it, is not
the real object in view. The man was condemned
because, instead of trying to satisfy the claims of both
mercy and justice, and so fulfil all righteousness, he had
allowed his own sense of obligation and the duty of
mercy to be crushed out under the claims of selfishness
disguised as justice, just as some people would allow
the claims of justice to be stifled under those of a
seeming love. There is nothing to show that our Lord
would have condemned the man if he had come to
some merciful composition with his fellow-servant on
the matter of repayment, and had offered it to his lord
as such part settlement of the debt owed as it was
within his power to make. We, under the limitations
of our nature, cannot always reconcile every moral
claim with those of other claims, and often have to
ignore secondary claims for those of a higher moral
value; but God, as almighty, omniscient, and loving,
may be confidently counted upon to reconcile all claims
and ignore none, and so "to devise means to fetch
home again his banished that he be not expelled from
Him."[1]

Our Lord's other two great parables upon forgiveness
equally represent that the necessary conditions must
be satisfied, the price paid, before it is granted. The
prodigal was not forgiven until he had first " come to
himself " in penitence, confessed " I am not worthy,"
and made what reparation he could by humbly returning home with the determination to render obedient
and loving service in future. And the father, on his
side, is not represented as moved by impulsive affection
to follow the prodigal with an offer of free forgiveness,
which, until the time was ripe, would have been scorned;

[1] 2 Sam. xiv. 12-14.

but as waiting strongly and patiently at home until his erring son had satisfied the conditions necessary for receiving it, and had paid the moral and spiritual price which true wisdom and love required of him.

In another parable, the publican in the same way obtains the justification which the Pharisee fails to receive, because his words and actions show on analysis that they include and express all the elements of a true repentance—contrition, confession, and such reparation as he had it in his power to make.

The Fundamental Condition for Forgiveness is the surrender of the Will to God.

Yet, to go back to what was said about forgiveness not being free, we must recognize that it is much more completely a gift than we have so far admitted, since the power to repent, in all its threefold aspects, is in itself a gift from God. The capacity for neither contrition nor even true confession is inherent in us, and much less the power to make adequate reparation. Repentance must come from God.

Yet it is not forced upon us. It is contingent upon our own freewill, upon our desire to repent. Unless we give our mind and will to it in the fullest sense, we shall never be able to receive that ability to repent which is necessary in order to obtain forgiveness. Fundamentally, then, this is what we give to God: what His holiness, including His love, requires of us, the free surrender of our will. And our will includes our whole selves. The price is, after all, that of our slavery—albeit a willing slavery—to God: a price most hard to pay, but found ultimately to be a slavery which is perfect freedom.

We Conclude that the Full Reparation due for Sin is both Necessary and somehow provided for.

We conclude that holiness must require men to make reparation for their offences, since if they are not willing to do so they are failing in one of the essential elements of repentance, which alone makes forgiveness right or morally possible.

We must further observe that if men desired to make reparation (and we cannot deny that every good man does desire it), but were permanently unable to offer it, then God would have failed to make provision for men to rise to the moral and spiritual plane they desire. At present it is impossible for us to rise to that level. We cannot offer adequate reparation because we are incapable of making the complete submission of our wills to God in actual obedient service. The most we can do is to set our wills in that direction, and progress some of the way. But, having done that time after time, we fail to make good our intention. We cannot love God as we should, nor serve Him even as we desire. Thus we are in a position which, if permanent, could not be reconciled with the hopes which the perfect love of God must cherish for men. This, obviously, would be an impossible *impasse*, and therefore we conclude that God's holiness must not only desire full reparation to be made to Him by men for their sins, but also have provided for its possibility. The thing itself must be possible in the fullest degree. We may be quite sure of that. God's love guarantees it. It only remains, therefore, for us to discover how it has been made possible and is to be attained by us, if it be God's will that we should apprehend it.

PART IV

HOW OUR LORD SATISFIED THE REQUIRE-MENTS OF DIVINE HOLINESS

CHAPTER I

WHY OUR LORD SUFFERED

Our Need of a Mediator.

WE have noticed man's inability to satisfy the require-ments of God's holiness. This makes it necessary for him to have someone to approach God on his behalf. The great public services of the Church teach the same lesson—firstly, by placing a general confession before the chief acts of worship, preceded in the Holy Com-munion by a form of self-examination; and secondly, in the purifying remission of sins which follows, and in which our Saviour is presented to us as the Mediator through whom sin is forgiven and approach to God made possible.

A mediator, or intermediary, is a sort of double ambassador, authorized to act for both parties. In the Old Testament Moses acted in this double capacity. He spoke both for the people to God, and also for God to the people; but later it was, broadly speaking, the priests who acted for the people Godward, and the prophets who acted for God to the people.

Jesus our All-sufficing Representative.

In our Lord we see the two offices again united. As perfect God and perfect man, He is a complete Mediator fitted to represent and act for both sides. In His self-imposed title, " The Son of Man," He claims to be our all-sufficing Representative before God. As Son of Man—*i.e.*, of mankind—He has inherited and contains in Himself all the qualities proper to humanity: of manhood and womanhood, of Jew, and Greek, and Gentile; and therefore, as the " all-inclusive Head " of humanity, He fitly represents mankind as a whole. Moreover, as the solidarity of the race is a real thing, He also truly represents each individual in the race. He is the Ambassador to speak and act for each one of us to God.

This truth has been much pressed in recent teaching on the Atonement, and far-reaching consequences have been deduced, and the fact that it was our Lord's own self-chosen title compels one to accord to it all the implications reasonably attached to it as probably intended by Him. But inasmuch as the realization of the solidarity of the race is a thing requiring thought and effort, whereas the sense of our separate individual existence is a natural, ever-present impression, and one not at all easily shaken off, we feel strongly, even though sadly, that it is only too easy for our Lord to have taken action for the race, and for ourselves person-ally to be outside the range of its benefits—that is, for us individually not to be in a position to base any moral claim upon it.

This impression is confirmed by the fact that, as the Lamb of God without spot or blemish, our Lord was entirely free from any stain of sin in which we are involved; so that it appears He cannot represent us as sinners in the same deep sense as He represents humanity in its innocent, God-given qualities acquired by Him at His Incarnation. Yet, since humanity is sinful, it seems to be almost necessarily implied by His self-chosen title that there may be some innocent involvement or contact of our Lord with human sin. At any rate, He certainly associated with sinners of even the worst type. There was at least physical

contact, and His conversations with sinners such as
Judas and the woman of Samaria suggest mental and
spiritual association also.   In this direction, revealing
the unspeakable love of God for man, we have some
shadowy indication of the way in which Christ was
" made sin for us," and it shows this to be much more
than a mere literary expression—to have, in fact, a
basis in reality.   The personalities of our Saviour and
sinners met, and impinged upon one another.

Yet it may well be questioned whether this association of our Lord as the " inclusive Head " of the human
race with sinful individuals is definite enough to justify
all the consequences based upon it by some writers on
the Atonement.   The moral sufficiency of His representative atonement to win forgiveness for sinners, if
based only on this ground, is doubtful.   For the present,
however, we need not consider this, and it will be
enough for us to recognize the uniquely representative
character of His human nature.

Jesus our Substitute.

In addition to being our Mediator and Representative,
it is claimed that our Lord suffered as our Substitute
also, and it is round the ideas connected with this word
that most objections to the Atonement have centred.
These kind of objections in their crudest form have been
forcibly expressed by Mr. Blatchford, who writes:
" God acts unjustly when He pardons for Christ's sake
. . . the fact that Christ is willing to suffer for another
man's sin only counts for the merit of Christ, and does
not in any way diminish the offence of the sinner. . . .
To forgive James because John had been unjustly
flogged would be to assert that because John was good,
and because the master had acted unjustly, James
deserved to be forgiven.   This is not only contrary to
reason and to justice; it is also very false sentiment."[1]

The surprising thing about such writing as this is

[1] *God and My Neighbour*, pp. 126-127.

that the authors do not see they prove a great deal too much, and that if this teaching really represented Christianity the existence of the Church for 1800 years, based upon such an immorality, would be the greatest miracle of history. Obviously it is impossible.

Yet it is unquestionable that our Saviour is frequently said in the Bible to have suffered for us, that He bore our sins, the Just for the unjust, and that with His stripes we are healed; and the explanation that these are only literary expressions, not to be taken literally, does not satisfy us, nor explain the whole underlying meaning of the Mosaic law and general Bible teaching. The doctrine is interwoven with the very core of Christianity. Nearly all the difficulties connected with teaching on Atonement centre round this question of justice, and so hardly any question can be more important for us to ask than: "How can Christ have suffered for our sins except in such a manner as to outrage our moral sense?" That is the question which men are putting with ever-increasing earnestness, and many answers have been given to it with the object of avoiding the moral dilemma Mr. Blatchford so forcibly states.

Reaction from Crude Substitutionism.

In the Middle Ages "substitution" of the crudest kind was taught. Our Lord was even said to have come under the malediction of the Father in the sinner's place. As a consequence there has been a very natural recoil from anything partaking of the nature of so artificial a "legal transaction." Going to the opposite extreme, some have claimed that our Lord's sufferings were in essence nothing more than the martyrdom which Plato long before had foretold would be the fate of God, or of any perfectly holy man who came to teach man righteousness in this wicked world.[1] Others

---

[1] This is practically the explanation of Canon Wilson in *The Gospel of the Atonement*. Jesus suffered in obedience to the great law of suffering necessarily obtaining the higher planes of holiness.

explain our Lord's death upon the Cross as being a confession, in the sense of acknowledgment, made on behalf of humanity of the justice of God's judgment upon sin;[1] and, lastly, Dr. Moberly has taught that it was a perfect act of penitence offered by our Lord as the inclusive head of the race for the sins of mankind.

Objections to Some Modern Teaching.

One great objection to all this teaching is that it has to ignore or explain away the natural meaning of a great mass of Bible teaching. One feels that it is a sort of mutilation of God's revelation forced upon us in order to make it fit our finite incapacity to perceive or grasp the truth.

Another objection is that when even this is done the moral difficulties with regard to vicarious suffering are only partially removed; for the Providence which demands or permits martyrdom still seems unjust. We feel things should be ordered better.

Vicarious Suffering not Unusual.

Yet, on the other hand, the principle of vicarious suffering is found everywhere in the world, as if it were an underlying principle of life. It is, indeed, probably true that all progress is made at the cost of more or less vicarious suffering, from the mother who suffers to give birth to her child, to the student or scientist who burns the midnight oil, or the inventor who gives his fortune and long years of painful labour to perfect his discoveries, or the aeronaut who is killed in trying a new machine by which to preserve the world's liberties. In the spheres of invention, of literature, and geographical discovery, we find the same thing. Everywhere the world's " frontiersmen " live hard and often die painfully, to open the way for others to advance to a larger life. Our Lord's saying, " Others laboured, and

[1] *Cf.* J. McLeod Campbell in *The Nature of the Atonement :* " The Cross was a great Amen to God's sentence upon sin."

ye are entered into their labours," might be written up over the door of civilization, and the road by which the car of progress has travelled is strewn with the bodies of those who prepared the way.

The same is true in the life of nations as well as of civilization as a whole. A recent article in the *Hibbert Journal* says: " . . . mankind proceeds on its upward course at the expense of individuals and nations. The French Revolution, which inaugurated a new era of general freedom, has profited France least of all; the lawsuit against Warren Hastings was unfair to him, yet for India it meant the greatest possible blessing; Belgium's heroism cannot possibly be recompensed. Metaphysically mankind represents an indivisible whole, and our enemies are one; there is no real separateness. Everybody is guilty for one single individual's sin, one person may save the world; every crime and every sacrifice is vicarious. Present humanity is being judged in the person of Germany; it is being redeemed to some extent in the person of France."[1]

But if what the *nations* do and suffer illustrates the fact that vicarious sacrifice is a principle of human progress, the Great War has brought its meaning home still more closely to the *individuals* who make up the nations. " Since every man who has come forward to serve his country knows that what he has done is right and noble, he must feel sure that a similar self-sacrifice is one of the attributes of the God Man."

So vicarious sacrifice is everywhere present in the moral life of the world, from the life of nations to that of individuals, from God on His throne to every mother in her home. It is only a question of degree.

The Morality of Vicarious Suffering.

Moreover, there seems to be something in it which raises it above the level of justice into a higher moral

[1] See article on " The Meaning of the War " by Count Herman Keyserling, in *Hibbert Journal*, April, 1915.

plane altogether. If it is not just it is because it is
more than just. We realize that the satisfaction of
the claims of justice is the *least* morality can demand,
while love and holiness require much more than what
is merely " fair." Applying this thought to our Lord,
we should expect His life to offer a supreme example of
this kind of morality, and to be more likely to find the
true explanation of the Cross in the direction of an
exalted supermorality than by seeking to palliate or
limit the suffering He was called upon to endure.

In any case our Lord suffered vicariously for human
sin, if only in the hardships of His life and His martyr's
death; and if it is only a question of " justice," this
was " unjust." From the point of view of " fairness,"
the morality of the way in which He "suffered for us "
and " bore our sins " is only a matter of degree. If it
is not an offence to justice for our Lord to be called
upon to be obedient to the Cross as a martyr, which no
one seems to question, then why should it be unjust
for Him to be called upon to endure any other vicarious
suffering in consequence of man's sin ? If the full
burden is intolerably unjust, the partial burden is
partially unjust.

The Question of Justice not Involved in our Lord's Vicarious Suffering.

The only answer is that in neither case does the
question come within the sphere of justice. It rises
above it in the moral world in the same way as an
explorer perishing in Antarctic cold in the interests of
science or a patriot dying for his country. The question
of justice does not apply. It is, then, in this direction
of idealism that we must look for the explanation of the
morality of the Cross, and practically all difficulty disappears if we view it as a divine adventure of sacrifice,
inspired by love, and voluntarily undertaken by our
Lord on behalf of His Father and fallen humanity: on
behalf of His Father in order that He might experience

10

the joy of seeing the children of His creation triumph over evil, and enabled to offer Him the reparation they owed; and on behalf of humanity in order that, freed from the guilt of sin, man might rise into the presence of God, and give Him that holy service love desires to render.

Our Saviour suffered no Punishment on the Cross, but passed through a Helpful, Qualifying Experience.

In studying the question of the morality of the Atonement the mind must be cleared of all idea of punishment in connection with our Lord's crucifixion; the conception of His being punished by the Father for human sin must be entirely eliminated. It was in no sense a case of punishment inflicted, nor endured.

For suffering only becomes punishment when inflicted and endured as such. It is not punishment when it has no connection with, nor reference to, wrong-doing on the part of the sufferer in the mind of either the person who inflicts or of him who endures it. In this case it is no more punishment than the pain inflicted by a surgeon for the benefit of a patient. In the latter case, even though the suffering be of a kind specifically connected with, and administered as, punishment for wrong-doing, yet it is not, and cannot be, punishment, because the wrong-doing does not exist, and the sufferer therefore cannot receive it as punishment. To him it is simply pain. An innocent person cannot, strictly speaking, be punished. He can only be made to endure pain which, if he were guilty, would be punishment.

For both these reasons, therefore, though our Lord endured the penalty due to sin, He was not punished. It was simply an experience that He decided to go through in penal suffering with the object of attaining a certain status, of being able to occupy a certain position, otherwise unattainable, which would enable Him to carry out the divine plan of salvation for man. This being the moral nature of His suffering, there was no injustice in it, but only self-sacrifice.

This is the view taken of the penal[1] suffering endured
by our Lord in this book. He experienced it, not, of
course, in order "to gain experience" in the usual
meaning of the phrase, but in order that He might be
in the position of one who had actually, as a matter of
historic fact, endured the consequences of sin naturally
flowing from the God in His relations towards evil as
part of the existing order of things. The only way in
which a man can become an Arctic explorer, and enjoy
the honours and personal knowledge which result from
such a position, is for him actually to undertake and
experience exploration in the Arctic regions. No mere
knowledge of, nor enthusiasm for, the work of Arctic
explorers, nor sympathy with the sufferings involved,
nor other subjective experience, however complete, is
enough apart from actual experience. Only this will
serve the purpose.

Or to take another illustration. The only rightful
way by which a citizen of the United States could obtain
for his children the pension voted to the descendants
of soldiers who fought for the North in the Federal and
Confederate War was for him actually to have enlisted
and served in its armies. No amount of sympathy for
the cause nor willingness to die for it would otherwise
be sufficient. Only by the thing having been actually
done could his children morally make out a claim.

So also with ourselves, and the benefit of the forgiveness of sins flowing to Christians from our Saviour.

1. It was only by actually dying Himself, and over-
coming in the experience of death all those temptations
of the soul connected with it, such as the temptation to
relinquish in that process the grasp of faith and loose
His hold on God; it was only by actual experience of
the spiritual weakness and disabilities arising from the

[1] The word "penal" is not used here to imply that these sufferings
were inflicted as punishment, but only suffering which under ordinary
circumstances would have been such. In our Lord's case, as we shall
see, it was simply "experimental." The word is used in this special
narrower sense in other places also.

alienation of the soul from God, and by actually rising above them, that He could communicate to others in and through union with Himself the status of one who had felt the full force of temptation, and could be in them the actual victorious power which man's necessity required.

2. Only in this way, by the experience of triumphant obedience and the practical achievement of perfect holiness whilst suffering under the full force of evil and the weakness of impending death, could He attain actually and in fact the highest conceivable standard of holy obedience, and so be able to transfer to those in union with Him similar qualities of perfected holiness.

3. Only in this way could He transfer to men through identification with Himself the moral and spiritual status of one who had already suffered the penalty due to sin.

So He offered Himself for the work of man's salvation by these means, and in His human nature actually experienced death in spiritual alienation from God. So henceforth He is in men who are in union with Him a power which, while suffering under all the disabilities which sin and death impose upon men, has yet overcome all their force of temptation, and can convey to Christians in union with Himself, not only the possibilities of a like victory, but even a share in His own, and a like achievement and share in His perfect, obedient holiness. Union with Christ is union with One who has suffered sin's penalty, has experienced the utmost temptation, has conquered sin, and attained holiness.

In no other way could these results have been attained, and in answer to the charge of the injustice of the Cross it is important to emphasize that this suffering of the penal consequences of sin was clearly, and in a true sense, not an experience of punishment, but simply of self-sacrificing achievement. And as this view of the Atonement has as its central feature the actual experience of the penal consequences of sin, as compared with those theories which, in the supposed interests of justice, deny that experience, it may fittingly be called " the experiential theory."

So, if it be asked, Why did Jesus suffer death and the penalties of sin ? the answer is twofold. He undertook to suffer them in His own Person in order that He might be to others in union with Him—

(1) The presence of one who has already suffered the penal consequences of sin, so that the Christian in effective union with His Saviour already has in him, through the presence of Christ, the real experience—at least, in embryo, and capable of being developed into its proper moral and spiritual effects—of the punishment of sin.

(2) A victorious power, a spiritual force which has actually and already overcome all the forces of sin and death exerted to their utmost capacity. For Christ is in men not only a power which can overcome sin and death, but a power which has already done so.

Thus, by identification with his Saviour a Christian has conveyed to him, and conveyed just in proportion as that identification is complete, something of the status of one who has already suffered the punishment of sin and attained the holiness of a perfect obedience.

Though such inclusion of the Christian in the sacrifice of our Lord, such co-operation with Christ in His crucifixion, may seem at first sight to be a fantastic impossibility, yet the reader is asked to remember that somehow and by some means St. Paul felt himself to have been really—if spiritually—sacrificed with Christ, and not definitely and finally to reject the suggestion as altogether unworthy of consideration until he has seen what can be brought forward in favour of such an identification combined with distinction of personality, as this would require, in Part V. of this book.

The nature of our Lord's sufferings and in what way they achieve His purpose will be dealt with later, but it may be said here that the view taken in this book is, as stated above, that they included the actual penalty of sin; but the fact of the voluntary nature of our Lord's undertaking, and that the part taken in it by the Father would be at least no less painful to Him than the Son's part was to our Lord, lifts the action far above those ideas of retribution by an angry God upon his innocent Son which occupy the minds of the more crude substitutionalists.

We may note further that the experience of this particular suffering was " necessary," because to God's omniscient holiness it was the very best way, the way most worthy of Him, and therefore the way He was bound to adopt for the salvation of man.

The Experiential Theory illustrated.[1]

An incident pictured by Charles Reade in his novel " It is Never Too Late to Mend " affords a helpful illustration at this point. The story is timed in the days before that prison reform which his book played no small part in helping to bring about, and describes how a prison chaplain set himself to work to cleanse the prison to which he was attached from the cruelties at that date often practised upon prisoners. He recognized that it was useless merely to draw the attention of the authorities to what was going on, because, being of the unimaginative, official, and commonplace type of men, they would only have replied that the disciplinary measures complained of were customary and necessary, and not so painful as the prisoners' cunning had led the inexperience of the chaplain to suppose. The only way open to him to impress upon the Commissioners the reality of the cruelties practised would be for him to be in a position to speak from personal experience, and, if necessary, invite them to follow his

[1] The word " experimental " is not used, because, although less clumsy than " experiential," it is commonly used with a different shade of meaning.

example as being, under the circumstances, a duty of their office. Accordingly he bribed the warders to lace him up in the straight-waistcoat, and let him endure the other punishments usually inflicted upon prisoners. As a result he was able to present his case to the prison authorities with a force otherwise impossible, and which convinced them of its truth and brought the prisoners the relief required.

In this instance one could not in any true sense say that the chaplain had been "punished," but only that he had gone through a certain experience, and the question of justice is not in any way raised. In the same way, without considering just *how* it brought it about, our Lord's experience of the penalty of sin put Him in a position—for very different and far deeper reasons than those of the story, as we shall see later—to save sinners from the penalty due to sin. And He achieved this, not by being punished, but by passing through a certain necessary, helpful experience.

But we need not go to fiction for illustrations, though the above in certain respects is particularly useful. Of all deaths, the death of a missionary by martyrdom comes nearest in its moral and spiritual likeness to our Saviour's. When Bishop Patteson's love of humanity led him to go to Melanesia to preach Christianity, and, owing to the sins of his own countrymen, he was killed by the natives, it is recorded that "His life was taken by men for whose sake he would willingly have given it."[1]

His death, therefore, gave the world an illustration of the sacrifices love asks of her children, since it was this which drove him to undertake the work which ended in his suffering the penalty of sin due to others. This punishment, deserved by the white traders, was experienced by him, but in his case it was not in any true sense of the word a "punishment," but a martyr-

[1] From the inscription on the memorial cross erected on the site of his martyrdom.

dom. Nor could it be *felt* by him as a punishment, since he was entirely innocent of the sin for which he suffered. It was an experience in " vicarious " suffering of the punishment deserved by sin.

We note that, though grieving, as they must have, at the death of such a man, yet the Society for which he worked regarded it as " the brightest crown of a life of Christian heroism " and as " an honour upon " the age; and it is noteworthy that his death effected what his life had failed to do. It put an end to what was in fact a slave trade.[1] Many other instances of the demands and vicarious sacrifices of love might be quoted, as, for instance, that of Father Damien for the lepers of Molokai, and of his peers elsewhere in the same heroic service; and as we view them we do not exclaim, " How unjust! How unfair !" but " How splendid !" In the same way our Lord's experience of sin-bearing to save mankind was not unjust, but refulgent with the moral splendour of love.

We may, however, carry the analogy further, and imagine these men to have had fathers who, when consulted as to whether their sons should follow the inward call to service, loved them too well to hold them back, and may even have encouraged them to undertake the burden of vicarious sacrifice. Again, in this case we do not say, " How immoral !" but, bearing in mind the suffering which the parental sacrifice involved, harder, perhaps, to bear in its quiet endurance than that of their children itself, we think how noble and even God-like it was to let them go.

No Dualism involved in this Theory.

In the same way God the Father, just because He loved His Son perfectly, was compelled by that very love to desire Him to achieve those sacrifices and endure the suffering which perfect holiness and love required. It was not only because He so loved the

---

[1] *S.P.G. Digest*, p. 449.

world, but also because *He so loved His Son*, that the Father gave Him, that men might have everlasting life.[1]

There is here none of that dualism, none of that clash of conflicting interests between an angry Father and a placating Son which some theologians have contemplated; but rather that perfect unity and co-operating love which St. Paul describes when he says that the Father was in the Son reconciling the world to Himself: both working together and suffering together to satisfy the exacting requirements of love with regard both to one another and fallen humanity. From one point of view our Lord's object was to win back for the Father the love of His children, of which He had been robbed, and to win it by showing them in this material world, in human flesh, how much the Father loved them. The law of $\delta\epsilon\hat{\iota}$ $\pi\alpha\theta\epsilon\hat{\iota}\nu$ is the law of love, and by virtue of His divine and infinite nature our Lord was able to do fully and completely what Bishop Patteson and his compeers could do only very incompletely. For He could bear the full weight of the burden of sin, while they, in the spiritual, mental, and bodily suffering endured, could bear it only very partially; He was able to help men to the uttermost, and make possible for all a full deliverance, while they could redeem men only in a very modified degree, and then only by virtue of what He had done before.

The Atonement is not a Desperate Expedient, but a Glorious Revelation.

It is a mistake to view the Atonement as if, in it, we see the Almighty reduced by the Devil to resort to a questionable or even unworthy expedient in order to counter a successful attack upon His creation. It is truer to regard it rather as an instance of the way in which God is able to bring good out of evil, and to see Him in the Atonement taking advantage of the oppor-

[1] John iii. 16.

tunity afforded by man's fall to originate a scheme for his recovery which exhibits to a wondering world unimaginable resources of wisdom and love. So far as we can see, it would have been impossible to conceive God's capacity for self-sacrificing love, or to imagine such a moral standard, unless it had been manifested upon the Cross. It is true the Greeks produced the beautiful legend of " Prometheus bound," but it is noticeable that his sufferings are represented as the involuntary and unforeseen, not the foreknown, consequences of his love for mankind. Moreover, he was a secondary deity, not the supreme power, whose character is rather typified by the chain which bound him to the rock and the eagle which tore his flesh. Plato's " righteous man," again, is but the martyr of his righteousness, and, high though his ideal is, it unquestionably remained for the Christ to reveal to mankind the perfect love and holiness of God.

Yet these missionary incidents do, to some extent, illustrate the part taken by God the Father in the Atonement, as well as that of His Son. For if it be assumed that Bishop Patteson consulted his father beforehand about his missionary plans, and received his approving support, then, in that case, his father was to some extent responsible for his son's subsequent sufferings, and also had some moral and spiritual share in his self-sacrifice. And, so far as the good results which followed are concerned, we may say that as in our Lord's case the Father was in the Son reconciling the world to Himself, so also was Bishop Patteson's father involved with his son's action in winning these heathen to a saving faith in God. The analogy holds good so far; but in the Atonement of the Cross, as we shall see later, there is reason to believe that the Father was much more deeply and more directly involved in the sufferings experienced by the Son, but yet without the introduction of any least trace of vengeful punishment. It was, as we have said, simply the experience of a certain kind of suffering which was necessary in order to put our Lord in a helpful position for bringing about the salvation of mankind—the position, namely, of being one who had suffered the penalty of sin.

It remains to ask: Do such views as these fit in, not only with the requirements of human nature, but also with the teaching of the Bible and the Church stated in her creeds and doctrinal pronouncements? Shall we be justified in concluding that these doctrines represent God's all-sufficient response to human need in the moral and spiritual sphere as conditioned by sin? Shall we be justified in supposing that our Lord Jesus Christ, Who " for us men and for our salvation came down from heaven, was incarnate . . . of the Virgin Mary, suffered under Pontius Pilate, was crucified, dead and buried," experienced these things, not at all as a punishment, but perfectly voluntarily, urged only by the demands of Divine Love, and because the experience of them was necessary for Him in order to attain a moral and spiritual position which would enable Him to bring about the salvation of Mankind in the best possible way? The main object of this book is to present for acceptance this view of our Lord's sufferings as the true one. Do we find sufficient ground in the facts connected with the conversion of souls and the doctrines of the Bible and Church to justify the belief?

A Caution.

In presenting this view of the Atonement to friends I have often found that at this point they anticipate what they think to be coming, and connect the statement that " our Lord experienced the consequences of sin in order to be in a position to help us " with preconceived views of what they think likely to follow. As a result ideas present themselves, such as those of vicarious or sympathetic sorrow or penitence for human sin, or substitutionary suffering, or example, etc., which in fact have no place in this theory. Such conceptions are confusing, and tend to make the view to be presented later on more difficult of apprehension.   It may therefore be useful here to ask that nothing of the kind be read into the above statement, but that it may be taken in its literal baldness—our Lord suffered in order to put Himself into a position to help us.   How this experience could help is a matter for later consideration.

CHAPTER II

WHAT OUR LORD SUFFERED

WE are now brought face to face with the question: What in its exact nature was this divine venture of our Lord—this mission of love ? Were His sufferings upon the Cross similar in their nature, though greater in degree, to those of any other missionary or leader in the world's advance, who dies as the natural result of his work[1] or by the hands of those he would help; or were His sufferings of an altogether deeper and more profound spiritual nature ? Was His physical death at the hands of the Jews all that He endured, aggravated by the intense sensitiveness of His refined and holy nature to an unprecedented degree of bodily suffering and by His profound sense of the true nature of sin which reached its climax of ingratitude, cruelty, hate, and injustice in this judicial murder ? Or beyond and in addition to all this, was He bearing the penalty of sin in the more direct and natural sense of the words ?

Our Lord's Death was more than a Martyrdom.

In trying to find an answer to these questions we may notice, in the first place, that our Saviour's death was evidently more than a martyrdom. As we view the agony in the Garden, the impression is forced upon us that our Lord was consciously facing much more than a cruel death at the hands of His enemies. If " heaven is the Cross "[2]—i.e., if heavenly joy consists

---

[1] As, for instance, the self-sacrifice of doctors in applying and studying the effects of radium upon cancer and lupus patients, or in sucking the poison from the throat of a diphtheria case.

[2] Temple, *The Faith and Modern Thought* (1914), p. 110.

in the sacrificing service of God—then, in some degree, it would also be true that " the Cross is heaven "; and in that case we should expect to find that our Lord would have been sustained to endure it with something more even than calmness.   But we find that on the contrary there was an overwhelming and unmitigated fear and horror, which has always been rightly described as " the agony "—an " agony " of anticipation, as the Cross drew near.

Our Lord's Mental Sufferings more than Natural.

We are told that it was the study of our Lord's agony in Gethsemane which led the scholastics and doctors of medieval theology to forsake Abelard's subjective theory for belief in that objective view of the Atonement culminating in teaching of an extreme type from which we shrink as unjustifiable, if not even blasphemous.[1] Yet the argument based upon our Lord's extreme suffering in the agony of Gethsemane has never been successfully controverted.   When it is argued that its overwhelming intensity and His prostration can only be explained upon the ground that He anticipated bearing the punishment of sin, it is difficult to refute the deduction; for no other sufficient explanation has been produced.   It is true that medical science has in recent times proved that among civilized races physical pain is much more severe than among savage people, and that we must therefore suppose that, in a nature so pure and refined as our Lord's, physical pain would be abnormally so, and unprecedently terrible either to bear or anticipate.   We recognize also that to His sinless nature the endurance of death in that form which men suffer as the consequence of, and as associated with, sin would be peculiarly shocking to Him.   We remember all this, but we remember also, on the other hand, that in His case there were forces which would have helped Him to sustain these special burdens.   His moral nature

[1] *Cf.* Canon Ragg, *Some Aspects of the Atonement.*

was perfect, and therefore He possessed unrivalled qualities of fortitude, strength of will, and sense of innocence to enable Him to bear up against them. When we remember the way in which martyrs, with all the weakness of our fallen human nature upon them, have gone to torture and death even with cheerfulness, we feel that there is something unnatural in the prostration by anguish of our Saviour in the Garden of Gethsemane, and are compelled to seek the cause outside His natural shrinking from death.

In addition to Mental there was also Spiritual Suffering— partly from an Evil Source.

We notice also that His sufferings were not only mental. There was a spiritual element in them. Our Lord's teaching about the Good Shepherd giving His life for the sheep involves that He had foreknowledge that, as the Shepherd, He would suffer from the wolf— *i.e.*, Satan; and that He would suffer what the sheep would otherwise have suffered.

Also His saying, " This is your hour, and the power of darkness," carries with it the same suggestion of suffering which would be spiritual, and proceed from an evil source.

This Spiritual Suffering was permitted by the Father.

Further, we notice that the source of these sufferings was in some sense dual. They were also at least permitted by the Father. Before coming into the world our Lord is represented as saying: " Lo, I come to do Thy will, O God," and it is impossible to read the Lamentations of Jeremiah, which are unmistakably Messianic, without feeling that our Lord's sufferings were to come chiefly from above.[1] Again, Isaiah prophesied: " The Lord hath laid on Him the iniquity of us all ";[2] and our Saviour had applied to Himself[3]

[1] *Cf.* especially Lam. i. 12-15, iii. 1-18.   [2] Isa. liii. 6.
[3] Matt. xxvi. 31, and Mark xiv. 27.

that other prophecy of Zechariah: " Awake, O sword, against my Shepherd, and against the man that is my fellow, saith the Lord of Hosts: smite the Shepherd, and the sheep shall be scattered."[1] And His prayer, " Thy will be done," is in accordance with this, as also His saying to the disciples, at His arrest: " The cup which *My Father* hath given Me, shall I not drink it ?" Later, also, He said to Pilate: " Thou wouldest have no power against Me except it were given thee from above "; and on the Cross, giving expression to His supreme suffering, He cried, " My God, My God, why hast Thou forsaken Me ?"

It also partly came from the Father.

All this unmistakably points to a feeling on our Lord's part that the cup of suffering was presented to Him by His Father, and the writer of the Epistle to the Hebrews in chapter x. 5-10, which supply matter for a whole theory of the Atonement in themselves, takes the same view, making " the offering of the body of Christ" to have been the response of the Son's perfect obedience to the will of His Father, in order to bring about our sanctification—*i.e.*, that the Father willed His Son's sacrifice as the means of man's salvation. We conclude that at the very least what God required from His Son as the reparation for our rebellion was a life, culminating in a death, of perfect obedience, and that this was offered by our Lord under conditions which, in that time and country, naturally led to the Cross. How this could affect us apart from an unreal or immoral substitution must be considered later; it is enough here to note the fact, as deducible from the evidence of Scripture, that such a life and death were offered.

[1] Zech. xiii. 7.

Our Lord's Death not Primarily Penitential.

But this only accounts for the outward circumstances of His death, and not for the inward spiritual suffering of which there is such clear evidence. And if we may deduce from the above passages, and especially from the sayings of our Lord, that to His consciousness the chief weight of this suffering came from without, then an important consequence follows—viz., that in that case His representative penitence as the inclusive Head of humanity cannot have been the chief and essential feature in the Atonement. For penitence cannot be imposed from without. It cannot flow from one person to another, nor be produced in one person by another. So that if prophecy and our Lord's sayings are a true index to the chief source of our Lord's atoning suffering, then the penitential theory—that Christ won man's forgiveness by offering for human sin a perfect penitence completed upon the Cross—falls to the ground. Not that the conception of our Lord's representative sorrow does not remain true to the extent that He might, and indeed would, feel sympathetic involvement in man's guilt, and that such sorrow was accepted by the Father as affording some ground for the forgiveness of human sin, but that this representative sorrow was not the whole nor the chief outstanding feature of His Atonement. It also follows that any theory maintaining that our Lord's sufferings were only of the nature of a supreme martyrdom at the hands of men, or any merely subjective view of the Atonement, is not a sufficient explanation of the facts. No doubt our Lord's sacrifice was all this, but it was also more than this.

Further Reasons for questioning the Penitential View— the Possibility of Vicarious Penitence.

In addition to these scriptural reasons for believing that our Saviour's spiritual suffering was not subjective

11

only,[1] there is also the evidence of reason. For it is questionable whether our Lord could, in the nature of things, offer a perfect penitence for human sin. For sorrow for the sin of others is not penitence. Contrition is essentially sorrow for one's own sins, and therefore Jesus' sorrow for man's sin would be lacking in the characteristic feature of penitence. It is not easy to see how it could in any sense be real contrition unless His identification with mankind was of a kind really to involve Him in human guilt, which it would be blasphemy to imagine.

It has been said that the Son of Man would feel shame and penitence to an infinite degree " for the sin of mankind which He bore, when He identified Himself in such a manner with our sins that it is said ' He was made sin ' (2 Cor. v. 21)."[2] But it has not been proved that we have any right to put such a restricted interpretation upon the meaning of St. Paul's expression. One can only say of such an identification that it must have been either based on reality or been one of sympathy only, to whatever extreme degree it extended. The first alternative is ruled out by the spotless purity of our Lord's nature. There was in Him no approach to the slightest stain of sin. To whatever extent, then, our Lord identified Himself with mankind in taking upon Himself human nature, it involved no stain of guilt. In that sense there can have been no real moral nor spiritual connection. There remains the other alternative, the self-identification of sympathy, and it is conceivable that this might, and indeed would, be so powerful as to impose a very heavy burden of sorrow

---

[1] The word " subjective " is used here and elsewhere in the sense of " that which arises and exists purely in the self-consciousness apart from any outside objective cause." Such experience, which to the person conscious of it would be " subjective," in this sense might be viewed as an objective fact by someone else. Thus God's object in His relations towards another person might be to produce in him joy or sorrow—to the man subjective conditions, but to God objective facts.

[2] *The One Volume Bible Commentary*, p. cxxix.

upon Him.   But, however great, it could not be truly
penitential in its nature.   Always at the bottom there
would be the consciousness that the sin and guilt of
mankind was not His own personal sin and guilt; that
His spiritual efforts and sufferings were not for Himself,
but for others.   To suppose otherwise is to imagine
that our Saviour allowed His loving sympathy to over-
ride His perception of the truth, and we cannot allow
such a failure for a moment in Him Who is the truth.
Love, however perfect, could not blind truth, and cause
our Lord to feel as if He had Himself sinned.   The
consciousness of innocence would be always His, and
is proved by His question, " Why hast Thou forsaken
Me ?"

Of sympathetic experience, however perfect, it cannot strictly be said that it can cause us to feel the joys
and sorrows of others " as our own."[1]   It may be said
" as much as if they were our own," or even " more
than if they were our own," but not " as our own ";
for there always remains the consciousness of personal
distinction.   For a man to lose this would be for him
to lose part of his personality—to be no longer a perfect
man.   When all is said, " feeling human sins as if one
had done them," even if it were possible, is not the
same feeling as that of conviction of sin.   If our Lord
had died of a broken heart due to His sympathetic
sense of what others felt in dying in alienation from
the Father, His death would have been in some sense
self-imposed.   But it was imposed from without.   As
we have seen, it was caused partly by " the powers of
darkness " and partly by His Father's will—His Father
Who He said had forsaken Him.   And since the Son
of God " loved us so perfectly that He willed for our
sakes to know what human suffering is to the uttermost,"[2] then He must have suffered the penalty of sin
not only sympathetically, but directly.   Otherwise He
has only suffered it at second-hand by sympathy, not as

---

[1] Strong, *The Incarnation of God*, p. 47.   [2] *Ibid.*, p. 48.

men suffer it. But He did not suffer only sympathetically. He did not cry, " Why hast Thou forsaken
them ?" or even " us " ? but " Why hast Thou forsaken
Me ?" We may believe, then, that our Lord's loving
self-sacrifice rose even to this higher, conceivable level,
and that He suffered directly in Himself the penal
consequences of sin as we ourselves do. He was made
in this, as in all other things, save only sin, like unto
His brethren, to make reconciliation for sin (Heb. ii. 17).
If it be true that " He had to bear the whole burden
of the sins, and the consequent sinfulness of the race,"[1]
then in His human nature He must have experienced
that divorce from God which is part of the burden and
consequence of sin. This was the last step in that
loving " self-emptying " begun at His Incarnation.

Vicarious Penitence inadequate to satisfy Divine Holiness.

But even though it had been possible for the Son of
Man by power of sympathy to have supposed Himself
involved in human sin, yet this could not apply to
God the Father; and in view of His knowledge of His
Son's perfect purity it would be impossible for Divine
Holiness to accept a sympathetic sorrow as a right and
sufficient atonement for the sins of others. Sin demands
at least a real penitence for forgiveness. It would be
still more impossible for Him as an onlooker and judge
than for the Son to impute conditions which did not
exist. Therefore the identification of our Lord with
human sin must either be real or inadequate. As the
first is impossible, we must conclude that any such
sympathetic sorrow as our Lord experienced would not
be in itself an adequate ground for Atonement, for it
could not be true repentance.

There is, however, another way of explaining our
Lord's sin-bearing. It is argued that when our Lord
took upon Himself human flesh He was " made sin "
in some deeper sense than " made to bear the penalty

---

[1] Strong, *The Incarnation of God*, p. 63.

of sin." It has been explained as meaning that when He became incarnate " He took upon Him the whole of our human nature and became flesh, conditioned though that fleshly nature was throughout by sin "; and that in this way, in spite of His personal sinlessness, He had laid Himself under " the curse."[1]

Incompatibility of this View with the True Doctrine of the Incarnation.

But if it be sought to justify morally our Lord's endurance of the penalty of sin on this ground, then it must involve that the flesh He took was morally tainted, or the expression " conditioned . . . by sin " must imply that our Lord was somehow, in some other way, however carefully the statement be minimized, involved in the guilt of humanity. But if, as seems to be the case, it only means that the state and circumstances of the humanity He lived among were such as resulted from sin, then no justification for the infliction of sin's penalty is afforded. If there were no moral nor spiritual contamination, then the words " conditioned though that fleshly nature was throughout by sin " really mean no more than that our Lord was brought into contact with sinful humanity, and suffered the natural consequences of living a pure life under impure surroundings—*i.e.*, martyrdom. The Creed tells us that He became " perfect God and perfect Man not by conversion of the Godhead into flesh," in which case it would perhaps have been necessarily involved in the faultiness of humanity; but " by taking of the manhood into God," so that as fire, when in the ascendant, will dissipate water, so the fierce white holiness of the infinite divine nature would burn out all impurity from the finite human nature He took into Himself, and only God's " very good " creation remained. Hence the term " second Adam," implying that Jesus was as pure as the first Adam before the Fall.

[1] *Lux Mundi*, p. 217.

On these grounds it does not seem possible to associate any real penitence with our Lord's atoning sufferings, yet so far as perfect sympathy and our Lord's representative Headship of the human race could make a form of sorrow for sin approaching penitence possible, it may be conceded as certainly present, but no farther. The Rev. E. L. Strong has pictured for us such a sorrow carried to its utmost length. He says that on the Cross Jesus at last " arrived at the awful condition of realizing man's sin as that which had made communion with God altogether impossible. . . . And then . . . longed for God with all the force of which His human nature was capable, and His heart broke because He could in no way and for no reason bear to be separated from His God."[1]

Here we have sympathetic sorrow for human sin such as Dr. Moberly writes of carried to its supreme limit, but still it does not and cannot include that element of personal sorrow for personal sin and personal guilt which lies at the centre of true repentance, and it also imputes to our Lord belief in a divorce which in fact did not exist. As being the Truth, it was impossible for the Spotless Lamb of God, however infinite His sympathy, to allow such feelings entrance to His mind and heart.

The Link between our Saviour's Sorrow and Man's Penitence.

Must we conclude, then, that all our Lord achieved by His sorrow for human sin was to give an example of what such sorrow should be for the sin which we see around us, and which is increased by our own falls ? This alone is indeed of great value, but is it all His sorrow could do in the work of man's redemption ? The answer to this question is " No ": it was only part of what He did. For though His sorrow, however intense, could never be the same thing as repentance

[1] *The Incarnation of God*, pp. 90, 91.

for sin, or take its place, yet, if transferred to the heart of a human penitent, it could supply just that necessary depth and completeness of abhorrence for sin which is beyond man's unassisted capacity to attain; and it also could, and would, automatically receive from the sinner that personal element necessary to change simple sorrow into penitence. Christ's perfect sorrow *plus* our personal penitence and sense of guilt complete a true contrition.

So the Son of Man, by virtue of His representative nature and perfect sympathetic grief for human sin, did all that was necessary in order to make it possible to present to God on behalf of each sinner a true contrition to set free the divine desire to forgive. All that is needed for this is that penitents should become identified with their Saviour's sorrow for their sins by means to be considered later.

In this way the first step necessary to an adequate repentance was made possible by our Lord's Atonement. The three steps necessary to obtain forgiveness are contrition, confession, and reparation. With the slight addition to Dr. Moberly's teaching mentioned above, we see how the first of these has been brought within our reach, and how and why we must fill up each on his part that which is lacking in the afflictions of Christ on our behalf.[1] Dr. McLeod Campbell has shown us, in his book upon the Atonement, how our Lord's submission to death satisfied another condition, inasmuch as it was a perfect acknowledgment or confession of the justice of God's sentence upon sin—a great Amen to His judgment. In this way our Lord satisfied the second condition for forgiveness, and there remains only the third—adequate reparation offered—for all three conditions to have been satisfied.

Did our Lord offer this also for our redemption? Did He in any way satisfy the just claims of God's holiness, and make it possible for penitents to overcome

[1] Col. i. 24.

the sentence of separation from God's fellowship to which sin condemns them ? The experience of all true penitents answers, " Yes, we know that it is possible. Somehow our Saviour has overcome this last difficulty and opened a way for us back to our Father."

We are approaching the supreme effort of God's love when we ask how this was done.

Was our Lord's Cry of Forsakenness on the Cross a Mistaken One ?

One of the ways in which our Lord's spiritual suffering has been explained is by supposing that under the agony of His crucifixion and its attendant circumstances He mistakenly felt Himself to be cut off from the Father. But here again there is no support for this view in His own sayings. All through He clung to God as His Father, and appealed to Him as present— " Father, if it be possible "; " Father, forgive them;" " Father, into Thy hands." There is no sufficient ground for explaining our Lord's agony of mind on the supposition of an imaginary separation having no basis in reality. The evidence is rather in the other direction, that His human nature clung desperately to a fellowship with His Father which failed Him, and that the severance broke His heart. Here one feels Dr. Dale is right when he says: " I shrink from saying that even in my calmest and brightest hours I have a knowledge of God and the ways of God which is truer than Christ had, even in His agony. I dare not stand before His Cross and tell Him that even for a moment He imagines something concerning God which is not a fact, and cannot be a fact. I prefer to believe that it was necessary for the great ends of human redemption that when Christ was on the Cross He should submit to the awful suffering arising from ' the loss of the sense of God's presence.' "[1]

[1] *The Atonement,* p. xli.

Examination of our Lord's Cry of Forsakenness on the Cross.

The cry of forsakenness from the Cross has always proved a difficulty in the way of those who have tried to form theories of the Atonement which exclude our Lord from the experience of the penalty of sin. Some of the most weighty writers explain it on the ground that it was only a quotation, and does not really express our Lord's real meaning.[1] Dr. Moberly in his great work, after carefully examining Dr. J. McLeod Campbell's argument in favour of this view, decides that it amounts to an explaining away rather than an explaining of Scripture.[2] But Dr. Moberly himself urges that there was no real experience of the separation which sin causes between God and the sinner, but only such a realization· of this as was possible to our Lord by virtue of His unique knowledge of the measure of God's holiness.[3] He says: " He [our Lord] did not— of course He did not—endure the damnation of sin. But in the bitter humiliation of a self-adopted consciousness of what sin—and therefore of what the damnation of sin—really is, He bowed His head to that which, as far as mortal experience can go, is so far at least the counterpart on earth of damnation that it is the extreme possibility of contradiction and destruction of self. He to Whom, as the Life of life, all dying, all weakness, were an outrage to us inconceivable bowed Himself to death—death in its outward form inflicted with all the contumely as of penal vengeance; death inwardly accepted as the necessary climax of an experience of spiritual desolation which, but to the inherently holy, would have been not only material but spiritual death . . . that dissolution was the consummation of penitence " (p. 133).

[1] *Cf.* J. McLeod Campbell, *The Nature of the Atonement*, chapter xii.
[2] *Atonement and Personality*, pp. 407-409.
[3] *Ibid.*, p. 130.

Inadequacy of the Penitential Explanation.

This is very subtle thought very finely expressed, but in its effect it seems to amount to very much the same thing as Dr. McLeod Campbell's view that our Lord's words did not express any real experience, but only His subjective feeling, a " self-adopted consciousness," a very perfect realization or apprehension. But even in this case, if His sympathy led Him so to lose all sense of the distinct, separate personality He possessed as perfect Man with a proper human soul as to become subjectively identified with sinners in their sense of loss of the Father's presence, then He actually was experiencing *part* of the penalty of sin; and whether by sympathy or otherwise makes no difference to the question of the justice of God, under whose providence this suffering was required of Him.

It is a little difficult to form a clear opinion as to the exact nature of the suffering Dr. Moberly would ascribe to our Lord, and perhaps one might be tempted to think he meant that He bore the real penalty of sin in the true, full sense by virtue of His power of perfect sympathy. But this would be an impossibility, and such a conception could only arise from confusion of thought. Moreover, his vehement denial quoted just above shows that this is not the case. He only claims that our Lord *realized* all that was involved in the penal averting of God's face, while not actually experiencing it.

Canon Ragg, who seems to accept and wish to interpret Dr. Moberly's theory, writes: " Is there not enough in the story of the Passion to convince us that Christ did, in some mysterious way, bear the burden of our sin; that He, the Sinless, did so identify Himself with sinful humanity as *to feel* the horror of it, to touch the lowest depths of the pit of woe that it opens up—to experience, *in feeling at least*, the terrible alienation from the Father that is the essence of its doom?"[1]

---

[1] *Aspects of the Atonement*, pp. 93-94. The italics are not in the original.

Mr. Strong writes to the same effect: Jesus experienced a literally heart-breaking sense of the separation existing between God and sinners, but was in no way really forsaken Himself.[1]   Mr. McDowall writes in a sense which is perhaps intended to involve our Lord in more than the mere feeling of sin's penalty: " It is the knowledge of consequences that is the punishment of sin, and may not we interpret the cry of loneliness from the Cross as the full entering into this knowledge by Jesus ?"[2]

When Mr. McDowall says that the knowledge of its consequences is the punishment of sin, this implies that a person who subjectively enters fully into the experience of another's punishment is, for all practical purposes, punished himself.   His argument is, in fact, a summary of Dr. Moberly's theory of sympathetic sorrow as the basis of our Lord's Atonement, and it calls for the same answer—namely, that such a conception is both inaccurate and unnecessary.

It is inaccurate because suffering and punishment are not identical, and therefore to suffer the pain of punishment is not necessarily the same thing as to be punished. There cannot be punishment without guilt.   In the same way that sorrow cannot possess the characteristic features of penitence where there is no sin, neither can suffering possess those of punishment where there is no guilt.   A sensitive child may cry at seeing another punished, and so prove he is enduring sympathetic suffering, but he will not feel that he is being punished himself.   Nor will he ask, " Why have you punished me ?" as our Lord asked, " Why hast Thou forsaken Me ?"   The reason is clear—namely, that the moral relations between the two classes of sufferers and the inflicter of the suffering are quite different.   In the one case there is the expression and realization of displeasure towards and by the sufferer; while in the other there is not.   It is only when by God's grace identifica-

---

[1] *The Incarnation of God*, pp. 73, 90, 91.
[2] *Evolution and the Need of Atonement*, p. 167.

tion is established between Christ and a human soul that, by virtue of the latter's guilt, Christ's sorrow for sin becomes in the sinner penitence, and Christ's suffering becomes in him punishment.

Again, Mr. McDowall's argument—as Dr. Moberly's also—is unnecessary. Its object is to evade the charge of injustice in the suffering of the innocent Jesus, but, as we have seen, there is no ground for this charge in connection with our Lord's voluntary experience upon the Cross.

Thus, the only practical result of the argument that our Lord suffered the penalty of sin by sympathetic insight only, and not by actual experience, is to depreciate the measure of Divine Love exhibited upon the Cross without any real moral advantage being gained. It is curious that these teachers who most insist upon making the love of God the only foundation and motive of the Atonement should end by limiting its range, and say in effect that it is too much to believe that God's Son suffered the penal consequences of sin—that Divine Love could not go so far. It seems preferable to believe that Perfect Love did not stop short even at this, and that there is nothing too much for the love of God to undertake, unless it be incompatible with His nature, such as involvement in the guilt of sin. Such a view best accords with a simple interpretation of Scripture language.

We conclude that our Lord actually suffered the Penalty of Sin.

All this is in favour of our Lord having experienced the penalty of sin rather than of only offering a representative penitence for it; and this conclusion is confirmed by the fact that in the Bible His sufferings are always spoken of as punishment borne by Him, rather than as an act of penitence offered by Him. Such expressions as " He bore the sins of many," " One died for all," " He tasted death for many," and " By His stripes we are healed," are frequent, but we never come across any expression which even suggests such a thought as " He made repentance for all," or " He confessed the sins of all." Without placing undue weight upon the argument from silence, yet, if the *primary and effectual* operative feature of our Lord's sufferings is their penitential character, this is very extraordinary, if not inexplicable.

The Evidence of Scripture as to the Penal Nature of our Lord's Sufferings and its Interpretation.[1]

On the other, positive side the Bible offers consider-able support to the view that our Lord experienced the actual consequences of sin. This, at least, is the mean-ing which naturally attaches itself to numerous passages which might be quoted.

Efforts have been made to alter them or deprive them of the sense which, under the historic evolution of Christianity, they naturally convey; but it is really begging the question to take it for granted that the sacrificial rites and terms arising from their use under the Mosaic law were not instituted under God's pro-vidence for the purpose of suggesting the very teaching these critics object to. So when we are told that we must not read them in the sense naturally arising from, and suggested by, their historic use, because they are connected with the sacrificial terminology of the people to whom they were in the first instance addressed, or that certain expressions must be interpreted only in a literary sense, we feel that these are unproved assump-tions. Somehow we are not convinced, and are probably right in supposing that it is better to fill the phrases with all the possible meaning we have learnt to asso-ciate with them, rather than empty them of any they

---

[1] The word " penal " here is not used to imply that these sufferings were inflicted as punishment, but only suffering which, under ordinary circumstances, would have been punishment. In our Lord's case it was experiential. The word is employed in this narrower meaning in other places also.

fairly suggest. Of the two courses, this seems the more reasonable in view of the profundity of God's plan of salvation, and of the fact that our present natural feeling and understanding with regard to them has been evolved under the guidance of His providence.

The Messiah as Sin-Bearer.

To enter into detail, there is, for instance, all that teaching given by the second Isaiah in chapters xlix. to lvii. upon the Suffering Servant of Jehovah, including the great passage containing " the vision of a personal sufferer and sin-bearer " in lii. 13 and liii., which teaches that " the spiritual salvation of Israel is (to be) accomplished by the vicarious conscience and sufferings of the Servant: . . . He . . . bears their transgressions, and iniquity . . . sinless . . . He submits in order to offer His life as a guilt-offering, and so wins righteousness for His people. Whether this figure be of the pious portion of Israel, or of one holy sufferer, the Christian Church has been right in finding its fulfilment in Jesus Christ."[1]

This represents practically the universal opinion of scholars on this passage, and it contains (Isa. liii. 12) perhaps the most familiar instance of the use of the expression " to bear the sin " in connection with our Saviour. Other instances occur in Heb. ix. 28 (" Christ also, having been once offered to bear the sins of many, shall appear a second time "), and in 1 Pet. ii. 24 (" Who His own self bare our sins in His own body upon the tree . . . by whose stripes ye were healed ").[2] Comparison with Lev. xx. 17, 20, xxii. 9, xxiv. 15; Num. ix. 13, xviii. 22, 32; and Ezek. xxiii. 49, shows that " to bear sin " undoubtedly means " to bear the

---

[1] Cf. article " Isaiah " in Hastings' Dictionary of the Bible, vol. ii. p. 497.

[2] If St. Peter had held " the martyr view," would he not have written " bare the sins of men," not " our sins." He would hardly have identified himself with his Lord's enemies.

punishment of sin." In any case, it must mean either to bear the guilt or the penalty of sin, and the former alternative is impossible in these instances.

Various Passages in the New Testament.

Other passages which seem to involve that our Lord suffered the penalty due to our sins are:

(1) " God, sending His own Son in the likeness of sinful flesh, and *as an offering* for sin, condemned sin in the flesh " (Rom. viii. 3). Since God condemned sin in Christ's flesh, then Christ's flesh has endured the condemnation of sin—*i.e.*, He suffered in His body God's punishment upon sin.

(2) " Christ redeemed us from the curse of the law, having become a curse for us: for it is written, Cursed is every one that hangeth on a tree " (Gal. iii. 13).

(3) " Him Who knew no sin He made to be sin on our own behalf; that we might become the righteousness of God in Him " (2 Cor. v. 21).

On this passage Dr. Dale says: " God made Christ ' sin for us,' not a ' sin-offering,' not ' a sinner.' . . . The sentence is intensely rhetorical. . . . But the rhetoric stands for something. . . . Great light is thrown on the whole passage by the closing words. The ultimate end of Christ's redemptive work is that ' we might become the righteousness of God in (Christ).' Righteousness is conceived, not as a mere quality of the redeemed, but as their very substance and life. . . . Had we not been saved, sin would at last have become . . . our very self. When sin and self become inseparable, then God deals with us as with sin. . . . He withdraws Himself from us, and His withdrawal is a mortal blow . . . what is commonly understood by ' the second death.' . . . God made Christ sin for us: withdrew from Him, as He must otherwise have withdrawn from us had we become sin. . . . I may say again this passage is intensely rhetorical . . . but . . . no such rhetorical conception of the death of Christ is possible to those who reject the vicarious or representative theory of His sufferings."[1]

We may add St. Paul had authority for the above teaching in our Lord's own likening of Himself upon the Cross to the brazen serpent—the representative of sin—upon the pole. The complete symbolism is of Himself as the Representative of sinful man enduring God's judgment upon sin on the Cross.

(4) " Him that loveth us, and loosed us from our sins by His blood " (Rev. i. 5). The expression to " be loosed from sin " might mean no more than " to be set free from the power of sin," but in the only other places where it occurs in the New Testament it means to be set free from the guilt of sin—*i.e.*, its liability for punishment (*cf.* Matt. xvi. 19 and xviii. 18). Granted St. John is the author of Revelation, this phrase is most likely connected with the saying of our Lord on the occasion recorded by him in John xx. 23, which would make an indelible impression upon his mind, and where the penalty of sin is clearly referred to. For other examples of the same thought see Eph. i. 7: " In whom we have redemption through His blood, the forgiveness of our trespasses, according to the riches of His grace "; Col. i. 19, 20: " . . . it was the good pleasure of the Father . . . through Him to reconcile all things unto Himself, having made peace through the blood of the Cross. . . ." Again, when it is said that our Saviour died " for our sins," or died " to save us from our sins," one feels, after making full allowance for the Greek idiom and the various shades of meaning in their prepositions, that they are not expressions which would be natural to use of any ordinary philanthropical work. One wonders, for instance, whether a Greek ever used them with respect to Socrates, or would have used them in connection with Bishop Patteson; and if not, why are they so naturally used of our Saviour unless it be that He saved

---

[1] *The Atonement*, p. 494, 495.

men not only from sinning, but also from the punishment of sin ?   Otherwise would it not have been more
natural—*e.g.* in Matt. i. 21—to have said that our Lord
was to be called Jesus because He would save the world
from " sin " or " sinfulness " ?   Does not " from their
sins " suggest, or at any rate include, salvation from
sins already committed ? and in that case only salvation from the consequences of sins can be meant.

Metaphorical Interpretation.

Of course, it may be said of all these and similar
phrases that they are the " language of metaphor " and
must be interpreted in " the literary spirit "; but even
when we grant this it still remains true that metaphors
have some real correspondence to the truths they
illustrate, and we ask, " What is the nature of this
correspondence ?"   Moreover, it is a historical fact that
in spite of every difficulty and much hostile criticism
a deep instinct in the human heart has lived on for all
these hundreds of years, which, refusing to be bound
by narrowing interpretations, has believed that God's
love cannot be narrower than men's hopes, nor less
generous than they have ventured to imagine.   No
doubt it is a fortunate thing, and another instance of
God's compassionate providence, that they who cannot
rise to the larger conception should be able to rest upon
the intermediate stage of metaphor; but we plead that
they should not try to bind down others to what are
felt to be more narrow views of what Divine Love has
done and suffered for us.

Divine Love is not Narrower than Man's Conceptions.

For if our Lord has not borne the penalty due to
human sin, then Divine Love has not climbed to the
heights that even the human mind has conceived as
possible; whereas it would seem that infinite love must
surely outstrip the conceptions of finite intelligence.

12

To some minds this thought in itself will appear to be a fatal objection to any theory which denies the penal nature of our Lord's sufferings.

No Moral nor Logical Advantage in Penitential Theory.

Moreover, there appears to be no gain, either moral or logical, in substituting a vicarious " penitence " for a vicarious " penalty." If it be immoral for God to forgive because Christ suffered for us, it is equally wrong to forgive because Christ repented for us. If it be answered, " But it is not wrong if we have transferred to us the perfect penitence of Jesus," then the question arises, as we have seen, as to the possibility of one being, even though divine, being able to repent for the sins of others. Moreover, our Lord certainly did not suffer only by sympathy, only feel what it is like for sinners to die. He suffered death actually, and He suffered it as conditioned by human sin. Therefore, He suffered at any rate some of the consequences of sin, either unjustly or not unjustly.

If, however, we believe that perfect penitence can be offered by our Lord for the sins of others, and that it is possible for us hereafter to be really identified with that perfect penitence, then it must be equally possible for us to be really identified with other features of our Lord's sin-bearing so far as they belong to His human nature, including a real suffering, a real experience of the Cross—a real participation in the perfect and sufficient sacrifice for sin. Such an identification we believe to be indeed possible, and claim that it admits us to a place not only in His penitence, but also in His " sin-bearing "—His endurance of all the consequences of sin.

Human Need requires our Lord to have endured Penal Suffering.

In connection with the question whether our Saviour only offered a penitence, or also bore other consequences which result from human sin, it is noticeable that the

Christian Church would suffer much spiritual loss if the first only were true. For a great part of human life is made up of the endurance of the suffering, moral and spiritual, as well as material, which follows as the penal consequences of sin, and the removal of our Lord from all touch with this large part of life would leave the Christian religion much the poorer.

In the prison scene in *Adam Bede*, where Dinah goes to visit Hetty Sorrel, and finds her seated on her pallet-bed in the gathering gloom of her cell sunk in the sullen silence of despair, feeling that her sin had cut her off from all hope and goodness, after her first kindly words and actions had brought them both to their knees, Dinah begins her prayer with these words: " O ever-present Jesus, Thou hast known the depth of sorrow; Thou hast gone into the darkness where God is not; Thou hast uttered the cry of forsakenness," etc. The incident, though taken from a novel, is true to human nature, and illustrates the fact that man needs a Saviour Who has not only sorrowed for sin, but Who has also experienced the penalties he himself is called upon to suffer. For how else can Jesus be our example in bearing them ? If He has not experienced that real divorce from the Father's presence which sin causes; if He has never known the temptations which then assail humanity, then, in that case, He has not " been tempted in all points like as we are ";[1] He has never been compassed with this infirmity;[2] and how shall He be touched with the feeling of it, or have compassion with them that are out of the way ?[3]

1. *Summary : The Experiential View meets the Requirements of Divine Holiness by our Lord's Death.*

For these reasons we believe our Lord suffered the full penalty of sin—viz.: (1) Death, as we have seen, is the penalty due, and our Lord endured it. The physical death which is sin's penalty is death as we know it—

[1] Heb. iv. 15.   [2] Heb. v. 2.   [3] Heb. iv. 15 and v. 2.

not as it would have been if there had been no sin.   In
that case there is reason to believe that under the
evolution of eternal life which our Lord in due time
would have brought into the world death would have
been a peaceful and even joyful occasion, looked forward to as a step upwards, and nearer to God.[1]   But
this was not our Lord's experience.   His approach to
death was as dreaded and at least as filled with fears
as that of any martyr expecting death by torture.   In
spite of the final calm, which men also often know, His
death as a whole was terrible, and sufficiently explains
the shrinking of " the agony."   It included many of
the characteristics of that of a sin-stained saint cut off
by his sin from the realization of God's presence and
forgiveness.   The difference was only in degree, not in
kind.   Not only in its inward, but also in its outward
circumstances, it included the consequences of sin.
Death by crucifixion was a criminal's death, both by
Roman law and also Judaic, and this adds significance
to Isaiah's prophecy: " He was numbered with the
transgressors."   Our Lord died as we sinners die.   This
brings us to the second great feature in His sin-bearing.

2. *Separation from the Father.*

(2) Our Lord suffered separation from the Father.
The characteristic of all death is separation.   Its loneliness is one of the things we most shrink from.   It
cuts off our physical senses from that communication
with the material world which makes up our experience
of life.   Darwin defined life as " response to environment."   The cessation of this physical response is the
first death.   But it still leaves room for the communion
of our spiritual life with God.   To be separated from
Him also is the second death.   It is absolute loneliness,
and that is why sin—which is self—when it is perfected

---

[1] See Appendix on " The Gospel of Creation " in Dr. Westcott's
Commentary on the Epistles of St. John.

bringeth forth death as its wages.[1] The completed
result of selfishness is to be left alone with self. This
also our Lord endured, as is shown by His cry upon the
Cross, which must always form the crucial test to apply
to any theory of the Atonement: " My God, My God,
Why hast Thou forsaken Me ?"

The Penalty of Sin is only Conditionally Eternal, not Absolutely.

It has been argued, in opposition to this view, that
our Lord certainly did not endure the penalty of sin,
since that is eternal, whereas His suffering was tem-
porary only. It is doubtful, however, whether the
penalty of sin is absolutely eternal, or only conditionally
so. It seems preferable to suppose it is a conditional
consequence of sin dependent upon the moral and
spiritual state of the sinner; and only eternal if or
because his sinful state is eternal. Our Lord's saying
about blasphemy against the Holy Ghost suggests a
spiritual condition in which the sinner, having quenched
and driven from him the Holy Spirit, has made repentance for ever impossible. In this case, as the sin is
eternal, the separation from God must also be eternal.
Or, looking at the matter from another point of view,
if, as Dr. Dale teaches, there is an eternal law of righteousness, then to break it eternally must involve eternal
penalty. But this is so, not because a temporal sin is
condemned by God to suffer an eternal penalty, but
because continuous sin necessitates continuous separation from God's purity. We may believe that the
instant a sinner repents and is absolved from his sin,
God desires to receive him back into communion. Thus,
if our Lord suffered any separation from His Father
at all, He experienced the penalty due from God's
holiness upon sin.

[1] Jas. i. 15.

The Separation required by Sin is (1) *Spiritual, and* (2) *not Absolute.*

When we speak of the penalty of sin being separation from God, of course this must be taken in the sense of spiritual condition, and not of separation by space. God is omnipresent, and even though hell were a place instead of a condition, it would exist by His permissive will, and therefore His personality would dominate it. But if hell be viewed as a state of existence, it is, if anything, still easier to understand that the realization of the presence of God is an ever-present condition of that state.   In this case the spiritual atmosphere of hell will be one of hopeless yet eternal hostility to an irresistible Presence.   But in either case there can be no such thing as absolute separation from God.   Apart from His will a hell, whether of place or condition, could not exist; and as will is the centre of personality, hell is in contact with God even though it is a contact of hostility.

It follows that the separation from God which sin causes is relative, not absolute.   It is a matter of degree and kind.   All of us have experienced to some extent the feeling of the withdrawal of God's approval. It is not uncommon in Christian experience to feel that heaven is shut to one's prayers; that one is cut off from communion with God; that He will not hear.   And this must be similar in kind, though vastly less in degree, to the extreme final state of divorce from God we describe as hell.

We know that between friends it is quite possible for a man, even though full of affection for his friend, for some reason he judges adequate, to block the invisible channels by which sympathy flows and the influences of personality interpenetrate.   In such a case the other man will be conscious of the change, will feel cut off from his friend, separated from him, and, maybe, greatly troubled about it.   And if this happens at a

time of trouble he may well feel that his friend has forsaken him, and ask the reason why.

In the same way we can understand that the Father
could check the intercommunion between Himself and
the human nature of His Son, and so cause Him to
experience that spiritual separation which is in very
fact the lessening of personal contact with God, and
in its extreme form the experience of the lost.

Such an experience would be in full agreement with
the facts conditioning our Lord's Incarnation.   For the
doctrine of the Incarnation teaches that, while possessing
permanently the whole nature and essence of the Godhead, the Second Person of the Holy Trinity added to
it human nature, and made it His own.   So that Jesus
lived on earth a truly human life with the limitations
proper to human consciousness, though found in Him
in its perfect development.   How He could possess at
one and the same time both His divine and His human
consciousness with the limitations inherent in the latter
is beyond our present powers of apprehension; but
Christianity is coming to understand that, as He possessed and possesses the two natures, human and divine,
without distinction or confusion, this involves that the
two consciousnesses proper to the two natures would
and do also coexist without distinction, and yet also
without confusion or intrusion upon one another's
spheres.

Therefore it does not follow that, because of the union
of the divine and human natures in Christ, His human
nature enjoyed the same experiences as the divine.   He
had both come down from heaven and was in heaven.[1]
" The human (nature of Christ) was not transmuted out
of its own character by its union with the divine."[2]
Therefore the spiritual bond between the Son of Man
and the Father could be broken while the divine unity
between the Son of God and His Father remained
undisturbed.

[1] John iii. 13.   [2] *The Incarnation of God*, p. 25.

In the self-emptying of Himself which the Incarnation involved we can understand also that our Lord might not be conscious in His human nature of the eternal, inviolable union still existing between the Father and Son in the eternal Godhead. If challenged on the point, He might have been aware of it as an intellectual truth, but it was in His human nature that He bore the penalty of human sin, and evidently that divine union was not present to Him. He was not conscious of it, when He uttered the cry of " forsakenness " upon the Cross. The dominating fact of the moment was the desertion of His human nature by God to which He gave expression, and we may be quite sure that, whether our Lord's cry was spoken as a quotation from the 22nd Psalm or not, it was in no sense artificial, but the natural and restrained expression of a real experience. It was a real separation, a real weakening of the personal bond between the Father and the human nature of the Son of Man. The enjoyment of God's approval, love, and support are all objective gifts of His grace flowing from Him into the soul. This flow of the divine grace into the human soul of Jesus had ceased, and the natural subjective results followed. All the personal relations of love are essentially matters of feeling. The very essence of the life of love is the assured sense of mutual trust and affection; and anything which weakens this does much more than intervening distance to produce anxiety and sorrow.

It was such a rupture of the sense of His Father's approving love our Lord experienced; and we can understand that in the case of one whose dependence upon and intercommunion with His Father had been hitherto so perfect that He could say, " I and the Father are one," and " He that hath seen Me hath seen the Father," the cessation of these relations might well prove a grief sufficient to break the heart.

Bodily Death is the withdrawing of a Divine Thing.

In addition to this there was another way in which
the communion between the Father and our Lord's
human nature was broken, and the consequences of sin
suffered by Him upon the Cross. Bodily life is communicated to us and maintained minute by minute by
God, " in whom we live and move and have our being."
It is continued by the maintenance of the chemical and
other natural and vital laws which emanate from Him,
and without which it would be impossible for us to live,
and which are kept in operation by the will of God with
regard to each one of us. Life, then, is a communion
to us of the power of God. It is an extension of the
divine life, and when our Lord felt the approach of
death by which this communion would be ruptured,
He, whose whole life was based upon the sense of
dependence upon, and union with His Father, would
apprehend it as a still further withdrawal of communion
and forsaking by His God. It was the removal from
Him of a divine thing which flowed from the life of God.

*The Separation required for Sin by Divine Holiness
Objective, not Necessarily Subjective.*

While speaking of objections to the " experiential "
view of our Lord's sufferings, we may deal with another
which might suggest itself. It might be argued that
one of the consequences of sin is the sense of God's
displeasure with the sinner, and that, as that was
impossible in our Lord's case, He did not and could
not endure the penalty required by Divine Holiness as
the consequence of sin.

It is quite true that the Father' could not possibly
have felt any anger against His Son, and that therefore
our Lord cannot have experienced the divine displeasure
felt by the ordinary sinner. This must be admitted.
But the objection based upon it disappears when we
remember that the sense of God's displeasure is only

an accompanying circumstance, and no integral part of
the original requirement of God's holiness with regard
to sin.   What this does require is that His purity shall
be separated from the contamination of spiritual communion with the guilty.   And though doubtless there
is displeasure, yet what is necessary to His holiness is
that it should be felt, and expressed by Him rather
than it should be felt by the sinner.   And so far as God
may wish the latter, the desire will be the outcome of
His love seeking to excite penitential sorrow, rather
than the sentence of His justice demanding punishment.
In our Lord's case what we have to consider is, not
whether He experienced the stimulus provided to
quicken human penitence, but whether He suffered the
penalty due to sin, and the above argument supplies no
sufficient reason to doubt that He did.

No doubt other objections to this view of our Lord's
sufferings may arise which perhaps will not be so readily
answered as these; but the evidence in its favour seems
so strong, and, moreover, it fits in so well with human
needs and instincts, and with the agelong conceptions
of Christendom, that it seems more likely to be correct
—at any rate, in its main features and so far as it goes
—than new theories which, though, maybe, difficult to
controvert, would require us to revolutionize our ways
of regarding the Cross.   On the whole it is a greater
shock to Christian instinct to be told that God's love
did not bear the penalty of man's sin than to be told
that, if He did, it was unjust.   Of the two, we feel that,
if only we could see clearly, the latter would be the
more likely to be found untrue.

The Experiential View completes the Penitential Theory.

In theories of the Atonement it is the negations which
generally fail to convince.   When we are told that our
Lord's was the noblest of all martyrdoms our heart
leaps in response, but when we are told that it was *only*
a martyrdom we are left cold and disappointed.   When

Dr. McLeod Campbell teaches that our Saviour made a full confession, in the sense of acknowledgment, of the justice of God's sentence upon sin, or Dr. Moberly that our Lord offered His Father a perfect penitence for sin, we gladly accept their teaching in so far as we can see truth in it.   But when we are told that God's love could carry Him no farther in identifying Himself with human experience than to feel a separation which was not actual, we are conscious, although these limitations are argued as an aid to faith, of a sense of disappointment rather than of relief.   In the things of God we cannot be enthusiastic about negations, for the truth concerning an infinite being cannot be limited.   It is an eternal Yea.   His holiness and love extend to the farthest horizon the human heart can imagine, and beyond it.   In God there is no Nay.   So in the Atonement God is just, and more than just; our Lord's death was a martyrdom and more than a martyrdom; His obedience to the Cross was an acknowledgment and confession of sin's desert to the fullest possible extent; and it was also an act of repentance for the sins of mankind of the fullest kind possible to Him.   The only limitations are those inseparable from the divine nature.

That is why we cannot limit it to penitence or contrition only.   A complete repentance includes " restitution " as well as contrition and confession; and, as our Church daily proclaims, our Lord's death was " a full, perfect, and sufficient sacrifice, oblation, and satisfaction for the sins of the whole world."   It included reparation, and full, perfect reparation, as well as contrition and confession.   All that is needed is to carry forward the " penitential theory " to make it include all that is necessary to, and involved in, a true repentance, and " repentance," as we have seen, " when carried to the uttermost, means death.   It begins with the confession of sin, but it ends with the endurance of sin's penalty," and this is separation from God.

CHAPTER III

1. *It satisfies Divine Holiness.*

We began by seeing what Divine Holiness requires
for the forgiveness of sin, and we have seen how our
Lord's sacrifice satisfies all those needs. Divine Holiness requires the separation of the sinner, and so our
Lord suffered "forsakenness" by the Father on the
Cross.

2. *It affords Reparation to Outraged Justice.*

Divine Holiness requires reparation in answer to the
demands of justice which form part of a holy character.
The reparation required for the rebellion and self-will
of sin is perfect obedience, and this was made by our
Lord in His submission to the fulness of sin's penalty
upon the Cross, experiencing both the first and also the
second death.

3. *It satisfies the Requirements of Love.*

Divine Holiness also requires the satisfaction of all
the demands of perfect love. This also our Lord
achieved upon the Cross. Looked at from the Father's
point of view, His Son, as all-holy and loving, ought to
have wished to make all the compensation possible for
man's failure, which, because of that failure, man had
become eternally unable to make for himself. To fail
either in the desire or achievement of this compensation
would be a failure in perfect love and holiness. The
Father, therefore, would necessarily desire His Son to

make this compensation; and also, on the other hand, it was the Son's " meat " to do His Father's will.[1] On both sides the requirements of love called for the same sacrifice. Just as a man seeing his mother grieved by the rudeness or neglect of a younger brother would be under a moral obligation, not of justice, but of love and right feeling, to make reparation so far as he could by some special act of kindness and courtesy for his brother's fault, so, in the same way, our Lord was under a moral obligation, not only nor chiefly of justice, but of holiness and love, to make reparation to His Father for the outrage of man's sin. His obedient self-sacrifice was a reparation for man's defiant self-will—" obedient " because He knew His Father was bound to wish to see Him attain this duty and perfection of right feeling and holiness. This in some sort explains why the writer of the Epistle to the Hebrews says our Lord needed to suffer to make Him perfect (ii. 10, v. 9), and our Lord Himself refers to His death as being His perfecting (Luke xiii. 32).

Driven by this holiness and passion of love, both for His Father and for His brethren, the Christ undertook His divine venture, and coming down into this world set His face steadfastly toward Jerusalem and the Cross awaiting Him there.

---

[1] Why the Father desired an act of sacrifice, as He unquestionably did (Matt. xxvi. 39 and par.), will appear later in the book. It is enough to say here that it was necessary for man's salvation, and represented the achievement of a perfect obedience.

PART V

HOW OUR LORD'S SACRIFICE CONCERNS US: THE LAW OF IDENTIFICATION WITH DISTINCTION

CHAPTER I

SOME OF THE WAYS IN WHICH OUR LORD'S LIFE AND DEATH CAN AFFECT US

WE have seen how, inspired by holiness, but especially by the holiness of love, our Lord undertook the great, divine venture of experiencing the penalties due to sin; and we can understand how, far from being in any sense unjust, such an experience was an act of supreme moral holiness. But the question arises: What has that to do with us ? Separated from the Cross, as we are, by 1900 years, how does our Lord's death concern us ?

The answer is, of course, that there is no necessary connection; yet in some ways the knowledge of our Saviour's sacrifice for sin tends very naturally and generally to affect us.

The General Appealing Power of the Cross.

Some heathen Esquimaux on seeing a lantern picture of our Lord's crucifixion burst out into cries of " What love ! Oh ! what great love !" and tears streamed down their faces. This is the natural effect upon the human heart of the story of our Lord's sacrifice, which in our case is apt to be much blunted by our familiarity with it from an age so early that at first we could not understand it. This natural effect is increased when we consider the deliberate voluntariness of the sacrifice. Our

Lord told His disciples beforehand in great detail what He would have to suffer, and this knowledge added greatly to the courage demanded. Yet, we are told, He steadfastly set His face to go up to Jerusalem. " No man taketh (My life) from Me," He said; " I lay it down of Myself."

The Natural Effects of Penitence and Aspiration Inadequate Grounds for Forgiveness.

The natural effect upon human nature is to stir us to penitence and aspiration to follow His most holy example. But both these fail to provide a satisfactory atonement for our sins. Contrition alone is not enough, because no repentance is complete which does not make restitution for past offences, and we are incapable of making the compensation to God which love would desire on our part to offer, and on His part to receive. And we are equally incapable of following the example of Christ's holiness. The greatest saint, bound most closely into spiritual communion with his Lord, is the man most sensible of his failure. " When we have done all, we are unprofitable servants."

The natural subjective effects, then, of our Lord's sacrifice upon our hearts cannot produce a satisfactory atonement for our sins, and we are forced to look elsewhere.

The True Answer found in the Unity betwixt Christ and His Church.

The true answer to the question what Christ's death has to do with us is found in one of the great paradoxes of Christianity—viz., in that union which is betwixt Christ and His Church, which St. Paul says is a great mystery. Christianity is full of paradoxes. St. Paul has given us a list of them in 2 Cor. vi., where he describes the Christian life as sorrowful yet always rejoicing, as dying and behold we live. So also we learn elsewhere of other paradoxes: that God is Almighty

and yet self-limited in the gift of freewill to man; that
" He that saveth his life shall lose it, but he that loseth
his life for Christ's sake and the Gospel's shall save it ";
that we pass through death to life, so that the grave
is the gate of heaven; that from the unity of God " in
the beginning " has issued the multiplicity of creation,
yet that finally all things are once more to be subdued
unto Him, that God may be all in all (1 Cor. xv. 28).
Again, just as even now, amidst all the multiplicity of
creation, scientists tell us that the ether penetrates all
matter and all space, linking star to star, and binding
the universe into one great whole, so St. Paul tells us
that all the many members of the Church form a unity
bound together by the pervading presence of Christ:
" He gave some to be apostles, and some prophets, and
some evangelists, and some pastors and teachers for the
perfecting of the saints . . . till we all attain the unity
of the faith . . . unto the measure of the stature of
the fulness of Christ." So in this Church, which is to
bind us all together in Christ, one great guiding principle
of its life is " unity in diversity "; or, as we may state
it for our purposes, *identification with distinction of
personality*.

Identification with Christ in His Sacrifice necessary to a Moral Share in its Benefits.

With regard to the Atonement it is not difficult to
trace the unifying influence of Christ's death down
through the 1900 years which have elapsed, and note
how His single personality affects millions; but it is not
so easy to see how that influence can rightly bring
individuals within the benefits of His atoning sacrifice.
We who stay at home have no moral right to share in
the benefits of the vicarious sacrifices of those who have
suffered and risked their lives to win liberty for our
country, unless we have in some way really identified
ourselves with them in their efforts and sufferings. So,
also, we have no moral nor spiritual claim to share in

13

the benefits of our Lord's Passion unless we are really identified with Him in His efforts to satisfy the requirements of holiness. How can this be attained ?

We have seen that the primary, outstanding feature in our Lord's crucifixion, which conferred its redemptive power, was that in it He passed through an experience which included that perfect obedience to His Father's will which is required by Divine Holiness as the reparation due for the rebellion of sin. This perfect obedience is the chief feature upon which emphasis is laid in the Bible. It is difficult, if not impossible, to provide scriptural proof of any penitential element in our Lord's death, as is noticeable by its absence from writings in support of that theory. But Biblical proof of the important place filled up by obedience is not difficult to find. For instance, the struggle to attain the spirit of complete submission to His Father's will is the main feature in the agony of the Garden, with its reiterated prayer, " Thy will, not Mine be done "; and the result of our Lord's victory was His obedience " even to the death of the Cross." He not only submitted, but submitted perfectly. So that we see here the perfect obedience of His life culminating in perfect submission to the hardest thing which could be asked of Him— viz., the experience of the utmost consequences of sin. A death has taken place, and not only an ordinary death, but the penal death upon the Cross under the circumstances required in order to make a just reparation, for the redemption of transgressions.[1]

It was therefore a " full, perfect, and sufficient . . . satisfaction " for the rebellion and self-will which are the essential characteristics of sin. Supposing it conceivable that God the Son had at any time failed to fulfil His Father's will in any degree, the obedience of His death would have made complete reparation for that failure.

[1] Gal. iii. 13 and Heb. ix. 15. The circumstances were those of suffering the " cause " of forsakenness and the offering of a perfect obedience.

Christ's Crucifixion was only a Potential Atonement to be completed by and in Each Believer.

Yet when we say our Lord's death was a " full, perfect, and sufficient sacrifice for the sins of the whole world," it does not mean that the necessary reparation due to God for our sins was then and there completed. It does not mean this, for what has one person's holiness to do with another man's sins ? but only that the means were then provided for atonement; and that it was then made possible, by the perfect obedience of that death, for each sinner, by its means, to offer a perfect reparation to God in the manner to be explained later.

If all sinners, inspired by Christ's example, could offer as reparation an obedience equally perfect with His, Divine Holiness would be able to accept such reparation as satisfactory. But man, corrupted by sin, is incapable of this. Our Lord alone could achieve it, and the entrance of this act of perfect obedience into the world of fact was the first necessary and preliminary measure towards making possible the extension of God's plan of salvation to all mankind. It provided the means of completion of the Atonement for and in each sinner. It opened a way to make possible the acceptance of each sinner by God. And it did it by presenting to the world a perfect obedience to God's will with which men could identify themselves in reparation for the self-will of their sins. The possibility of identification with Christ's holiness is the alternative offered by God in view of man's incapacity to produce any perfect obedience from his own unassisted nature. If man can be truly involved in, and identified with, Christ's perfect obedience, then, as one with Him, he will be able to offer the reparation due to God which he cannot produce by himself. So that, regarded from the standpoint of the individual sinner, our Saviour's death was a potential rather than a completed atonement for the sins of the world. It was indeed a sufficient sacrifice, but its efficacy, so far as each sinner is concerned, depends upon himself—*i.e.*, upon his succeeding, with God's help, in so identifying himself with His Saviour that, one with Him, he is involved in His obedience and His sin-bearing (John xvii. 21).

To make this possible was the second and enabling step required and taken by God in His plan of salvation.

So the Atonement falls into two parts: First, there was provided an act of perfect obedience, as a possible reparation to God for each man's sin; and, secondly, God provided means by which men might identify themselves with Christ's perfect holiness. The first was mainly the work of God the Son; the second is mainly the work of the Holy Spirit.

Doctrine of Sanctification through Union with the Obedience of the Cross.

Of these two sides of the Atonement, emphasis in recent years has inclined more and more to be laid upon the latter. The moral difficulties connected in the past with our Lord's sin-bearing have caused attention to be directed more and more to the thought of man's forgiveness and acceptance by God on the ground of his sanctification by union with our Lord's perfect, obedient holiness through the work of the Holy Spirit. Bishop Wilkinson, indeed, sees in this one of the laws of God's spiritual kingdom, and calls it " the law of acceptance in the Beloved."[1]

Doctrine of Christian's Union with Christ generally accepted.

There is no need to prove the doctrine of the union which is betwixt Christ and His Church, or of the Saviour with the individual Christian soul. It may be a patent fact with regard to some of the Greek prepositions that they " had lost all their distinctive meaning in the days

[1] *Some Laws in God's Spiritual Kingdom*, chapter ii.

that the Gospels were written,"[1] but at any rate the meaning of ἐν χριστῷ, etc., is not doubtful; and the whole of the New Testament is so charged with the teaching involved that to give a list of Biblical proofs would mean quoting a great part of the Epistles. Nearly every writer on the Atonement says that it contains a great mystery which probably will never be wholly solved, and no doubt this is true; but there is reason to think that the heart of the problem lies in the mystical union which is betwixt Christ and His Church. If all the language dealing with it is only symbolical and literary, as some assert, then there is really very little that is mysterious about it. It is not beyond the power of man's mind to grasp it. Yet St. Paul says it is " a great mystery "—the great mystery of our religion, and there is reason to believe that when, on the Great Day, this " great mystery " is made plain, the Atonement will no longer be an unsolvable difficulty.

Union with Christ the Basis of Recent Theories of the Atonement.

It is in this direction, then, that the solution must be sought, and it is noteworthy that among recent writers on the Atonement there is universal agreement as to the crucial value of the doctrine. It is made the main basis of all their theories.

Dr. McLeod Campbell writes: " . . . it is in the Son . . . we are approaching the Father. . . . He, who made atonement for our sins and brought into humanity the everlasting righteousness of sonship, is not the mere pattern of life, but is Himself that life in us in which we are able to confess our sins, and to call God Father. . . . He is the vine . . . we are the branches."[2]

Dr. Dale also carefully argues that when St. Paul wrote, " If one died for all, then all died," this was not

---

[1] Cf. *The Atonement and Modern Thought*, p. 100.
[2] *The Nature of the Atonement*, p. 304. See also pp. 138, 251, 266, 271.

merely " a strong rhetorical argument "[1] or " repre-
sentation,"[2] but is " explicit " teaching that the " destruction of evil within us is the . . . fulfilment in
ourselves of the mystery of Christ's death," and a statement of fact avouched by the experience of many who
are " conscious that in the death of Christ their old
and evil life perished." . . . " We died in His death "
on the Cross,[3] he declares; and in another passage
writes: " In His death our sins die, and in His life the
very life of God is made our own. How . . . we may
be unable to tell. . . . But it is enough that in God's
idea, and according to the law of the kingdom of heaven,
we are crucified with Christ. Sometimes through our
union with Him sin may seem to perish as by a sudden
blow. More frequently it dies slowly . . . as . . . by
crucifixion. . . . But it is actually crucified, if only
our union with Christ is complete. . . . The death of
Christ is the death of sin."[4]

Dr. Moberly insists that likeness to Christ depends
upon incorporation with Him,[5] and says: " Everything
turns, in the exposition of the Atonement, upon the
reality of our personal identification with Him,"[6] and
later uses such an expression as " identification with
Christ of the very inmost personality of each several
man,"[7] and speaks of being " really . . . translated into
Christ " in order to find " the ultimate reality of our own
individual being."[8]

Necessity of Distinction of Personality as well as of Identification with Christ.

It is noticeable how these writers exhaust language
in their endeavours to describe the closeness of the
union existing between our Lord and the Christian;
and in later writers a new feature is observable, which
naturally follows upon the teaching of a union which

[1] *The Atonement*, p. 425.   [2] *Ibid.*, p. 426.   [3] *Ibid.*, p. 427.
[4] *Ibid.*, pp. 429, 430.   [5] *Atonement and Personality*, p. 284.
[6] *Ibid.*, p. 276   [7] *Ibid.*, p. 284.   [8] *Ibid.*, p. 285.

amounts to identification. Whilst maintaining, or indeed, if possible, emphasizing still further, the closeness of this union, they at the same time teach that the separate personality of the individual must be preserved. Man is not—must not be—absorbed in His Saviour.

Dr. Hitchcock emphasizes our Lord's identification with the human race rather than with the individual. He writes: " His [Christ's] sufferings, sorrows, and penitence were neither penal nor substitutionary, but were the expression and result of His realization of His solidaric oneness with humanity in humanity, who summed up humanity in Himself, apart from whom humanity has no purpose, no way of redemption, or achievement."[1] This racial view of the entire oneness of Christ with mankind in which " our identification with Christ, the federal Head of the race . . . is consummated by the Spirit of Christ," is balanced by the words " who enables us *one by one* to say, ' I have been crucified with Christ, yet I live, and yet no longer I, but Christ liveth in Me.' " And he adds later: " The sacrifice consecrated on Calvary is consummated in the Christian's conscience. The *personal identity is maintained* all through. If Christ is in him, he is also a man in Christ."[2]

We have here the idea of identification combined with distinction of personality clearly expressed as an important, possible, and actual feature in spiritual existence. The qualification of " distinction " is obviously necessary. For to teach the identification of our personality with that of Christ apart from the doctrine of distinction would be blasphemous. But to accept it so conditioned is to have opened up for one's apprehension a supreme manifestation of the love of God.

---

[1] *The Atonement and Modern Thought*, p. 106.
[2] *Ibid.*, p. 109. The italics are not in the original.

CHAPTER II

THE DOCTRINE OF IDENTIFICATION WITH DISTINCTION OF PERSONALITY

The Doctrine stated.

THIS conception is the main basis of the view of the Atonement taken in this book, and may be stated as follows: In spiritual existence it is possible for separate persons to be so identified in a common life as to be really and morally involved in the consequences of one another's actions, whilst at the same time maintaining the distinctness of their several personalities; or, to put it more concisely, for there to be *a real identity combined with real distinctness of personality.*

The passages quoted above seem to lack little in definiteness, but as the word " identification " is capable of a weaker meaning, it will perhaps be best to say that, in the above definition, it is intended to carry all that it can be made to contain. In an identification of this kind with our Lord, it is meant to imply that, in so far as Christ has died, the true Christian is involved in His death; and that, in so far as His death was a sacrifice for sin, so far also the Christian is involved in His sin-bearing. This inclusion is real, though in the first instance it is only potential, and not fully developed until later—possibly not until after death. Yet, as the seed in every part of its development contains the full plant, so the Christian in union with His Lord contains all the reality and moral consequences of His life, death, and present existence so far as that is possible in view of His personal distinctness and divine transcendence.

Difficulties of Spiritual Conceptions mainly due to Limitations of our Material Condition.

A recent writer has declared that for the Christian Church seriously to put forward the doctrine of the unity of the Holy Trinity for acceptance is an insult to intelligence,[1] and no doubt it is in the difficulty of realizing, under our present conditions, the possibility of plurality in unity that the chief obstacle to the acceptance of modern views of the Atonement arises. Yet it is a very hasty utterance for anyone to assert that it is an insult to present the idea of the identification of personalities for serious consideration as a possible truth of spiritual existence. If the objection to it really lies in its profundity, it is a compliment rather than an insult to present it for men's apprehension.

Our chief difficulty lies in our very strong consciousness, under our present predominatingly materialistic conditions, of the distinctness of our personality. It is especially at this point that this theory of the Atonement is most likely to fail in carrying conviction; yet this distinctness of personality is not questioned by the law of identification as we conceive it. It is only that an additional claim is put forward for personality— viz., that, while maintaining its distinctness, it can yet become really identified with another or other personalities. It is this further capacity which at first sight appears to be directly contrary to reason, and tends to provoke an outburst of denial. Probably, in most cases, no logic, but only some measure of actual experience, will ever win any measure of acceptance for this view of the " great mystery." " To know God," says Illingworth, " is a process which . . . involves the action of our entire personality, both in its extent and its intensity, its wholeness and its oneness."[2] No

---

[1] H. G. Wells in *God, the Invisible King*.
[2] *Personality Human and Divine* (Cheap Edition), p. 67.

merely intellectual apprehension is sufficient for this
purpose. Nothing less than experience will enable a
man to realize the possibility of union with God.

Shakespeare's Conception of Unity with Plurality.

But man has powers of intuition which outrange the
capacity of reason, and have enabled philosophers and
poets to forestall the discoveries of science and the
deductions of logicians. As one of the greatest, if not
the greatest of these, Shakespeare conceived the possibility of plurality in unity as a condition natural to
personality when raised to its highest point of development by love, and has expressed it in " The Phœnix
and the Turtle." Of this poem Mr. John Masefield
says: " In dark and noble verse it describes a spiritual
marriage. . . . It is the work of a great mind trying
to express in unusual symbols a thought too subtle and
too intense to be expressed in any other way. Spiritual
ecstasy is the only key to work of this kind. . . .
Poetry moves in many ways . . . it may give to
thoughts such life as thoughts can have, an intenser
and stranger life than man knows with forms that are
not normal, and a speech unintelligible to normal
moods."[1]

In the poem thus described these verses occur:

> So they loved, as love in twain
> Had the essence but in one;
> Two distincts, division none:
> Number there in love was slain.
>
> Hearts remote, yet not asunder;
> Distance, and no space was seen
> 'Twixt the turtle and his queen:
> But in them it were a wonder.
>
> So between them love did shine,
> That the turtle saw his right
> Flaming in the Phœnix' sight;
> Either was the other's mine.

---

[1] *Shakespeare* (The Home University Library), p. 249.

Property was thus appalled,
That the self was not the same:
Single nature's double name
Neither two, nor one was called.

Reason, in itself confounded,
Saw division grow together,
To themselves yet either neither,
Simple were so well compounded,

That it cried, How true a twain
Seemeth this concordant one !
Love hath reason, reason none,
If what parts can so remain.

Whereupon it made this threne
To the phœnix and the dove,
Co-supremes and stars of love
As chorus to their tragic scene.

It is evident that here Shakespeare is contemplating no ordinary kind of union, but one in which each of two separate personalities both interpenetrates and is absorbed by the other; so that, though two, they are also inseparably one. You have two " co-supremes "; " two distincts, division none." It is a case of perfect unity in plurality. In Shakespeare's own words, " Reason " is " in itself confounded."

Such Conceptions transcend rather than insult Reason.

Yet one would not say that in presenting the thought for public acceptance and appreciation Shakespeare was offering an insult to human reason. Mr. Masefield on the contrary calls it " noble verse," " the work of a great mind." It is a surpassing of, a challenge rather than an insult to, reason, if only to reasonable humility in the presence of spiritual phenomena. We have, then, here the intuitive conception of a great genius, and it should be allowed full weight. But still one might ask whether any solid grounds can be adduced in support of such a conception of spiritual conditions, and in that case confirmation is not lacking.

Philosophy's Support of such a Conception.

We have, for instance, the irresistible tendency to union found in human nature. As gravitation rules in the material world, so an impulse to union rules in the world of personality, and may be traced in an ascending scale. Dr. Illingworth says: " We desire to incorporate and to assimilate with ourselves the various contents of our material, moral, and intellectual environment. The twofold process of desire, acquisitive and active, irresistibly impels us into communion with other persons. . . . We press on . . . till we have found persons like ourselves with whom to share it " (*i.e.*, our experience), " and then we are at rest. Thus all persons are ends to us, when compared with impersonal things, but in different degrees," and " . . . only partial ends. . . . But we instinctively seek more than this. We require to find in other persons an end in which our entire personality may rest. And this is the relationship of love. . . . It is our very self, and not a department of us that loves."[1] " Our own personality . . . is incomplete in itself, and must go beyond itself for completion, as, for example, in the family."[2] Carrying this thought forward from the human to the Divine Personality, he adds later: " But union with God can neither be attained nor yet declined by man; it is felt to be imperative, yet seems to be impossible. And hence issues the universal cry of all true religion—' Make me a clean heart, O God, and renew a right spirit within me.' That may be done from the divine side which cannot be done from the human. And from the conviction that this cry is answered comes the assurance that we are in contact with a personal God."[3] And again: " . . . we find the desire for union with God to be at the very basis of our being . . ."[4] so that " . . . the highest personal religion always tends to mysticism,

---

[1] *Personality Human and Divine*, p. 26.   [2] *Ibid.*, p. 41.
[3] *Ibid.*, pp. 65, 66.   [4] *Ibid.*, p. 93.

a sense of spiritual communion which lies too deep for words," and it is in the Divine Person alone that our personality finds its home.[1] Another authority, W. McDougall, says: "Hence, it is argued, it is reasonable to believe that this religious experience, of which the fullest or completest type is the mystical sense of the absorption of the self in a larger whole, is what it appears to be to those who best know it—namely, an actual union or communion of the human mind with the divine mind."[2]

The Confirmation of Science.

In these quotations we find man's instinctive desire traced up from his receptivity of material things to the spiritual communion with God which lies too deep for words; and the whole movement points forward to a perfecting of that communion which would conceivably amount to that " identification combined with distinctness of personality " we have ventured to postulate. We have here, then, some foundation for this theory, and it is supported from various directions.

Science itself tends to make the doctrine of identification combined with distinction in a future consummated bond of union with our Lord more easy of realization.

Illustrations in the Human Body of Plurality in Unity.

It helps one to grasp the idea of " plurality in unity " or " identification with distinction " when we remember that our own physical life includes many separate lives. Our blood is certainly an essential part of our personality. We commonly speak of it as our *life*-blood, and we are told that " the blood is the life."[3] Yet in the phagocytes which act as its scavengers we have an innumerable host of separate living creatures, each

---

[1] *Personality Human and Divine*, p. 68.
[2] *Psychology*, Home University Library, pp. 225, 226.
[3] Lev. xvii. 11 to 14; Deut. xii. 23.

with an independent life of its own. They are a part
of our physical nature, and a necessary part, yet each
of them is " a living creature endowed with powers of
locomotion, of assimilation, and of reproduction . . .
by fission."[1] So the position is that we and they are
necessary to, and yet in a sense independent of, one
another, and together form a complete whole.

In somewhat the same way, but carrying the thought
farther, it has been said: " God is the centre, and the
manifestation of God the circumference of all existence.
Within this vast circle lies the whole creation, like the
myriad cells in the human body. Each of these cells
in our body has a life of its own, yet all are related to
a unitary consciousness, a personality which far transcends the life of each cell. Thus, also, we may conceive the human race as the constituent cells . . . of
the One Body to which all are related, and yet all
transcended in the one supreme ineffable Being."[2]

Science combined with philosophy helps us again in
its teaching upon what we may call the " immateriality
of matter " when it proclaims (1) that matter is fundamentally only a form of electricity[3] or energy in motion;
(2) that the ultimate reality is personality,[4] of which
(3) the predominating element is the will.[5]

So the thing necessary for the perfect union of personalities is mainly an identification of their wills, such
as is indicated in our Lord's sayings as existing between
Himself and His Father: " My meat is to do the will
of Him that sent Me ";[6] " The words that I speak unto
you I speak not of Myself; but the Father that dwelleth
in Me, He doeth the works;"[7] " The word which ye

---

[1] Sir Oliver Lodge in *Raymond*, pp. 385, 386.

[2] Sir William Barrett in *On the Threshold of the Unseen*, p. 290.

[3] *Cf. Introduction to Science*, by J. A. Thomson, Home University
Library, p. 136.

[4] *Personality Human and Divine :* " Personality is our canon of
reality " (p. 28). Also Note 8: " Personality the ultimate reality."

[5] *Ibid.*, p. 63.

[6] John iv. 34.   [7] John xiv. 10.

hear is not Mine, but the Father's which sent Me;"[1]
" I and My Father are one."[2]

As opposed to the dictum of philosophy that the
ultimate reality is personality, we on our part feel, as
one of our most certain convictions, that the impersonal
world about us is also " real," in the sense of really existing; but the two views may be reconciled if all things are
real by virtue of our and their union with the personality
of God. Mr. McDowall, in his study on *Evolution and
the Need of Atonement*, is led to feel that the science of
evolution is in favour of, rather than opposed to, such
a union. He argues that some form of union with God
is necessary. " The creation must eventually work out
its own salvation . . . and appear at length in the
likeness of God, the primal Cause. To assist this
development the Godhead limits itself by the Incarnation, making it possible . . . for man to . . . enter
into perfect union with Him (*i.e.*, Christ) . . . for He
is of the same nature;" and " when this union is consummated . . . it is indissoluble. . . . Here is no
substitution, but identification. Identification not only
of God with manhood, but of manhood with the Incarnate God—a reciprocal process. . . . As man draws
nearer to perfection, so he enters into closer communion
with God, and we believe that he too shall eventually
enter into the category of the timeless or eternal, when
his will shall be wholly united with the will of God,
while yet his personality shall remain in its own identity.
. . . In time there is pluralism, in eternity God is the
great I AM, with whom the personal souls of men will
at length be joined in full communion of will and love;
no longer pluralism, in the ordinary sense of the word,
because their experience will be the experience of God;
for them reality will hold the same content, if only
partially, as for God."[3]

[1] John xiv. 24.   [2] John x. 30.   [3] P. 173.

The Evidence of Psychology.

The study of psychology also supports the view of the interpenetration of personalities. We are told that we must " recognize the existence in a certain sense of over-individual or collective minds. . . . The thinking and acting of each man, in so far as he thinks and acts as a member of society, is very different from his thinking and acting as an isolated individual. . . . Every normal human being grows up under the constant influence of the society into which he was born, and his mental development is moulded at every point. He becomes the heir to an intellectual and moral tradition which has slowly been built up, bit by bit, through the efforts of thousands of generations." Each of us is moulded by suggestion, " in virtue of which beliefs are induced in, or communicated to, the subject independently of all logical reasoning to a solution," and this is brought about by sympathy, which is " the tendency to experience in the face of the same object the same emotions and impulses that are revealed by the behaviour of our fellows "; and by imitation, which is " the tendency to direct in detail the bodily movements to which our impulses prompt us, according to the pattern set us by our fellows."[1] Owing to the interpenetration of these personal influences, " each member of a crowd tends to lose to some extent his sense of personal identity and responsibility," and " the collective life of a well-organized society commonly attains a higher level, both intellectually and morally, than could be individually attained by its average members, and raises many who participate in it to much higher levels of thought and action."[2] " A nation with a long past and a vast system of living traditions and institutions has a character which is not by any means merely the sum or resultant of the characters of all its component units."[3] But if the

[1] *Psychology*, Home University Library, pp. 228-235.
[2] *Ibid.*, pp. 241, 242. [3] *Ibid.*, p. 247.

nation moulds the individual the influence is reciprocal, and the individual man also moulds the nation. " Metaphysically mankind represents an individual whole, and our enemies are one; there is no real separateness. Everybody is guilty for one single individual's sin, one person may save the world; every crime, every sacrifice, is vicarious. . . . Unity in diversity . . . is the distinguishing mark of human beings. . . ."[1]

The Evidence of Sociology.

The two seemingly antagonistic principles of personal independence and authority are found in human nature as far back as history goes, each struggling for predominance, and first one and then the other gaining ascendancy. In the early dawn of civilization the personality of the tribal chief dominated everything, but under his rule the tribe was everything and the individual did not count where the two interests clashed. This lived on into the very considerable civilization of the Greeks who " had very little conception, if any, of spiritual individuality."[2] Among the Semitic peoples the rights of a father to sacrifice his son did not seem strange even to such a man as Abraham, and it was not until the times of the later prophets that the individual rights of the children were beginning to be recognized, as witnessed by Ezekiel's protest against the proverb, " The fathers have eaten sour grapes, and the children's teeth are set on edge."[3] Coming down to later times, we find that individualism found one of its strongest homes in England, became very marked in the time of Queen Elizabeth, and reached its highest point in public recognition by the law under the influence of the Manchester school during the latter half of the nineteenth century.

In France Balzac recognized that the Revolution

[1] Count Herman Keyserling in *Hibbert Journal*. April, 1915.
[2] Temple, *The Faith and Modern Thought*, p. 127.
[3] Ezek. xviii. 2.

14

was an irruption of individuality in victory over the suppressive forces of feudalism; but in view of the weakening of the family or patriarchal bonds which he saw would follow, did not altogether welcome it as an unmitigated blessing. " As the law now stands, the father is no longer responsible for the son's crime, and the father's guilt does not attach to his children, a condition of things which . . . (has) weakened the paternal power and contributed to the triumph of that individualism which is eating the heart of society in our days. The thinker who looks to the future sees the extinction of the spirit of the family; those who drew up the new code have set in its place equality and independent opinion. The family has always been the basis of society, and now the family, as it used to be, exists no longer. . . . With the solidarity of the family, society has lost that elemental force which Montesquieu discovered and called ' honour.' . . . Can the general welfare take the place of the welfare of society ?"[1]

This movement towards an unrestricted personal freedom, with the danger of individual licence it involved, has wrought out its own cure, though the new controlling force does not now reside in the old family authority of the father so much as in the social power of the State; and at the present time this reaction is so strong that many fear it will seriously affect personal liberty, and reduce individuals to being mere cogs in the State wheel. Some feel that the war points forward, not only to a time of State Socialism, but of world-wide Socialism, when " the solidarity of the race," in at least its outward organization, will have become complete.

So we find these two principles of human nature persisting through the centuries, first one and then the other having the upper hand; but neither ever com-

[1] *The Country Parson*, Eng. Translation, Everyman's Library, p. 106.

pletely dominating the other; and the reason probably is that both conceptions are true, and each is necessary to our proper development. Man in his nature is both distinct and homogeneous. The solidarity of the race is a fact, but so also is the distinctness of the individual.

Identification with Distinction in the Common Experiences of Life.

But we need not go to history in order to trace the influences and alternating movements of these two rival forces. In the experiences of ordinary life we find support for the view of the interpenetrability of personalities. A thing we have all met with is discipline, and discipline is simply the invasion of one personality by another. It may be so slight and insidious as to be scarcely noticeable, or so overwhelming as to amount to the breaking of a person's will or individuality; and there is no more difficult question in practical life to decide upon than the kind and degree of discipline it is justifiable to enforce or submit to.

In the Principles of Government.

In the State we recognize that that form of government is best which produces the most orderly corporate life combined with the least interference with individuals—*i.e.*, with personality; and it is because up to now in Great Britain we have attained an unusually fair balance in both these directions, and carried, even though unconsciously, these ideals with us into our administration abroad, that we are able to pride ourselves upon our special love of liberty. The British Empire aims at identification of interests combined with distinction in the life of its separate units, at orderliness with liberty for individual development. That is to say, in governing human beings we work, in our national affairs, on the line of God's own laws, and our Empire is the result.

In the Discipline of School Life.

But the character of a nation, which produces its laws, is moulded in its schools; and here we find the same principle of government at work—viz., a discipline which, while producing obedience, does so with as little compulsion and while permitting as much liberty as possible. In England a schoolboy is not kept always under the master's eye, so he can easily break the rules if he wishes to, and is prepared to receive the punishment which may follow. The object is, not so much to break his will to obedience as to encourage his character to develop in the right direction and train him to discipline himself. Dr. Arnold, who best represents our public school system, strongly denounced the objection to corporal punishment as originating in " that proud notion of personal independence which is neither reasonable nor Christian, but essentially barbarian."[1] Yet he refused to use corporal punishment with pupils beyond a certain age, preferring expulsion, as giving the culprit a chance of voluntarily making a fresh start elsewhere. It was in harmony with this same conception of human nature that one of his guiding principles was to put considerable responsibility upon, and so develop, the personality of his elder pupils, a method which has been almost scientifically developed in the training of the younger officers of our navy, with results which speak for themselves.

The practice, if not the understanding, of this principle of training is transmitted from the masters through the prepostors to the school at large; and, moulded by its influence, later the boys, on leaving, carry the same spirit with them into the public administration of the country, its colonies and dependencies. As a result, where Britons rule, the unnecessary use of force has come to be regarded as the sign of an incapable or bullying disposition. Yet it is recognized that infant

[1] *Miscellaneous Works*, i. 365.

races and young children are not capable of responding to reason—the other great alternative in regulating the action of freewill—so that in these cases an additional measure of force has to be used. It is this same principle underlying human nature, and producing the best methods for its development, which explains the fact that certainty of punishment rather than severity gives the best results. For this in a sense, and to a certain extent, permits while at the same time it discourages disobedience, and stimulates right action. The personality is left free to choose.

In the Married Life.

Another instance of the intermingling of personalities is furnished in the relations of a true marriage. " The truest marriages are the marriages of completest union— of soul, of mind, of body. . . . In this life lovers never quite annihilate the barrier between themselves. . . . Marriage is not an end; it wants more. Lovers desire a union which shall be endless . . . always at the summit of elation. . . . The union must be such that they must inevitably be two, yet at the same time one. Of this perfect union lovers get an occasional gleam which opens to them quite a new world. . . . Yet their glimpses point to a beyond towards which true lovers ever press. And analogous all the way is the union between God and a soul."[1]

In the Influences of Friendship.

But we need not go to the special relationship of marriage for an instance of the interpenetrability of personality, for we find it in the mutual influence of friends upon one another. Whenever we speak of the importance of keeping good company we are bearing passive witness to this truth. " Personality has been defined as ' the capacity for fellowship '—that is, the

[1] W. J. Carey, *Prayer and Some of its Difficulties*, pp. 37-39.

capacity for self-communication to persons, communion, mutual response, mutual indwelling, real union with persons.[1] . . . Influence is the pouring in of personality into personality; it is the interpenetration of souls. An officer is in a trench with his men, and the order comes to make a charge. He leads the way with the courage of a true man, shouts a rousing word of encouragement, and pours courage into the whole of his company. But think what that means. Courage is not an unreal abstraction, but, on the other hand, it is not a thing in itself with an existence apart from the officer. It is *his* courage which he pours into them, an ingredient of the person flowing into other persons. . . . Courage does not leave the officer. On the contrary, his courage grows, because in rousing his men to courage he in turn receives theirs poured into him."[2]

Another good description of this side of friendship is offered by Canon E. A. Burroughs: " . . . there are a few—perhaps only two or three in a lifetime—whose influence upon us is of a different order. It goes on; we carry them about with us; the thought of them is continually modifying our thoughts and actions; their will, so far as we know it, is to us even more than our own. Somehow our friend, though he, too, began as a force outside us, has found a way in; and now, instead of being one influence among many, he has become a part of our very self. The relationship is no longer external, but internal; such that each party to it begins to live in, and through, and therefore also for, the other. . . . An *alter ego*, the significant old Latin term for a friend, has suddenly appeared at the very centre and source of personality, and the dethroned *ego* loves to have it so."[3]

[1] A. H. McNeile, *Self-Training in Prayer*, p. 12.
[2] *Ibid.*, p. 25, 26.
[3] The *Guardian*, July 2, 1914.

A danger of even Undue Influence recognized by our Lord.

We all recognize this as a real possibility of friendship, and, indeed, the influence of friends is so great that even when it is for good it may amount to an " undue influence "—that is, an influence which overpowers, and so threatens to injure and weaken, or even destroy, the personality subjected to it. In such cases the separate personality is too much absorbed; the " distinction " too much lost. It is a case of too complete identification, obliterating the proper distinction of personality. Dr. Latham has shown us how carefully our Lord, in His great love for souls as priceless, guarded against this danger. " Our Lord never transforms men so as to obliterate their old character and substitute a new one: new powers and a new life spring up from contact with Him, but the powers work through the old organs and the life flows through the old channels; they would not be the same men or preserve their individual responsibility if it were otherwise. . . . Christ's particular care to leave the disciples their proper independence is everywhere apparent. . . . He cherishes and respects personality."[1] Therefore our Lord teaches and trains men by parables, by silences,[2] by deeds rather than by more definite methods or commands,[3] thus giving full scope to individual capacity, initiative, and freedom of choice. He " refuses to employ moral compulsion."[4]

Nothing could better bring home to us the real efficiency of personal influence and the reality of its powers of interpenetration than our Lord's perception of the danger of undue influence, which He recognized and practically guarded against in this way. He, who was to provide for the salvation of the world through communion with Himself, provided also that through that identification the distinctions of individual personality should be preserved.

[1] *Pastor Pastorum*, pp. 4-6. [2] *Ibid.*, pp. 346, 354, 415, 449.
[3] *Ibid.*, p. 4. [4] *Ibid.*, p. 24, 463.

Evidence derived from Abnormal Psychical Conditions.

The instances we have been considering so far have all been taken from the ordinary experiences of life, but psychical research affords us very striking suggestions of the interpenetration of personalities in connection with telepathy, suggestion, and hypnotism. It is true that official science still regards these subjects with a certain amount of suspicion, but in recent times there has been a considerable change of attitude among leading scientists on the subject, as may be seen when we turn to the records of the Pyschical Research Society, and find such names as Sir William Crookes, Dr. A. R. Wallace, Sir Oliver Lodge, Sir J. J. Thompson, Lord Rayleigh, Mr. W. E. Gladstone, and Rt. Hon. A. J. Balfour, among those who have either taken some part in the experiments and investigations, or at least an interest in the proceedings of the Society.

Sir William F. Barrett, F.R.S., writing upon Psychical Research, says that our conscious life may be compared to islands which rise above the level of the ocean, but rest upon invisible, submerged parts, which, like our hidden subliminal life, are in their turn united together in the vast bed of the ocean, which represents the fount of life. Sleep and waking are the tides of life, which cover or expose our conscious life; death, represented by the subsidence of an island, is the withdrawal of human life from our present superficial view.[1]

Our Subliminal Self.

Mr. Myers in like manner says that our conscious self " is but a portion of ' a more comprehensive consciousness, a profounder faculty, which for the most part remains potential, so far as regards the life on earth,' but which may be liberated in full activity by the change we call death."[2] In the same connection

[1] Barrett, *Psychical Research*, pp. 35-6.
[2] See Barrett, *Ibid.*, pp. 34-36.

Sir John Herschel also said " there was evidence of a thought, an intelligence, working within our own organization, distinct from that of our own (conscious) personality."[1] It certainly seems that the existence of a subliminal self, in closer and more direct communion with other personalities than is possible in normal life, is required by the facts, which have been carefully verified by qualified observers in connection with telepathy, hypnotism and suggestion; but whether we accept such a view of life or not, the phenomena connected with these abnormal experiences appear to be inexplicable except on the ground that there is such a thing as interpenetration of personality. For instance, there appears to be abundant evidence that the characters, tastes, habits, and even bodies of persons have been affected, sometimes temporarily and sometimes permanently, sometimes for good and sometimes for evil, by " suggestion," which appears to be a form of interpenetration of personality, and it is difficult to see how these things can be accounted for in any other way.[2]

Unity in the Plurality of National Life.

In the history of recent events we can trace among nations and empires, as representing the larger organized units of humanity, equally as among individuals, the working of the law of " identification with distinction." It can be traced in our opponents, where the unity of several nationalities under the dominating German Empire was perhaps the chief factor in the great resist-

[1] *Psychical Research*, p. 38.

[2] The classical instance of the effects of mind upon matter is the " stigmata " of St. Francis of Assisi. The evidence for the truth of the fact is of a nature that has compelled even the incredulous to accept it. Granted that the stigmata were the result of the effect of St. Francis's own mind upon his body, it still remains true that it was our Lord who affected St. Francis's mind and whole personality to the degree required to produce this phenomenal result. It was an instance of interpenetration of personality (*cf.* Sabatier's *Life of St. Francis of Assisi*, chapter xvii. and the Appendix).

ance they offered to the world in arms against them; but perhaps the British Empire is the most conspicuous example of this kind of unity in plurality. For here the unity is one of freedom and national instinct, not of enforced military methods, and therefore more closely identified with the personalities of the separate individuals. It is a less artificial and more real, deeper-seated unity. The existence of this vast, complex human unit, compounded of numerous very distinct parts, its real unity, and the distinct diversity of its parts, are all equally unquestionable; and an organization on this greatest scale perhaps helps us to realize the peculiar and advantageous features underlying the law of identification with distinction more clearly than in its application to mere individuals. In the case of empires and nations one realizes how necessary the whole of its parts are to one another for their respective highest development. One sees how, through identification with the larger whole, the life of the smaller units of nationality is quickened, and ideal conceptions become potential realities. Each separate part of the empire, with its hopes and aims enlarged and purified and its forces strengthened by the support derived from the one great whole, can conceive and attempt developments of its own national life which would have been impossible either to imagine or secure in a state of isolation. In this way fresh power of national life is infused into the community and national liberty increased.

On the other hand, vital energy is concentrated, thought and feeling vivified, and, above all, interest strengthened, and all brought to a point of concentration under the impulse of the organization of the smaller units of national and local life, to an extent which could never have been possible under the more diffused life of the empire; and in this way the local life of these smaller units of organization become assets of increased value, making again, in their turn, for the larger life of the whole world-wide organization. Indeed, when regarded in its national and imperial forms, it is not difficult to realize how human life interpenetrates and reacts upon its various units; and in this way we are helped to grasp the truth of the " solidarity of the race," and that each separate human organization is very greatly the product of its environment. The national assemblies, local governments, schools, societies, clubs, trading councils, unions, etc., are all influenced in form and spirit by the history, circumstances, laws, and power of the nations and empire as a whole.

Then, if we remind ourselves that the national, local, and social life is but the result of the lives of the individuals who make its laws, customs, and public opinion, and how these in their turn react upon individuals— *e.g.*, through education or the nature and conditions of work, so that none of us are the same characters we should have been had we been brought up in some other country, such as Greenland or Persia—when we remember this, it begins to come home to us that many lives have entered, and are entering, into our life to make us what we are; that personalities, for all their seeming distinctness, interpenetrate one another; and that our identity overlaps and is overlapped by that of others. Yet, at the same time, it is clear that we must each have a distinct self. Otherwise the individual would have no contribution to make to the common stock; all would be of one uniform type, which is clearly not the case. But, as things are, communion with distinctness is clearly a general law of human life; it is only a question of the degree in which these two things simultaneously coexist.

Probable Alteration at Death in our Perception of the Relative Values of the Constituent Elements in Man's Composite Personality.

We have been considering a number of facts bearing upon personality in connection with the solidarity of the race, with the object of getting help to enable us to overcome that overpowering sense of our individual separateness which impresses itself upon us under present conditions of existence. In this relation it is interesting to remember that under other conditions— *e.g.*, less material and less shut off by sin from the influences of God's supreme being, or even of other great spiritual personalities—our impressions as to the place filled by our individual soul in our own personal life might be reversed.

The first of these two conditions—viz., that of a less material existence—reminds us that our bodies are probably the cause of the greatest of the difficulties we have to overcome in realizing the possibility of identification between separate personalities. For during the present stage of existence they are felt to be so predominant a part of our nature that it is difficult to conceive of existence apart from them; and a material body is at the same time so obvious a difficulty in the way of complete personal identification with other people. Nothing is more distinctive under present conditions than our bodies. Our thumb-marks alone separate us off, not only from some of our fellow-men, but apparently from all of them. It is important to remember, therefore, that our present bodily condition is only a passing phase; that philosophy does not recognize the material body, but the immaterial will, affections, and reason, as forming the foundations of personality; and that under the conditions obtaining in eternity our material bodies will have become spiritual bodies, and that it is these, together with the immaterial elements of our nature, which will need to be identified with our Lord Jesus Christ.

It is not so difficult to conceive that when all the hard lines and limitations of our material body have been exchanged for the immaterialism of a spiritual body, that then our wills, affections, and reason may be able to be interpenetrated, mingled with, and permeated by the infinite divine will, affection, and reason, and that, provided they are set in the same direction, the contact with, and rush of, the power of the divine character will carry us forward and upward to heights of moral and spiritual perfection, and make us like unto Christ to an extent now inconceivable.[1] In this connection St. Paul's teaching that " the first man (*i.e.*, our present bodily nature) is of the earth, earthy (*i.e.*, material); the second man (our future spiritual nature) is the Lord from heaven,"[2] is of very glorious significance. In any case, it seems that such a change would necessarily involve the satisfaction of the second of the two conditions we noted above as necessary to the reversal of our present impressions as to the predominating place filled by our distinct individual soul in the composite whole of our personality. We should surely under these conditions be also less shut off by sin from the influences of God's being, and consequently become more aware of the relative importance of the place filled by His presence in our lives.

A person on the earth finds it difficult to realize that the sun is not smaller than the world. In our own case, in accepting this truth, we have behind us the advantage of the knowledge of past generations, and it has grown up slowly with us from childhood; but history records how difficult our forefathers found it to grasp. Yet an observer placed halfway between the earth and the sun would, on the contrary, find it difficult to imagine that any inhabitant of the world could imagine for a minute that the earth is the larger of the two.

In the same way it seems more than probable that those who by death have changed their point of view and been brought into closer, clearer perception of God's infinite being, and fuller realization of their position as members of His Son's mystical body, are overwhelmingly conscious of *His* personality rather

---

[1] John iii. 2.

[2] 1 Cor. xv. 47. The R.V. omits " the Lord," though retaining it in the margin.

than of their own, and of their necessary involvement in all that He is, including those actions of His life and death which have helped to make Him what He is. Even now on earth the result of the true Christian life is for a man to become less and less conscious of himself, and more and more conscious of others and of God. He dies with his face set in that direction, and who can say what altered perception of the relative values in the elements making up his own composite personality is forced upon him when the spiritual world and the vision of God bursts upon his view, and he becomes aware of his true relation towards them and in them ? The true Christian may perceive then that at the centre of his personality, in his spiritual life and will, Christ fills a far larger place and his separate self a relatively smaller space than he had supposed possible.

It is at this point that we reach mysticism; and though the name and thing is antipathetic to a certain class of mind, yet it should never be forgotten that there is a true mysticism—that of St. John, and St. Paul, who found his life hid with Christ in God—as well as a false. To work out the thought of identification of the Christian with his Saviour from this point of view in connection with the Atonement would not be incongruous in a book upon this subject, but it does not fall within the plan of this work, and is beyond the ability of the writer. It must therefore suffice to refer back to the quotations from such men as Drs. Moberly, Dale, and McLeod Campbell, given in the last chapter, and to remind ourselves that in dealing with the mystery of the union which is betwixt Christ and His Church[1] we are not dealing with anything misty or unreal, but with the practical core of Christianity. For the main object of Christianity, as our Lord's last great prayer shows us, is that by advancing from glory to glory of spiritual life into the image of Christ men shall at last become one in God, as the Father is in the Son and the

---

[1] 2 Cor. iii. 18.

Son in the Father (John xvii. 21-23).   This is what I have
tried to express when speaking of identification with
Christ in the innermost shrine of our personality.   As
the centre of personality our wills must become the will
of Christ.   We must not only be conformed to His likeness, but His mind must so be in us that, as St. Paul
found later, it is not so much a question of what Christ
will have us to do as what He will do in us as His
members.   He is our environment.   " Lo, I am with
you always,"[1] and " our life is hid with Christ in God."[2]
And just as a living thing absorbs, and is affected by
its environment, so that in a true sense it becomes the
old creature plus its environment, so we in Christ Jesus
are changed,[3] and the second man is the Lord from
heaven.[4]

[1] *Cf.* Matt. xxviii. 20.   [2] *Cf.* Col. iii. 3.
[3] 1 Cor. xv. 52.   [4] 1 Cor. xv. 47.

CHAPTER III

THE DOCTRINE OF IDENTIFICATION IN RELIGION

The Possibility of Identification more easily realized in the Spiritual Sphere.

So far we have been considering the interpenetration of personality under our present normal conditions of life, which, owing to our invincible sense of the finiteness of our material bodies, presents special difficulties to realization. But in considering the extension of the moral and spiritual consequences of our Lord's Atonement to ourselves, what is required is chiefly identification of the *spiritual* part of our nature with our Lord's sacrificed and now spiritualized human nature. It would appear, moreover, that the necessary identification need not be perfected until after death, when everything material on our side will also have been left behind, and only the spiritual remain. Under these circumstances the possibility of the identification of two spiritual personalities is not so difficult to realize as it would have been under material conditions. If identification is possible to so great an extent as we have seen it to be under our present conditions of existence, much more will it be possible under the less restricted conditions and enlarged capacities of spiritual life.

And in Connection with God's Omnipresence.

Moreover, when the Second Person of the Holy Trinity first allied Himself to human nature, it was " not by the conversion of the Godhead into flesh, but by the taking of the manhood into God "; and if we may assume that this is still the method by which our Lord lifts up men into union with Himself (and certainly the grace of attachment must flow out from God and not *vice versa*), then it is not so difficult to think of ourselves being involved in the spiritual, infinite, and all-pervading personality of our Lord, Who is in all things, by Whom all things consist, and Who made atonement for us on the Cross.

Identification and Natural Religion.

In its basic idea the old Greek religion of Pantheism is by no means opposed to Christian theology, which only insists upon adding to the doctrine of the immanence of God the necessary corollary of His transcendence. That is to say, in its true form, Pantheism is a doctrine of unity with distinction—God in and above all. " Lift the stone, and there thou shalt find Me; cleave the wood, and there am I," is a Christian saying, claiming for itself the highest of all authority, that of our Lord Himself.

The immanence of God in matter is seen in the laws which govern it. The existence of the rule of law in relation to matter is unquestionable, and the existence of law itself has been shown by Dr. Mozley to be only explicable on the basis of the existence of a personal God, from Whose intelligence and will the laws of nature emanate. Law cannot exist by chance. " If double-six were thrown fifty times running it could not be by chance. We should say the circumstance was the result of some law, yet at the same time there is no physical, no mathematical obstruction to the throw. The disposition, the arrangement of certain particles of matter is no mathematical demonstration. But when there is manifold coincidence and adaptation to an end we say that it is manifestly impossible that such machinery should not be by design."[1] That is to say, with regard to any regular and orderly sequence of events human reason asks why it should be, and we

[1] *University Lectures.*

15

are so constructed that our personality demands an explanation of it. It would amount to a denial of personality, to a denial of reason amounting to insanity, to accept the possibility of double-sixes being thrown fifty consecutive times without there being a reason for it—that is, an ultimate, reasoning, controlling force issuing in the form of law. And the only conceivable source of such a force is personal will—*i.e.*, personality.

Therefore it is reasonable to conclude that the properties of matter being inseparably bound up with the laws of nature which coexist by and with them—for since these laws only operate in connection with matter it could not be asserted that without matter the laws would actually exist either—since this is so, it follows that in matter we find the will of God immanent in the laws of chemistry, heat, light, motion, and the other laws of physics which control it. When we say " God is a God of order," we are stating that law is God's will, and so in the operations of nature we find the divine personality manifested and immanent in creation.

God, then, through His will, which is the centre of personality, is immanent in matter. Natural law is God's will in matter, and if in dead matter, how much more so in living, which manifests even more clearly the operation of laws issuing from His reasonable will. And if the life in every living thing be His life, it is incredible that He should be absent from human beings, who are most fitted of all created things, by their likeness to Him,[1] to receive His indwelling Presence.

One can conceive of all creation as having a graduated consciousness of its union with God. In inanimate nature the stars in their courses sing together in His praise; dead matter, by its obedience to His laws, pays a real homage to its Creator; and in living things there is more or less conscious enjoyment of the God-given life in them. Their very happiness is a form of praise to God, though they have no perception that that life is from Him—that, in a sense, it is God's life in them.

1 Gen. i. 27.

Man alone in the Material World conscious of God's Immanence.

Man alone, in the material world, is *conscious* of God, and has had revealed to him his union with God. In the spiritual world this consciousness may exist in countless forms of life. We know it is in angels of various orders. But this communion, and the perception of it in all its fulness, is perfect only in the Holy Trinity. Man, however, already has his share, and presses forward to attain the full measure assigned to his nature—" My soul is athirst for God."

Man aspires to Fuller Communion with God.

Man " moves in another world than that of sight and sound—a world wherein he feels himself to be but a beginner . . . our personality lays claim to a loftier method of appreciation (than material modes of measurement), based upon its infelt capacity for intercourse with God. . . . The sense of divine nearness . . . is no invention of Christianity . . . we find the desire for union with God to lie at the very basis of our being."[1] " There is a certain infinite element in man . . . if he cannot adequately comprehend the idea of infinity, he cannot get along without it. There is infinity in his intelligence, for his mind seems, in its way, to mirror the universe. He actually weighs the stars. . . . There is infinity also in the heights and depths of his conscience, of his loyalty, of his faith, of his love . . . the best in man is always growing, but has never attained his growth. The ideal, the true and perfect self, is always above him. There is in him the self that is always being built up . . . into the image of the originating kernel of the life."[2]

[1] Illingworth, *Personality Human and Divine*, pp. 92-3.
[2] *Cf.* article on " The Divine Unity " in the *Hibbert Journal* for January, 1912, pp. 450-452.

Christianity requires the Identification of Christians with their Lord.

In other words, the instinct of aspiration after God is intended to find satisfaction in Him. And this is necessary, for when we leave natural religion and enter upon the consideration of the definite doctrines of Christianity, identification with our Lord is demanded by the insufficiency of any purely human penitence, obedience, and holiness, as found in the actual experience of life, to afford an adequate basis for a doctrine of Atonement. We are bound to admit, without any question at all, that no merely subjective human penitence, nor human holiness standing by itself, is sufficient to give us a claim to God's forgiveness. Experience protests that in every case man is deeply imperfect in both. Our penitence and holiness are utterly inadequate. It is only " in the Beloved " that we can be accepted; and if our acceptance is not to be of a " transactional " character, it is necessary that we should not only have placed ourselves under Christ's personal influence, or be merely in touch with Him, or connected by any merely superficial union, but that, while still retaining our identity, we should be involved in an identification with Him extending to the innermost shrine of our personality.

The Church teaches and aims at the Union of Christians with Christ.

In the doctrines and rites of the Christian Church it is such a union as this which is taught and aimed at.

The Incarnation of our Lord proves that there is nothing incompatible in the union of the two whole and perfect natures of the Godhead and the manhood in one Person; so that our Lord, though He is God and Man, is not two, but one Christ; and " one altogether: not by confusion of substance but by unity of person."

The Church aims at extending the Incarnation.

The Christian Church next seems consciously and deliberately to set herself the aim of extending the Incarnation to humanity at large by bringing every individual into oneness with our Lord by means of a union with Him as nearly identical in its nature to this as possible. From the beginning the Church has based its hopes of final salvation on such a union with our Lord, initiated, continued, and perfected by the power of the Holy Ghost operating through the holy Sacraments instituted by Him for that very purpose.

Through the Sacrament of Baptism.

So we find that the Apostles were commanded to baptize " every creature " for his salvation (Mark xvi. 15, 16) " into the Name " (*i.e.*, the Person) " of the Father, and of the Son, and of the Holy Ghost " (Matt. xxviii. 19); and they taught, therefore, in accordance with the wording of this command, that baptism was a real initiation, a real entering " into the Name "—*i.e.*, the Person of the Lord Jesus (*cf.* Acts xix. 5; Rom. vi. 3; Gal. iii. 27); that it was a death unto sin by participation in His death (Rom. vi. 3, 4; Col. ii. 12); so that in baptism there is remission of sin (Acts ii. 38; xxii. 16) and salvation (Tit. iii. 5; 1 Pet. iii. 21), and also a putting on of Christ (Gal. iii. 27; Eph. v. 30), who, by His resurrection, and our participation with Him in it, raises us with Himself into the life of righteousness (Rom. vi. 4-11; 1 Pet. iii. 21).

Confirmation and Holy Communion.

This new life begun at baptism is renewed by the Holy Ghost (Tit. iii. 5), given to dwell in man (1 Cor. iii. 16, vi. 19) as the spirit of Christ (Rom. viii. 9; 1 Pet. i. 11); by the laying on of hands (Acts viii. 16-18; xix. 6) and also by the constant renewing of the life of Christ in them by the partaking of His body and blood in the sacrament of the Lord's Supper (John vi. 35, 49-58; Luke xxii. 19, 20; 1 Cor. x. 16). In fact, the whole Christian life was habitually viewed by the Apostles, and planned out to be a dying with Christ unto sin (Rom. vi. 6-8; vii. 4, 6, viii. 10; 2 Cor. iv. 10, v. 14; Gal. ii. 19, 20, v. 24, vi. 14; Col. ii. 20, iii. 3; 1 Pet. ii. 24), and a rising with Him to a life of righteousness lived in Him (2 Cor. iv. 10; Eph. i. 3, 4, ii. 5-6; Phil. iii. 10; Col. ii. 12, 13, iii. 1; 1 John v. 11, 12), the end of which was to be a further rising into His likeness when He appeared (1 John iii. 2). So that it is not too much to say that the whole object and method of the religion founded by our Saviour is to save men by bringing them into vital union with Himself. We may define Christianity as " a system for identification with Christ."

The Christian's Identification with Christ a Progressive Life.

No weaker term than identification satisfies the requirements of the case. The Christian Church is not merely a building in which the stones are fitted together one after another about the " Corner Stone," and connected by the cement which surrounds each, running from stone to stone and binding all into one great whole. It is all this, but it is also more. It is not a rigid, stationary union, but vital and ever-growing. It is not so much the unity of different parts of a building as that of a living tree and its branches. As we read our Lord's Parable of the Vine there is pictured to us the curve and unity of line as the stem flows into the branch; and we realize the significance of it—the continuity of life; the flow of the sap under the bark; the reflow into the heart of the vine; the carriage of the vine's life and vitality; the substance and nourishment of the deeply sunk root to the farthest extremity of the branches, breaking forth in leaf, and flower, and fruit; the bleeding of the parent plant if a branch be injured; the failure, collapse, and withering of the branch if broken or cut off from the vine. St. Paul uses the grafting of a wild into a cultivated olive-tree to illustrate our union with Christ; but when the union is with a branch having no foreign origin, nature and source of life, the analogy is still closer; and bearing in mind man's creation and Christ's Incarnation, our Lord's illustration comes nearer to the essential truth of things.

The " Literary Theory " an Inadequate Explanation of Bible Teaching.

Dr. Dale forestalled Canon Wilson's argument that the language of St. Paul must be taken in the literary, and not literal, sense of his words, by showing that careful arguments were built upon the phrases involving identification between the Christian and his Saviour.[1] Still more strongly do we feel the force of this argument with regard to our Lord's own teaching. The communion taught in the Parable of the Vine and its Branches cannot be satisfactorily explained away, our Lord's words cannot be emptied of their obvious significance in this manner. Even if it were granted that they only taught the flow of the divine grace to the heart of man, yet grace is not an impersonal thing. It has been defined as " the life of God in the soul." It is the love, strength, faith, and holiness of God, His life and character, infused into men; and therefore the grace of God is a real importation into us, not in thought or intention only, but in reality, of the righteousness and personality of God. We are the " temple of God," and He dwells in us.

Our Lord's Teaching in His Great Intercessory Prayer.

But there are some still more solemn words of our Lord giving direct teaching which certainly cannot be explained away on the ground of rhetoric or literary

[1] *The Atonement*, pp. 222, 425.

style.   St. John records that our Lord in earnest communion with His Father in heaven said: " I pray for
them . . . that they all may be one; even as Thou,
Father, art in Me, and I in Thee, that they also may
be one in us. . . .   And the glory which Thou hast
given Me I have given them; that they may be one,
even as we are one: I in them, and Thou in Me, that
they may be perfected into one " (John xvii. 20 *ff*.).
Here we see that in the same breath our Lord likens
the union of Christians with Himself to that of Himself
with the Father, of which He said: " I and the Father
are one," and " He that hath seen Me hath seen the
Father."   The union between the Father and the Son
is not one of mere feeling or harmony only; and in these
words union is presented to us, and pleaded for, in
that utmost perfection demanded by the fundamental
character of God as love.   It has been said that our
Lord's saying, " I am in the Father, and ye in Me, and
I in you," is the core of all we know of the Atonement,[1]
and we can understand how this is so.   Love craves
for union.   Absolute love craves for the absolute union
expressed by the word " identification," whilst at the
same time demanding that " distinction " which is
necessary to the divine transcendence, and without
which love would be deprived of the separate personality
which is its object.

Identification with Distinction in the Doctrine of the Holy Trinity.

This saying of our Lord reminds us that in the Holy
Trinity we have a perfect example of that absolute
identification combined with distinction of personality
for which we are contending.   If anyone, in contemplating the doctrine of the Atonement, is tempted to
say that it is impossible to be crucified with Christ, or
to rise with Him, and sit in heavenly places with Him;
that such an identification of personality is impossible

[1] Basil Matthews in *The Fascinated Child*.

even in the spiritual sphere, one would urge him especially to consider the doctrine of the Holy Trinity, in which we are taught to "worship one God in Trinity, and Trinity in Unity, neither confounding the persons nor dividing the substance." Dr. Illingworth says, referring to crude attacks upon this doctrine: "However much it transcends intelligence, (it) distinctly claims to be the most intelligible mode of conceiving God as essentially personal,"[1] and this reasoned opinion, carefully led up to, by so careful a thinker, is not to be lightly set on one side. If, however, we accept it, then it follows that God combines in Himself a plurality of persons forming a unity—*i.e.*, that in the divine spiritual sphere identification with distinction of personality is a fact: "The Father that dwelleth in Me, He doeth the works." And then, turning to ourselves, we remember we are created in His image. It may be possible, therefore, for human personalities to interpenetrate one another, and, since our Lord is perfect Man, for there to be interpenetration of Christians with Him. Thus St. Paul out of his spiritual experience asserts, "I am crucified with Christ"; and "I live, yet not I, but Christ liveth in me." Our bodies are not our essential selves, but rather our wills which form the core of our moral and spiritual personalities; and in the spiritual sphere experience asserts that personal identification with our Lord, including all that He has done and is, is both possible and a fact.[2]

The Need of Expressing this Doctrine in the Church's Worship.

But if Christianity is in this way a system for the identification of souls with Christ a further consideration

---

[1] *Personality Human and Divine*, p. 42.

[2] Since sending the MS. to the printers I have come across another passage stating this same doctrine very explicitly, and as the matter is of importance, and the support it lends considerable, representing as it does three confirmatory opinions, I have quoted it very fully in Appendix B at the end of this book.

arises.   It would appear certain that the proper, general appreciation of any religion must inevitably be injuriously affected if its main purpose and principles are ignored in its regular, public presentations.   Surely then, since the Christian religion is in its essence a system for the salvation of men by their union with Christ, and participation through that union in His life and death as the just consequence of and reparation for sin, the worship of the Church should in the main clearly express these principles for the benefit of all her members. Especially among a people who have a marked distaste for giving their attention to abstract teaching, it is in this way that the truth will be most readily assimilated and the guiding principles and meaning of the Christian religion grasped by them.

CHAPTER IV

HOW IDENTIFICATION WITH OUR LORD DEVELOPS

UNDER our present material conditions our sense of distinctness from everyone else is so overpowering that when the thought of identification with another is presented to us our natural instinct is to say: " In spite of everything which science, philosophy, or religion may say, I cannot accept it. The thing is impossible. How can it be ?"

Many Demonstrated Facts surpass our Powers of Realization.

It is helpful, therefore, to remind ourselves that many facts are being forced upon our acceptance as true which it is quite impossible for us to grasp, so that men have to choose between accepting the assertions of their reason or the negations of their powers of realization. " When we leave the realm of matter and attempt to penetrate into that of electricity and the ether, the highest intellect feels the need of models, and the impossibility of obtaining even the raw unfinished material out of which to construct them. . . . Our most fundamental conceptions are, like ourselves, material . . .; their simplification to suit the immaterial world . . . is difficult almost to impossibility."[1] Certainly most of us feel that when we are told by a high authority that the charge of electricity carried by 1 gram of hydrogen would, if free, charge the whole world up to a potential of a million volts, and would require a steel cable capable of carrying 35 tons to

[1] Soddy, *Matter and Energy*, pp. 164, 165.

keep two such quantities from flying farther apart, though already separated by the distance of the North Pole from the South;[1] when we are told that an electron possesses mass without matter, that its size is $\frac{1}{2500}$ of a hydrogen atom;[2] and that electrons oscillate and return round their particles of matter at the rate of 185,000 miles in a second—then we have to admit that we cannot realize them, and that to our powers of conception it appears impossible for the optic nerve to receive sixteen million impressions in a second, or for matter to exist without mass.

No more Unreasonable to accept Spiritual than Scientific Mysteries.

But so long as the highest class of human intelligence accepts these marvels as being facts in the material world, it seems unreasonable to deny the possibility for identification to coexist with distinction of personality in the spiritual world.

We can the more easily urge this since the identification of self with another personality is, as we have noticed, mainly spiritual. The will, which is the centre of personality, is at least not material, and in the thought that such identification is primarily immaterial or spiritual we undoubtedly find considerable help. A spiritual identification is easier to conceive than a physical one.

Identification with our Lord a Gradual Process completed after Death.

Moreover, this process is a gradual one, which is only begun here on earth to be completed hereafter. Yet we have some experience of it even now. Every time a man says, " I am ready to identify myself with you in the matter," he bears witness to the possibility in some degree of what we are considering. Again, in his struggle against selfishness, the Christian is conscious

---

[1] Soddy, *Matter and Energy*, pp. 166, 167.   [2] *Ibid.*, p. 175.

of a double personality within himself, and a desire to merge his lower will in the higher will of Christ. In our own unity there is even now evidence of a plurality. But this capacity for merging our self-will in Christ's will is only in a limited and initial stage during our present life. We have already noticed how Mr. Myers said that our conscious self is but " a portion of a more comprehensive consciousness, a profounder faculty which for the most part remains potential, so far as regards the life on earth,"[1] but may be liberated in full activity by death. Dr. Moberly thought that even in the act of dying a greater development of self-surrender to God and more complete identification of our personal will with His may be possible than during the former period of life: " What is going on throughout the life . . . is not unfrequently more conspicuous still, under . . . conditions of sickness, decay, and death . . . there are long silences, the silences often of enforced reflection . . . which we who stand by feel to be characteristic. . . . We have not measured, neither is there any man living who is capable of measuring what those silent moments of pain, and growing weakness, and conscious ebbing away, and dying are capable of being . . . the self, in them, is developed, not revolutionized; and yet, what their possibilities of developing discipline may be we have no power . . . even of conceiving . . . in those moments in which they are drawing very near to the threshold of His Presence !"[2]

A Scientific Analogy.

There is also a passage in Mr. McDowall's book on the Atonement which is very suggestive on this point. In writing upon the gradual emergence of human personality by evolution from the lower forms of existence, he says: " Now let us imagine a ' receptive ' organism—that is, an organism capable of large re-

[1] Barrett, *Psychical Research*, p. 34.
[2] *Atonement and Personality*, pp. 293, 294.

sponsiveness to environmental change, an organism on the main line of evolution—suddenly drifting to a new threshold, and . . . left stranded on a shore where new conditions, not of sun and air, but of supersensual influences, act on it. . . . Is it not possible, at the very least, that the reason for the appearance of moral and spiritual phenomena . . . may be that the organism has developed to a stage when . . . a fresh factor of the total environment has become operative owing to the organism having reached a stage where it can be influenced by that factor ?"[1]

If we take this thought and apply it to that other change of death, in which we drift beyond the threshold of this life into eternity, and are cast upon the shores of a new life and a fresh environment " of supersensual influences " operating upon us with a new degree of force, it becomes less difficult to realize that rapid developments in spiritual capacity may take place, and the possibility of being able completely to identify our personality with that of our Lord's human nature does not appear so incredible.

Personal Distinction increased rather than diminished by Identification.

But the difficulty of realizing our personal distinctness under these conditions still remains, or is even added to, when Identification is granted. It seems that in this case we must be lost " as a drop of vinegar in the ocean." There is reason, however, to think that in reality self-sacrifice helps rather than, as seems at first probable, blurs the distinctness of personality, and this thought has been most helpfully expressed in an article appearing some time since in the *Church Quarterly Review*.[2] One would like to quote it all; but as space does not permit, the following is offered as its substance.

[1] *Evolution and the Need of Atonement*, pp. 14, 15.
[2] O. C. Quick, " Self-Sacrifice and Individual Mortality," January, 1916.

The essence and significance of the Christian religion is that it is a dying in order to live eternally—" dying, behold we live." All self-sacrifice is a form of dying— a denial and surrender of self. The Christian life is a continuous development of dying by self-surrender to God's will in Christ. The remarkable feature in Christian self-sacrifice is that the more the will, the basis of personality, is sacrificed, the more it develops. Among degraded and savage peoples, most incapable of self-sacrifice, there goes along with that incapacity the smallest development of distinct personality. " True self-sacrifice can only be found where the individual is intensely conscious of his own absolute distinctness, and being so conscious determines to give his distinct self to serve another." Our present self is imperfect. Our full personality is a far-off goal towards which we must progress by the giving of ourselves in self-surrender to others. The more selfish a person is, the less he develops. Selfishness is essentially commonplace, and ends in loss of individuality. " Just in proportion as we succeed in giving ourselves to another we become more fully and distinctly ourselves." That is, the more we identify ourselves with another, the more distinctly our personality develops, until at last it attains its summit in the whole surrender of oneself to God in death, which must therefore be the entrance to a fuller, more complete personal life.

Identification with God's Will in Death completes our Personal Distinction.

Physical death is the culmination of self-sacrifice, of the surrender of our whole personality to the will of God; a complete and final death to Self; a merging of our will in another's; an absolute identification of self. Physical death is our divinely planned opportunity for a culminating and decisive act of self-sacrifice. " Death is the most dreadful and inevitable of all realities." Therefore, to submit when God asks us to experience it is the supreme test of obedience in this life, and herein lies its spiritual significance. Suffering and death " are the outward and visible signs . . . of the complete surrender and self-sacrifice that are needed before this mortal can put on immortality." Physical death " marks the culmination of the process of sacrifice upon earth." " And so to St. Paul the true death . . . is not simply the death of the body, but the complete self-sacrifice," and for this reason " the death of the body is needed to complete the Christian's sacrifice of himself." This does not involve that no further demand for nor development of the self-surrender of our personality to God's will will be made beyond the grave, but that *this* demand is so crucial a one that it is decisive as to the further direction of the soul's progress. This true death is an adequate giving of himself by the Christian to God in time and for eternity; and " evidently the claim to give eternally must involve a claim to an eternal distinction for the person that gives. For it is on the personal distinctness of the giver that the very possibility of giving depends . . . life eternal is the realization in complete individual distinctness of our union with Christ and with each other." Therefore, by death we enter upon new conditions of life, a fresh environment from which materialism has faded out, and spirituality is everything; in which the personality in its completed distinctness is identified with the human personality of Christ our Lord.

This conclusion fits in with Mr. McDowall's theory, and is natural if God is the true end, object, and goal of human life as well as its source—if the true end of life is union with Him. For in this case the right direction for human energy and development is towards Him. Other efforts are in the wrong direction, and must make for limiting and degrading our true nature instead of developing it. On the other hand, all effort towards God is in the right direction as opposed to the blind alleys of which Mr. McDowall speaks, and leads to evolution as infinite as is necessarily involved by union with an infinite God; we " are changed into the same image from glory to glory." So that the more we are identified with God, the more our distinct personality is developed.[1] Mr. McDowall's theory applies to the evolution of the race, not of individuals, and the need for the latter to attain in one lifetime the proper far-off end of humanity explains the need for the Incarnation. By union with our Lord's perfected humanity the individual anticipates in the unit of his own personality the proper end of far-off generations— so far off that there might not be time for their evolution during the world's lifetime, even granted that the operation of freewill did not make it for ever unattainable for the race.

[1] *Evolution and the Need of Atonement*, pp. 11, 12, 153 *ff.*

CHAPTER V

THE APPLICATION OF THE LAW OF IDENTIFICATION:
HOW IT WORKS

Our Involvement in Christ's Perfect Atonement.

In the second part of this book we noticed what our
Lord achieved for us in His atoning life and death.
We saw that He experienced that separation from the
Father which is the consequence of sin; that He achieved
that perfect obedience which in the case of a sinner
would be the proper reparation to Divine Holiness for
the rebellion of self-will, the essence of sin; and in this
manner opened a way for the satisfaction of the desires
of Divine Love both on the Father's part and His own
that a due reparation should be made by us. In this
way our Saviour offered a full, perfect, and sufficient
sacrifice, oblation, and satisfaction for the sins of the
whole world; and we hold that by a real identification
with His personality each faithful Christian soul is
involved in the atoning benefits of His life and death.

Our Great Advocate's Plea.

For this enables the Son to plead: " Father, only
look on them as found in Me. Accept them in Thy
Beloved. Their unrighteousness is covered by My
perfect obedience, which is now also theirs. The consequences of all sin have been endured by Me, and by
them in Me. The spiritual death of separation from
Thy life and presence which the law of righteousness
enforces, and which both love and justice claim as due,
has been experienced. That experience is in Me, and
I in them. They too have now died *for* sin, as well as

to sin. In Me they live to righteousness. Their second death would be another death for Me also. Their penalty would be My further suffering. It would be an injustice to Me. I am the life; and one with Me—members of My body—in Me they must enter that eternal life which is Mine by right."

Co-operation of the Church in Christ's Intercession.

This we can conceive is the everlasting plea presented by our Saviour before the throne of God. Just as, in the prophetic rite of the Judaic law, the high-priest on the Day of Atonement went behind the veil into the Holy of Holies carrying the blood of the chosen victim, and poured it out before the mercy-seat of God to make propitiation for the sins of the people, so did our Lord at His Ascension penetrate into the most holy place of heaven, to plead eternally and to make reparation for sin by the presentation before the Father of the perfect obedience of His sacrificed body, as repre-senting all true believers contained and involved in Himself and His action upon the Cross. And as He pleads above, the Church, as His visible body on earth, co-operates with Him below. For the sacraments He has ordained are made effective instruments by the Holy Ghost, through the repentance, faith, and love He bestows, to weld continually new souls into identi-fication with their Saviour and His all-sufficient sacrifice. Holy Baptism initiates the union, and the laying-on of hands confirms it; but unquestionably the most signi-ficant and all-inclusive rite of Christianity is the Holy Eucharist. For there we have not only the renewal and strengthening of our union with Christ, but we also join in pleading with and in Him before the Father the merits of His sin-bearing and perfect, all-satisfying obedience upon the Cross—the sacrifice made once for all, yet eternal in its ever-renewed application and appeal. And how much that appeal is weakened, it would seem, both for the Father and ourselves, if it be the appeal, not of sin-bearing and sacrifice in its fuller sense, but only of a sorrow for men's sins—perfect, indeed, as far as it goes, but falling short of making that restitution for wrong inflicted without which no repentance is complete !

Even granted that in the case of the Son of Man such sorrow might possibly contain the personal element necessary to give it the character of repentance, yet many will feel that more than this is needed in order to charge with their fullest meaning many expressions found both in the Bible, and in the service-books of the Christian Church.   For while voluntary sin-bearing is truly a sacrifice of love in the fullest sense, penitence is but a duty, however incurred, and has not the same claim to the supreme adoration of heaven and earth which the former naturally calls out.   Moreover, the penitence in question which is presented for acceptance is an incomplete thing, since no sin can be taken away, no wrong rightly counted atoned for, until the fullest possible restitution has been made.   For these reasons the " penitential theory " will fail to commend itself to many.   But we, for our part, hold that the penitential theory does not contain the whole truth of divine love and achievement.   We hold that the necessary reparation has been achieved, the sacrifice made, and that it is the " great glory " of God on high, and on earth the basis of His peace among men, and the inspiring motive of the highest Christian worship.

The Influence Natural to a Suffering Mediator.

Dr. Mozley has shown how naturally a mediator who has suffered on behalf of an ill-doer can plead, and as a matter of fact does plead, even under ordinary circumstances of human justice.   He says: " There is obviously an appetite in justice which is implied in that very anger which is occasioned by crime . . . we desire the punishment of the criminal as a kind of redress, and his punishment undoubtedly satisfies a natural craving of the mind. But . . . it is undoubtedly the case, however we may account for it, that the real offering . . . of a good person for a guilty one will mollify the appetite for punishment. . . . It is undoubtedly a fact of our nature . . . that the generous suffering of one person for another affects our regards for that other person. . . . There is something which truly passes from suffering love to him for whom it suffers; something which is communicated to the criminal; a new regard to him which is an advantage to him . . . it is rank to him; a new position; that the love of another to him can move towards pardon is a fact of our nature. . . . This kind of satisfaction to justice is involved in the scriptural doctrines of the Atonement."[1]

The Reasonable Basis of it.

Dr. Mozley does not show why the suffering of another should have this effect, but it is probably due to the fact that by his suffering the mediator sets up a sort of moral claim to have his way, to have his method tried for the reclaiming of the wrong-doer. Moreover, if punishment were inflicted in spite of his sacrifices, then the mediating sufferer would be robbed of the reward morally due to his unselfish act, and the suffering would fall upon the innocent as well as the guilty. The argument would hold even in such a case as Dr. Mozley imagines, but it would hold even more strongly where the personal relations between the mediator and the wrong-doer were of such a nature, amounting to a perfect identification, as exists between the penitent, believing Christian and his Saviour.

This gives Christ's plea for the members of His mystical body additional weight.

And in addition to this relationship we must add a

[1] See Mozley's University Sermon on the Atonement, which does not seem to have generally received the attention it deserves. In places the order of this quotation is reversed in order to bring out the sequence of the argument to suit our purpose.

further consideration—viz., the moral influences resulting from the circumstances connecting our Saviour and
His Father in this work of man's redemption. For it
was undertaken in accordance with the Father's will,
at His desire, and that gives our Mediator's plea still
more force.

For imagine the case of a family which by carelessness
or other fault of its own had got into a bad way, and
was connected with a high official from whom it hoped
for help, but who, though personally interested in his
relations and desirous to aid them, found it inadvisable
for various reasons to act directly in the matter; and
under these circumstances asked a kind-hearted friend,
whom he could trust, to do what he could in their case.
If his friend threw himself heartily into the affair, and
at considerable personal sacrifice and some risk to his
own reputation was able to extricate the family from
some of their difficulties, infuse them with a better
spirit, and put them into a position to advance still
further if only their relative would countenance them
in some particular matter—then, in such a case, the
mediating, self-sacrificing friend would have a very
strong moral case in appealing to their relative for the
support needed. The fact of his self-sacrificing exer-
tions having been undertaken at his friend's request
would give such an appeal almost irresistible moral
force.

So also in the case of our great Mediator's intercession
for fallen humanity. It is hardly necessary to prove
at this time that the Father was in the Son reconciling
the world to Himself;[1] that the work of man's redemption was undertaken by the Son in accordance with
and in obedience to His Father's will;[2] and this fact
gives our Lord's plea for man's forgiveness a moral
force which would seem to make it even an immorality—
an injustice to our Lord—to resist. The Father, having

[1] 2 Cor. v. 19.
[2] Cf., for instance, Matt. xxvi. 42; John iii. 16; Heb. x. 7-10.

put His Son into that position of a suffering Mediator, is morally bound to grant what is necessary in order to complete and crown His Agent's work. To refuse would be a wrong to His Son, a repudiation of the moral consequences of His own action in desiring the work of redemption to be undertaken by Him. Even if we were to admit that to grant His Son's plea would entail some omission of strict justice, yet to reject it would be a greater immorality.

But we do not admit that any least failure in perfect holiness is involved. If it be argued that, under the circumstances, the Father should never have desired such a work—involving His own moral indebtedness— to be undertaken by the Son, we hold that it has already been shown that the highest morality—viz., the demands of the mutual love of the Father and the Son—made the sacrifice morally necessary;[1] and that, as far as the justice of man's forgiveness is concerned, this depends entirely upon the reality of the Christian's identification with His Saviour's perfect obedience, and of his endurance in Him of sin's penalty and involvement in His holiness.

God's Infinite Omniscience connects Christ's Atoning Life and Death with Subsequent Events.

But if in spite of all that has been urged it is still claimed, " But the death of our Lord upon the Cross is a far-off event of history, and we know we did not suffer with Him there. *Our* bodies never hung upon the Cross "—if this be urged, there is a further consideration still to be borne in mind—viz., that to God's eternal, omniscient nature time is an everlasting present. A thousand years past are to Him as one day, and He foresees the future as an immediate present. It is quite impossible for us who live in time and not in eternity to realize altogether, or even partially, what this means in practical effect, but we are not quite without help

[1] *Cf.* pp. 37, 152-3.

from our own experience.   Dr. Moberly has said: " The future in practice means the continuance of the present —the present carried on from moment to moment. Power to live sinlessly is . . . present power continuing continuously onward—a perpetual and unbroken present. . . .   Again, there is a sense, much more real than we had sometimes thought, in which the past also is really an aspect of the present.   For the past . . . concerns me as it affects what I now am, as it remains in me still, an abiding, alas ! an inalienable present."[1]

Our Lord's Teaching upon Man's Moral Involvement with the Past.

And that later ages may be morally involved in the actions of those who have gone before our Lord Himself has shown where He said to the Pharisees: " Ye witness to yourselves that ye are the sons of them that slew the prophets. . . .   Therefore, behold, I send into you prophets and wise men, and scribes: some of them shall ye kill and crucify; and some of them shall ye scourge in your synagogues, and persecute from city to city: that upon you may come all the righteous blood shed on the earth."[2]   Because they were the sons of their fathers, and because they had, by their own actions, given their assent to and identified themselves with the deeds of their ancestors, they would be held guilty not only of their own crimes, but also associated with the guilt of all the murders committed by their fathers in bygone ages.   This is our Lord's declaration as to the working of divine judgment; and if God acts so with regard to sin, doubtless in His mercy the same principle will also hold good with regard to virtue.   Where present moral conditions identify a person with the virtues of the past, we may believe that the blessings attached to those past virtues is extended into present and future ages.   This, after all, is only the teaching of

---

[1] *Atonement and Personality*, p. 33.   [2] Matt. xxiii. 34-5.

the Second Commandment: God visits the sins of the fathers upon the children unto the third and fourth generation of them that hate Him, and shows mercy unto thousands of generations of them that love Him. It is this teaching our Lord confirms. In God's court the present aider and abettor, whether of good or evil, is held to be morally involved in the original action. But we can go further than this.

Our Relation to the Atonement through our Crucified Lord.

If we take this true thought of human existence and apply it to our Saviour, then His present personality is part of His past, and we in Him, identified with Him in His mystical body, have part in His atoning life and sacrifice upon the Cross. And when it is protested, " But our bodies never hung upon the Cross," the fact that our bodies are not the most essential part of our personality makes the objection seem somewhat superficial. One might answer: " What you say is, of course, true; but are you quite sure that no part of our being, nothing in us from God, nothing that is perhaps far more essential to our personality than our bodies, none of that true light which lighteth every man coming into the world " (John i. 9), and therefore " lights us, has not been involved morally and spiritually in the crucifixion ?"

Wordsworth, speaking of our birth, says:

> Trailing clouds of glory do we come
> From God who is our home.

May it not be that some of that glory, some of that true light which lighteth every man as he cometh into the world, is reflected from the wounds of Christ ?

It cannot be questioned that our souls are from God, the Father of spirits (Heb. xii. 9). It seems, too, that in this work of ever-fresh creation the Son, as the Creative Word, has His share no less than in the original work of creating the world: " My Father worketh hitherto, and I work " (John v. 17). And again: " This (Creative Word) is the true light which lighteth every man as he cometh into the world " (John i. 9); so that our souls have in some true sense come from the Son as well as from the Father. When, also, we bear in mind the reciprocal nature of our union with Christ; that we need not only dwell in Him, but He also in us; that the sap of the Vine feeds the branches; that we are temples of the Spirit of the Son; that God makes His abode (John xiv. 23) and dwells and abides in the faithful Christian (John xv. 4); and the insistence in the Epistles that Christians are members of the crucified Christ, of His flesh, and of His bones (Eph. v. 30), it appears that he would be a bold man who should positively assert that there is in Christians nothing which involves a real objective connection with their Saviour's atoning sacrifice; which, when precipitated, as it were, by repentance and faith, justifies them in saying, " I am crucified with Christ." It would indeed seem that such a connection is not only possible, but necessarily involved—a necessary result of these relations with our Saviour. For if Christ be in us at all, it must be the Christ who died upon the Cross.

Our Present Participation in Christ's Atoning Work.

And for the rest, we know that though our Lord's sacrifice was in itself perfect and complete, yet, if its benefits are to be associated with us, our lives and deaths, inspired by faith, must move in unison with His, in order that we may fill up in our own body that which is behind in the sufferings of Christ on our behalf (Col. i. 24). We too must be moved by true penitence to make the reparation to God's holiness which love as well as justice demands; we too, in the measures possible for us, must offer a full obedience; and we too in due time must make that complete surrender of ourselves, our bodies, souls, and spirits, in death to the will of God which our Saviour has made before us, and in this way add our Amen to the great Amen He uttered to the sentence of God's holiness upon sin. In all the essential features of the Atonement we have our part to bear; otherwise we have no place in the sacrifice of Christ on our behalf. But when we have done our part, then, by the power of the Holy Spirit, our imperfect sacrifice is identified with His perfect sacrifice, our personality with His personality. He becomes, in fact, our "Kipper," our propitiation, because His perfect sorrow for sin and obedience " covers," and so crowns, completes, and perfects, our imperfect penitence and obedience, and we are " accepted in the Beloved."

To some this may seem mere transcendentalism, but as our hold on the material elements of life grows weaker, and the veil between us and the spiritual world more transparent; as death draws closer, and we gaze forward into the resurrection life, there is ground for confidence that to those who hold this creed it will loom ever clearer upon their vision as the great fundamental truth of Christian life and hope; and that when we see Christ as He is we shall become like unto Him, and our vile bodies be changed like unto His glorious body (1 John iii. 2, and Phil. iii. 21).

This View of the Atonement includes the Chief Positive Teaching of the Past.

It has been said that in all great questions the affirmations of men are generally true, and it is the negations which are finally found to need correction. This seems to hold true with regard to the doctrine of the Atonement, and the view of it taken in this book finds room for the more helpful leading thoughts of all the great teachers upon it.

We may notice, in the first place, that there is a real connection between St. Paul's teaching on " justification by faith," and the view that Christ's Atonement is effective for our salvation by virtue of the Christian's personal identification with his Saviour. The connection between the two views, indeed, amounts to a degree of similarity deserving of attention. St. Paul's position is that— (1) God cannot accept men as righteous by virtue of their actions, because none can fulfil all the requirements of the law (Rom. ii. 12 to end, iii. 10-20, 23; Gal. ii. 16, 19, iii. 10, 11, and 22, v. 3); but (2) God can and does accept men on the ground of faith in Him (Rom. i. 17, iii. 26-28, iv. 3-5, 20-24, v. 1; Gal. ii. 16, 17, 20, iii. 6-9, 11, 18, v. 6).

If we ask, What is there in faith that makes it morally justifiable for God to accept men on this ground, the general line of his teaching may be paraphrased and explained as follows:—

If men trust to be accepted by God on account of the holiness of their deeds (works), their hope is vain, for no one does or can keep God's law. And if this was true of the Judaic law, much more is it true of the new revelation of God's law given by Christ; for that is on a much higher moral and spiritual plane, and therefore much more difficult to keep. Tried by it, we all fail miserably. We have all sinned and come under the condemnation due to sin.

Thus, so far as our *actions* are concerned, God has to condemn us. He cannot permit our guilt to be condoned by His holiness. But though He cannot accept our actions as praiseworthy, He can accept men's aspirations after holiness. Those who recognize the claim of His moral and spiritual laws, and desire to observe them, in that recognition and aspiration possess something worthy of divine acceptance. The desire to obey and practice these laws may and does fail miserably, but the recognition of and desire for holiness is altogether admirable, and, what is still more important, it is potential of perfect goodness.

These things, therefore, are acceptable to God both because of their character and of what they lead on to, and if we examine them we find that they are the component elements in that faith which St. Paul teaches is the ground of man's acceptance by God; not because God imputes to men moral and spiritual excellences they do not possess (which would be a pretence), but because it is in itself a holy thing, and in the end brings about the identification of their personalities with the perfect holiness of Christ.

For what is faith, and what does it involve ? When we analyze it we find that it includes, in the first place, the recognition of the existence of a personal God, and the acceptance of the moral and spiritual law as representing His will; secondly, the acceptance of them as the rule of life—*i.e.*, the dedication of the personality in trustful surrender to God's law as being the rule of life most conducive to man's proper development and eternal welfare; and, thirdly, the life of practical obedience and effort to obey God's laws as the moral and logical outcome of this attitude of the soul. Of these three steps, the crucial one is the act of trust or faith in God by which, without anything in the nature of compulsion, the soul decides to surrender itself in trust to divine wisdom and goodness. This really involves both the prior recognition of, and the subsequent obedience to, God's law, and for this reason the whole threefold attitude and movement of the soul is rightly included under the single designation of " faith."

Why this faith should have saving power and be regarded by St. Paul as the ground of our justification or acceptance by God in the Beloved is not difficult to understand. For the obedience which is part of it (Jas. ii. 17, 20) involves the confiding of our whole personality to Him, and the use of the sacraments and all the other means of grace, in accordance with the will of God expressed through Christ and the Holy Ghost, which result in that gradual union of the soul with Christ's perfection, and that inclusion in His righteousness which requires from God's loving justice its due reward (Rom. iv. 11; 2 Cor. v. 21). In this way the Christian is justified by faith expressing itself in works of obedience.

If, passing beyond St. Paul, we take the classical definition of faith given in Heb. xi. 1 as " the assurance of things hoped for, the proving of things not seen," we arrive at much the same conclusion by a different road. For this definition regards faith as a realization of spiritual truth which has the strength of practical certainty in its influence upon the decisions of life. But this is not all. Christian faith goes beyond any mere intellectual certainty. It " does not import mere ' belief ' in an intellectual sense, but all that enters into an entire self-commitment of the soul to Jesus as the Son of God, the Saviour of the world,"[1] in such a way that the believer is made " possessor before the judgment-seat of God of the alien righteousness wrought out by Christ."[2] Christian faith, then, is an activity of the will as well as an intellectual apprehension. It is an " entire self-commitment "—an attitude of the soul taken up by virtue of that power of self-determination which is " the very nerve of personality "[3] by which the Christian commits himself in trust to Christ.

Thus, practical faith in Christ is self-surrender to Him; it is the decision to identify our will, the centre of our personality, with His; to become one with Him, identified with Him. Conversion, therefore, as an act of faith, can justly be called " a decision for Christ," and St. Paul's doctrine of " justification by faith " be viewed as in full harmony with our conception of the Christian atonement as achieving salvation from sin by a process of identifying the believer's personality with that of his Saviour.

Leaving the Bible for the teaching of the Fathers, we may note that this view is based upon the belief

---

[1] See article on " Faith " in Hastings' *Dictionary of the Bible*, vol. i., p. 831.

[2] *Ibid.*, p. 838.

[3] See Illingworth's *Personality Human and Divine*, Lecture II., Note 6.

in our Lord's representative Headship of the human race taught by St. Irenæus and St. Athanasius. It finds room for Anselm's assertion of God's justice and the need of reparation for the injury done Him by human sin: it harmonizes with the later medieval teaching of the schoolmen upon the " rectoral satisfaction " God was morally bound to require as the official ruler of the world; it agrees with McLeod Campbell's teaching that in His atoning life and death our Lord uttered a great Amen to God's sentence upon sin; it accepts Dr. Dale's view that our Lord really suffered the penalty of sin upon the Cross in His conscious separation from the Father, and that the faithful Christian is by faith included in that sin-bearing. It is also in harmony with Dr. Moberly's view that our Lord offered a perfect penitence for sin; and that by the work of the Holy Spirit, operating in the Church and her sacraments, that penitence may become ours also. But it completes this penitence and increases our conception of God's love by adding to it perfect obedience in actual bearing of sin's penalty as that reparation made to God without which no repentance is perfect. Further, by accepting the view of the possibility of a true identification of our personality with God, towards which Mr. McDowall has shown the law of evolution points, and emphasizing it, it shows how, while maintaining our distinct personality, we may be involved by a true identification with our Lord in all the elements of His one perfect and sufficient sacrifice for the sins of the whole world—in His perfect obedience and in His sin-bearing.

It meets Difficulties as to the Justice of the Atonement.

In addition to being in harmony with the chief features of the great theories of the past, it may be held that the principle of " identification with distinction " combined with the " experiential " view of our Lord's sufferings meets certain difficulties very generally felt as to the justice of the Atonement. These, as a rule, come under one of three heads. It may be argued—

(1) It was not just that the innocent should suffer the penalty due to the guilty.

(2) It is not just that the guilty, who deserve punishment, should escape.

(3) It is not just that God should accept the suffering of the innocent as a satisfactory settlement of the claims of justice.

In answer to the first of these difficulties, we have seen that if the experiential theory be correct our Lord did not suffer any punishment at all. He only underwent voluntarily an experience of the penal consequences of sin—*i.e.*, " sin-bearing "—in order to attain a position which would enable Him to save mankind. Just as a missionary prepares himself to help and save the heathen by the self-sacrifice involved in study and the renunciation of home-life, so our Lord made an unspeakably greater sacrifice in order, as it were, to qualify Himself to save humanity.

The second difficulty is met by the fact that it is a mistake to think the guilty escape the penalty of sin. They must really be involved in Christ's sin-bearing if they are to be saved. Even in the case of those who come within the atoning influence of the Cross it is still true that their life is a continual dying for their sins. They "die daily" (1 Cor. xv. 31); they are always being called upon to die to self in reparation for their sins of living for self. They experience the fellowship of Christ's sufferings, being made conformable to His death (Phil. iii. 10). They always bear about in their body the dying of the Lord Jesus (2 Cor. iv. 10); they " are crucified with Christ " (Gal. ii. 20). They know what it is to be separated from God by the guilt of sin; to be dead spiritually; to be incapable of responding to their spiritual and divine environment, or of making spiritual effort; to be, to some extent, forsaken by God because their sinfulness limits the possibilities of divine communion. They know also what it is to die *to* sin. They are continually sacrificing themselves, using and giving up their life to do the will of God; constantly drinking the cup of hard obedience He offers them in the experiences of life; being baptized with His baptism of suffering, so that their life becomes more and more one of absolute surrender. And since they cannot do all this of themselves, but only in so far as the Spirit of Christ and His grace animates, inspires, and directs them, it is true as a very fact of existence, and not of mere literary expression, that the life they live is the life of Christ lived in them. They not only " become like unto Him " (1 John iii. 2), but the life as well as the death of Jesus is verily made manifest in their bodies (2 Cor. iv. 10, 11). That is to say, if we are to be saved the crucifixion of Christ must be re-enacted to some real extent in our lives, and our actions and character must be inspired by the virtue of His life in us. He must really live in and act through us.

When this conception of the Christian life is grasped, the third difficulty we have mentioned dies away. For it becomes clear it is not the suffering of the innocent, but of the guilty—not of Christ, but ourselves—which satisfies the claims of justice. One perceives that, to use St. Paul's expressive phrase, penitent sinners " fill up on their part that which is lacking of the afflictions of Christ in their flesh " (Col. i. 24, R.V.). In Him they truly experience the penal consequences of sin, and not altogether unconsciously. As their union with Christ becomes perfected, their sense of the guilt of sin increases; and the enlightened Christian recognizes, in the sufferings demanded of him in life, his progressive crucifixion, so that he finds himself truly involved in the sin-bearing of his Lord. In the discipline and suffering he experiences; in the weakness, inability, and deadness of his spiritual life; in the darkness of faith

17

which limits or refuses him all heavenly vision, he recognizes, and submits to, the separation between himself and his Father which is the consequence of sin, and which Jesus experienced in completed measure on his behalf. As a partaker in Christ's sufferings (1 Pet. iv. 13) he knows himself to be drinking some few drops from the full cup his Saviour accepted. But though, in his sin-blunted capacity for spiritual suffering, he can but taste what his Master drunk to the dregs, yet, by his identification with Him, he is no less fully involved in that completed experience, although too insensitive to feel it. If our experience can fill up what is lacking in the suffering of Christ for us, much more do His sufferings make good the deficiencies in those of His disciples.

The Joy of making Restitution to God through Christ.

It is hoped that in another direction also this view of the Atonement will be found to meet a real need of the human heart. Penitent men who love God cannot rest satisfied with offering Him nothing but contrition, however deep and sincere it may be, however perfected by a possible union with that of Christ. They desire, just in proportion to the depth of their penitence, to make some reparation for the wrong they have done God. Their own sacrifices are limited by the conditions and duties of life, and at the best are wholly inadequate. We feel profoundly that in our " sacrifices and oblations " God can " have no pleasure." Then to us in our naked inability, comes the possibility of identification with the acceptable and all-sufficient sacrifice of righteousness—the perfect obedience and service of God's Son—and our heart leaps at the thought. It lifts up our religion to another plane. It makes the Christian sacrifice of ourself in union with that of our Lord to be no longer a vain oblation, but glorious; and its offering becomes no longer merely our ground of chastened hope, but also our joy. Our religion is transfused with splendour. The infinite love of our heavenly Father has found for us a way of escape from the ignominy of owing Him an eternal debt of injury; He has made possible for us a worthy reparation; and we are left only with the debt of an eternal gratitude, which is love's joy rather than her shame.

Description of a Christian's Atoning Life in Christ.

One of the best descriptions of the practical working of the Atonement has been given in *The East and the West*, in the January number for 1918.[1] After saying that sin is a condition " of depravity of will " and consequent " alienation from God," and that we all " inherit this damaged will-power, with its tendency to make wrong acts of choice " the writer continues:—

" As regards the application of the Atonement to the individual, we note that there is no arbitrary remission of penalties justly incurred, no fictitious undoing of what is really done, no bartering of justice. It is the painful remaking of a man's character that is to result from forgiveness, the straightening of the distorted will, the slow growth of the God-given life within, the enlightening of the conscience, the breaking down of old bad habits, and the persevering development of goodness—a lifelong struggle to surrender the whole nature to the will of God, and to use it in His service. The process is twofold: on man's part repentance; on God's, forgiveness. Repentance begins with a genuine sorrow for sin, not remorse for the consequences, nor shame at exposure, but a genuine sorrow for the sin itself. This is an experience which those who have not known it are not in a position to estimate . . . it is wont to bring with it such a sharp and penetrating pain that to find relief from sin becomes thereafter a compelling necessity, to be attained at the cost of any humiliation and any effort. It springs from the vision of holiness, it deepens as love for the sinless Saviour deepens, and

[1] *Cf.* article " Forgiveness versus Karma," by Sister Dora.

its reality is proved by the transformation of character that is its invariable result. . . . The forgiveness with which God meets repentance looks both backward and forward. By it He removes the guilt of the past, and restores the soul to that state of union with Himself which its own acts had interrupted. He also grants a fresh infusion of divine strength with which to renew the victorious struggle of the future. God is, and has been, always ready to do this for all men. He does not need to be induced to do it. But He can only do it when man's will has repented, and has turned from sin to desire to serve Him. This is the meaning of the Atonement."

The writer here does not deal with the difficulty presented to God in dealing with " the guilt of the past," which is only just glanced at. We realize, however, that it must be dealt with somehow, and, it would seem, necessarily through an intermediary. That just as a person needs an instrument or gloves to touch some unclean thing, so man's guilt must be " covered " before God's purity can come into communion with him. There must be an intermediary, a " Mediator with the Father," to make a " covering " (*cf.* Heb. *kipper* to atone by covering) for our sins. If we view this as attained by our Lord's incarnate life and death, and combine it with the above description of its application to the individual, we shall possess a working theory of the Atonement.

Summary of the Experiential Theory.

It would perhaps be useful now to summarize the conclusions we have arrived at :—

1. Our Lord did truly suffer the penalty of sin upon the Cross by the breaking of the spiritual communion which had hitherto united Him to the Father.

2. He suffered this, not as a punishment, but as an experience which would give Him a certain helpful and necessary status for the work of man's salvation.

3. It helps in this work—(*a*) By putting Him in the position of one who has already suffered the penalty of sin, and (*b*) because in this way, upon the Cross, He also achieved in actuality in His human nature perfect obedience to the will of the Father in conflict with the utmost powers of evil, and under conditions which made it a supreme test and attainment of perfect positive holiness.

4. Man's salvation is brought about by a true identification with Christ which involves him in His sorrow for man's sin, His sin-bearing, and His perfect obedience, so that—(*a*) In Christ man's imperfect penitence is perfected; (*b*) in Christ he suffers the penalty due to his sins; and (*c*) in Christ is able to offer God a perfect obedience as reparation for the disobedience of his sins.

5. This perfect union with Christ amounts to a real identification of personality, so that our imperfect atonement for sin is perfected and made part of Christ's perfect atonement; and is brought about by the power of the Holy Spirit working through the various means of grace, and especially in the sacraments of the Church. Yet, though these are the normal methods of the Holy Spirit's working, He is not limited to their use.

Salvation, then, is not to be found in any system of thought or practice only; not merely by accepting and assimilating any form of teaching, but in assimilating Christ Himself; not in accepting His doctrine merely, but in union with His personality—His life and death. This is our religion, our Gospel. Christianity needs to be rebuilt upon the Cross of Christ. This is what the world needs, and it is for us as members of Christ's Church to go forth and proclaim it in tones to which the world cannot be deaf. To work out our salvation from sin and the penalties of sin is no light task, to be easily achieved. It is no small matter. For there is no salvation save in union with the crucified Christ; save in such an identification of ourselves with Him, by the power of the Holy Spirit working through faith and the means of grace, that in some real sense there is brought about a union between ourselves and Jesus so true and vital that in Him we really suffer the penalty of sin, and in Him offer God the reparation of His perfect obedience. However imperfect, however dimly realized, there must be for our salvation some real involvement of ourselves in His atoning life and death. It may be brought about by means and connecting-links we cannot trace; its existence may be by us imperceptible, but it must be recognizable by God, and be no unreal imputation.

The Ideal and the Actual : Is it Possible?

The conception of such an identification with our Lord, however, suggests one arresting thought: Is not the ideal presented us too high for practical life ? Who dare say that his faith and conduct are such that they have welded the connection between himself and his Saviour formed by the sacraments and other means of grace, into a real, vital union such as we have been contemplating ? We ask: " How far have I attained that effective union and identity of personality, of heart, will, and body with my Saviour upon which hangs my eternal salvation ?" It is a humbling question, but perhaps one much needed in view of the general self-satisfaction which is the world's greatest danger in its religious life to-day. But though it is a humbling question, it is not one which need bring despair. Even now many Christians have experienced some intimations of the divine life working within, and we know how this " earthy " body limits our spiritual capacities.

Now we can only see spiritual realities dimly, as in a glass darkly, and our spiritual life can move but feebly, as an infant wrapped in swathing-bands; but when these restrictions are removed by death, if only our life be sincerely set in the right direction, we may hope to burst through into that other world where the spiritual forces of divine mercy, love, and life have their full sway, and where, seeing our Lord as He is, under the influence of that environment, we shall become like unto Him.

The Bow on Earth and in Heaven.

In the early stages of the Bible we read that God set His rainbow in the cloud as a symbol of mercy, and a sign that His justice would no more destroy all flesh from the earth. In that bow the red, always typical of anger and death, is uppermost, and fades through the glory of the mediating gold into the greens and blues of mercy and purity[1] which lie below. Again, in the last pages of the Bible we have a bow set: this time not on earth, but round about God's throne in heaven. And now the red of divine wrath has altogether disappeared, for the offering of love by the Son of Man has perfectly satisfied the claims of holy justice and smoothed out " the dark line in the face of God." The golden glory of Christ's mediation has also faded in fulfilment, having coalesced with the azure of God's purity to form the prevailing background of His throne in heaven. For the flood-tide of mercy has risen above the submerged red of divine antagonism to sinful man, so that now there is but one colour, the colour of mercy, and the rainbow round about the throne is " like unto an emerald to look upon."[2]

And before the throne, and Him who sitteth thereon, the four-and-twenty elders fall down, and worship the Lamb, saying: " Worthy is the Lamb to receive honour, and glory, and blessing, for Thou wast slain, and hast redeemed us to God by Thy blood out of every kindred, and tongue, and people, and nation: and hast made us unto God kings and priests." And ten thousand times ten thousand angels, and thousands of thousands, and every creature which is in heaven, and on earth, and

[1] The Blessed Virgin is always dressed in blue to represent her purity as that of the cloudless sky

[2] Rev. iv. 3.

in the sea, join in the hymn of praise. This is the triumphant vision of atoning love wrought by Him who " was made a little lower than the angels, because of the suffering of death . . . that by the grace of God He should taste death for every man: that every man might die in Him. For the love of Christ constraineth us; because we thus judge, that one died for all, therefore all died; and He died for all, that they which live should no longer live unto themselves, but unto Him who for their sakes died and rose again."[1]

Heb. ii. 9; 2 Cor v. 14, 15.

APPENDICES

APPENDIX A

A CATENA OF PASSAGES BEARING UPON THE TEACHING OF OUR LORD AND HIS APOSTLES ON THE VINDICATIVE CHARACTER OF GOD'S PUNISHMENT OF SINNERS

PERHAPS no better introduction to illustrate their character could be found than the words of St. John the Baptist, the forerunner divinely appointed and inspired to bring the world into moral tune for the reception of Christ's teaching:—

"O generation of vipers, who hath warned you to flee from the wrath to come ? Bring forth therefore fruits worthy of repentance, and begin not to say within yourselves, We have Abraham to our father: for I say unto you, that God is able of these stones to raise up children unto Abraham. And now also the axe is laid unto the root of the trees: every tree therefore which bringeth not forth good fruit is hewn down, and cast into the fire " (Luke iii. 7-9).

The tone is unquestionably in startling contrast with much recent religious reconstructionist effort. But it was justified by the divine teaching it prepared the way for, and to put it aside as behind the religious conceptions of the present age would be an act of great spiritual presumption.

In our Lord's parables we have the following passages:

"But the king was wroth: and he sent his armies and destroyed those murderers and burned their city " (Matt. xxii. 7, Parable of the King's Son).

"The king said to his servants: Bind him hand and

265

foot, and cast him into outer darkness: there shall be weeping and gnashing of teeth " (Matt. xxii. 13).

" His angels shall gather all things that do iniquity, and shall cast them into the furnace of fire: there shall be weeping and gnashing of teeth " (Matt. xiii. 42, Parable of the Tares).

" The angels shall come forth and sever the wicked from among the righteous, and shall cast them into the furnace of fire: there shall be the weeping and gnashing of teeth " (Matt. xiii. 49, 50, Parable of the Net).

Note.—Except in connection with smelting ore for purification the idea connected with burning is final destruction.   It is all the more significant that our Lord uses the metaphor of burning rather than of smelting in His teaching.

" Howbeit, these Mine enemies which would not that I should reign over them, bring them hither, and slay them before Me " (Luke xix. 27, Parable of the Pounds).

" . . . the lord of the vineyard will come and destroy those husbandmen, and will give the vineyard to others " (Luke xx. 16, Parable of the Wicked Husbandmen).

All these sayings suggest the ideas of retribution rather than restoration as God's primary attitude towards the sinner.   They make against the idea that God always loves everybody; and this still holds true even when we remember that the parables use the language of metaphor, and had an immediate and local meaning as well as teaching for all time.   The very fact that the instinct of divine love is to save the sinner shows that he has already incurred a fate he needs to be saved from.

Our Lord's General Teaching.

But even though this were not so, we find the same kind of teaching in other sayings of our Lord.   For instance:

(1) " Whosoever shall speak against the Holy Spirit, it shall never be forgiven him, neither in this world, nor in that which is to come " (Matt. xii. 32).

(2) " If thy hand or thy foot causeth thee to stumble, cut it off, and cast it from thee: it is good for thee to enter into life maimed or halt, rather than having two hands or two feet to be cast into the eternal fire. And if thine eye causeth thee to stumble, pluck it out, and cast it from thee: it is good for thee to enter into life with one eye, rather than having two eyes to be cast into the hell of fire " (Matt. xviii. 8, 9). The parallel passage in Mark ix. 48, 49, adds: " Where their worm dieth not, and the fire is not quenched. For every one shall be salted with fire, and every sacrifice shall be salted with salt."

Note.—Even though we render αἰώνιον as " age-long " instead of " eternal," that does not get rid of the thrice-repeated formula in St. Mark, nor remove the impression that the Speaker was thinking of retribution rather than of the promotion of penitence.

(3) " Ye are the salt of the earth: but if the salt have lost its savour, wherewith shall it be salted ? It is thenceforth good for nothing, but to be cast out and trodden under foot of men " (Matt. v. 13).

(4) " Ye serpents, ye offsprings of vipers, how shall ye escape the judgment of hell ? Therefore, I send unto you prophets, and wise men, and scribes: some of them shall ye kill and crucify; and some of them shall ye scourge in your synagogues, and persecute from city to city: that upon you may come all the righteous blood shed upon the earth. . . ." (Matt. xxiii. 33-35).

(5) " . . . it were good for that man if he had never been born " (Matt. xxvi. 24 and Mark. xiv. 21).

(6) " . . . Unto them that are without all things are done in parables: that seeing they may see, and not perceive; and hearing they may hear, and not understand; lest haply they should turn again, and it should be forgiven them " (Mark iv. 12).

Note.—Unforgiveness seems to be contemplated. Granted that the passage is ironical, with a reference to Isa. vi. 9, it still remains a solemn warning, and it cannot be claimed that St. Paul also quoted it ironically at Rome (Acts xxviii. 26, 27).

(7) " . . . I will warn you whom ye shall fear: Fear Him, which after He hath killed hath power to cast into hell; yea, I say unto you, Fear Him " (Luke xii. 5).

(8) " I tell thee, thou shalt not depart thence until thou hast paid the very last mite " (Luke xii. 59).

(9) " Ye shall see Abraham, and Isaac, and Jacob, and all the prophets, in the kingdom of God, and yourselves cast forth without " (Luke xiii. 28).

Note.—The context shows the reference is to a shutting out from God's presence at the judgment-day in spite of appeal, and it is represented as a final judgment.

(10) " I say unto you that none of those men that were bidden shall taste of my supper " (Luke xiv. 24).

(11) " Every one that falleth upon that stone shall be broken to pieces; but on whomsoever it shall fall, it will scatter him as dust (Luke xx. 18).

(12) " For these are days of vengeance, that all things which are written may be fulfilled. Woe unto them that are with child or to them which give suck in those days ! for there shall be great distress upon the land and wrath unto this people (Luke xxi. 22, 23).

N.B.—Our Lord plainly speaks of the punishment of sin as a vengeance proceeding from God's wrath.

The Evidence of the Epistles, etc.

In view of this language of our Lord, it is not surprising to find the same kind of teaching in the writings of our Lord's followers.

St. Paul teaches that " the wrath of God is revealed from heaven against all ungodliness and unrighteousness of men " (Rom. i. 18); and since the restoration of the sinner proceeds from loving sorrow, the whole expression suggests a penal attitude towards sin both in this and the following passages.

(1) " . . . in the judgment of God, they who commit such things [*i.e.*, sins] are worthy of death " (Rom. i. 32).

(2) " Unto them that are factious and obey not the truth, but obey unrighteousness, shall be wrath and indignation, tribulation and anguish, upon every soul of man that worketh evil " (Rom. ii. 8, 9).

(3) " Is God unrighteous who visiteth with wrath ?" (Rom. iii. 5). The Greek is ἐπιφέρων τὴν ὀργήν, and the A.V. renders " with vengeance." Liddell and Scott show that the common meaning of ἐπιφέρειν in combination with other words is one of attack, and instance the expression " ὀργὰς ἐπιφέρειν τινί " as meaning " to minister to, to gratify his passions."

(4) " The law worketh wrath " (Rom. iv. 15).

(5) " Saved from the wrath of God through Him, [i.e., Christ] . . . we were reconciled to God through the death of His Son " (Rom. v. 9, 10).

(6) " Behold then the goodness and severity of God: towards them that fell severity; but towards thee, God's goodness, if thou continue in His goodness: otherwise thou also shalt be cut off " (Rom. xi. 22).

(7) " Vengeance belongeth unto Me; I will recompense, saith the Lord " (Rom. xii. 19; quoted from Deut. xxii. 35).

(8) " If any man destroyeth the temple of God, him shall God destroy " (1 Cor. iii. 17).

(9) " Because of these things cometh the wrath of God upon the children of disobedience " (Eph. v. 6).

One cannot question that the impression produced by these passages is that St. Paul conceived the primary attitude of God towards the sinner to be penal, and the writer of the Epistle to the Hebrews is, if anything, still clearer.

(1) Heb. vi. 4-6 teaches that persistent wilful sin produces a spiritual condition in which repentance becomes impossible, and where there is no repentance all agree there can be no forgiveness either.

(2) " If we sin wilfully . . . there remaineth no more a sacrifice for sins, but a certain fearful expectation of judgment, and a fierceness of fire which shall

devour the adversaries. A man that hath set at nought Moses' law died without compassion . . . of how much sorer punishment . . . shall he be judged worthy who hath trodden under foot the Son of God . . . ? For we know Him that said, Vengeance belongeth unto Me, I will recompense. And again, The Lord shall judge His people. It is a fearful thing to fall into the hands of the living God " (Heb. x. 26-31).

" Our God is a consuming fire " (Heb. xii. 29).

Again, in the last of the Epistles St. Jude writes: " Behold, the Lord cometh with ten thousands of His holy ones, to execute judgment upon all, and to convict all the ungodly of all their works of ungodliness which they have ungodly wrought," etc. (Jude 14, 15).

Even the Apostle of Love emphasizes the retributory aspect of God's dealings with sin. This is, indeed, nowhere more plainly taught than in our Lord's messages to the churches, in one of which He speaks of " the second death " (Rev. ii. 11) and the blotting out of the sinner's name from the book of life (Rev. iii. 5) as the penalty of sin. It is true that repentance is repeatedly urged upon the churches as a means of escape, but it is made clear that the primary demand of God's holiness is for retribution, and that penitence is a secondary alternative. Except they repent, God's punishment will fall upon them. It is in this book also that we read of " The wrath of the Lamb " (Rev. vi. 16); of the " Seven bowls of the wrath of God " (Rev. xvi.); of the cup . . . of the fierceness of God's wrath " (Rev. xvi. 19); of the " winepress of the fierceness of the wrath of Almighty God " trodden by the Word of God (Rev. xix. 15); and of the lake of fire which is the second death (Rev. xx. 14), into which all sinners are cast (Rev. xxi. 8). It is remarkable that there is no book in the New Testament which dwells so insistently upon the judgment of God's holiness upon sin as the Revelation of the Apostle of Love; and nowhere is there found expressed more severe judgment upon sin unless in some of the sayings of the King of Love in the Gospels. Yet as one reads them it is impossible to avoid the impression that there is something behind them besides love. An unbiassed judgment cannot help but ascribe them to some other source. We feel that "the fierceness of the wrath of Almighty God" must have some other origin besides love, however exacting ideal love may be; and that that source is the terrible holiness of God, before which even the angels hide their faces. This holiness is asserted by His vindicating omnipotence when He makes evil to perish from before His face, as the sun destroys darkness or health disease.

Unquestionably the language used in the Bible to describe God's attitude towards sin is opposed to the general trend of recent thought, and the opposition is symptomatic. Men do not deny God's hostility to sin—that would be too openly immoral—but they do not like to think of it as a personal thing, nor as a very passion of hatred, and a destructive energy such as Biblical language implies. We find it difficult to conceive such an abhorrence of sin. Our shrinking from such plain language (the truth of which, however, we do not deny, whether it be described as the wrath of God or the action of divine law) may be due to high moral and spiritual instincts, or to some less praiseworthy tendency; but in either case there is always danger in giving way to the natural dislike, and even irritability, we are all inclined to feel when required to face unpleasant facts, or hear them called by their plain, unpleasant names. Whether we view God's dealings with sin as the natural consequences of the operation of law, or as His personal intervention, the result in either case is punishment, traceable to His hostility; and honesty requires that the truth should not be veiled, nor refused acknowledgment. Why, after all, should we shrink from saying plainly to ourselves: "God 'hates' sin: He abhors my sins"; for the more His hatred, the greater His love in providing an atonement.

APPENDIX B

IDENTIFICATION WITH DISTINCTION OF PERSONALITY

In Chapter X. of the book *Naval Intelligence* the above theory is expressed very exactly by " A Chaplain of the Fleet." After referring to Sir Thomas Browne's saying in *Religio Medici* that " united souls are not satisfied with embraces, but desire to be truly each other," the author quotes Rupert Brooke as teaching positively what the doctor-divine only ventured to conceive as an ideal impossible of realization:

> " Manua, there waits a land
> Hard for us to understand.
> Out of Time, beyond the sun
> All are one in Paradise.
> You and Purpure are one,
> And Taü, and the ungainly wise."

He then continues: " Were it not that you can drag isolated texts of Scripture into proving anything there would be a strong temptation to adduce certain texts to support the thesis . . . that the final consummation of all things will be a state in which each soul, while preserving his individual personality, will be identified and unified with every other living soul; and all made one with God. Possibly we are intended to deduce this from the Doctrine of the Trinity. . . ."

There seems, indeed, to be crystallizing in the minds of men a movement in favour of this doctrine which may shortly lead to its general acceptance in Christian thought. The doctrine of the Holy Trinity appears to afford strong support for such teaching.

GENERAL INDEX

INDEX OF AUTHORS
REFERRED TO, QUOTED, OR CRITICIZED

INDEX OF TEXTS

281

BILLING AND SONS, LIMITED, PRINTERS, GUILDFORD, ENGLAND